S0-BMC-589

The Doctrine of Regeneration

Stephen Charnock

BAKER BOOK HOUSE
Grand Rapids, Michigan

Reprinted 1980 by
Baker Book House Company

ISBN: 0-8010-2462-5

First published in 1840

PHOTOLITHOPRINTED BY CUSHING - MALLOY, INC.
ANN ARBOR, MICHIGAN, UNITED STATES OF AMERICA

L.I.F.E. College Library
1100 Glendale Blvd.
Los Angeles, Calif. 90026

CONTENTS

FIRST GENERAL TOPIC

NECESSITY OF REGENERATION

CHAPTER I

CHAPTER II

CHAPTER III

CHAPTER IV

SECOND GENERAL TOPIC

NATURE OF REGENERATION

CHAPTER I

CHAPTER II

CHAPTER III

031941

L.I.F.E. College Library
1100 Glendale Blvd
Los Angeles, Calif. 90026

THIRD GENERAL TOPIC

AUTHOR OF REGENERATION

FOURTH GENERAL TOPIC

INSTRUMENT OF REGENERATION

FIRST GENERAL TOPIC

NECESSITY OF REGENERATION

CHAPTER I

Man in a state of sin or righteousness —His apostacy from God —Its effects on the character and condition of Man — Regeneration universally necessary —The Law requires it —Man's happiness depends on it — Christ's work had a special reference to it — The mission of the Holy Spirit designed to effect it — Necessary to every faculty of the soul —Natural reason assents to its necessity.

THESE words contain the foundation of all practical religion here, and happiness hereafter. It is the principal doctrine Christ, as a prophet, came to teach; and as a king, to work in the heart.

The text proves the indispensable necessity of regeneration, by which I mean not a relative, but a real change of the subject, wrought in the complexion and inclinations of the soul. As in the restoring of health, there is a change made in the temper and humours of the body.

As mankind were changed in Adam, from what they were in a state of creation; so men must be changed in Christ, from what they were in a state of corruption. As that change was not only relative, but real, and the relative first introduced by the real; so must this. The relation of a child of wrath, was founded upon the sin committed. Without a real change, there can be no relative. Being in Christ, as freed from condemnation, is always attended with a walking in the Spirit; and walking is not before living. For the better understanding this point, I shall lay down some propositions concerning the Necessity of Regeneration.

There are but two states, one saving, the other damning; a state of sin, and a state of righteousness. All men are divided into two ranks. In regard of their principle, some are in the flesh, some in the spirit. In regard of their obedience, some walk after the flesh, some after the spirit. Some are slaves to the flesh, others are led by the Spirit: some live only to self, some live to God. In regard of the exercise of their minds, their nobler faculty; some mind the things of the flesh, others the things of the Spirit. Some indulge themselves in sin, others place the delights of their spirits upon better and higher objects.

The scripture mentions no other. A state of enmity, wherein men have their inclinations contrary to God. A state of friendship and fellowship, wherein men walk before God unto all well-pleasing, and would not willingly have an inward motion swerve from his will. One is called light, the other darkness; you were sometimes darkness, but now ye are light: one, the children of wrath, the other, children of God. There is no medium between them: every man is in one or the other of these states. All believers, from the bruised reed, to the tallest cedar; from the smoking flax on earth, to the flaming lamp in heaven; from Thomas, that would not believe without seeing, to Abraham, who would believe without staggering, all are in a state of life. And all from the most beautiful moralist, to the most venemous toad in nature's field; from the young man in the gospel, who was not far from the kingdom of heaven, to Judas, who was in the very bottom of hell; all are in a state of death. Mere nature, though never so curiously garnished, can place a man no higher. Faith, though with many infirmities, puts us in a state of amity: unbelief, though with many moralities, continues us in a state of enmity. These two very opposite conditions mentioned, include all the human race. The highest endowments of men in a state of nature cannot please God. The delight of God then, supposeth some real change in the object, which is the ground of that delight : for God is wise in his delight, and could not be pleased with any thing which was not fit for his complacency. Since original nature in a man, cannot displease God, unless it be changed by some fault, because it was his own work ; so our present nature cannot please God, unless it be changed by some grace, though it be otherwise never so highly dignified. Whatsoever grows up by the new Adam, in us, is the offspring of the Spirit ; and upon these two stocks, all men in the world are set. Since therefore one is utterly destructive, and cannot please God, though never so well garnished, (for being utterly contrary to him, it cannot be approved by him) the other is absolutely necessary to salvation.

It is necessary upon the account of the fall of man, and the consequences of it. In Adam we died, " As in Adam all died :" therefore in Adam we sinned. 1 Cor. xv. 22. " By one man's disobedience, many were made sinners." Rom. v. 19. Man cannot be supposed to sin in Adam, unless some covenant had intervened between God and Adam, whence there did arise in the whole human nature a debt, of having righteousness transfused from the first parent to all his posterity : the want of this grace, wherein his posterity are conceived, is a privation, and a crime which was voluntary in the root and head. This privation of righteousness must be removed. The institution of God stands firm, that Adam, and his posterity should have a pure righteousness. It is not for the honour of God to enjoin it so strictly at first, and to have no regard to it afterwards. Now this privation of righteousness, and the unrighteousness which hath taken place in the sons of Adam, cannot be removed without the infusion of grace. For without this grace, he would always want righteousness, and yet be always under an obligation to have it : he would be desirous of happiness ; but without

it, and under an impossibility of attaining it. Were the
soul of man indifferent to good and evil, the writing
of moral precepts upon it, by good education, would
sway it to walk in the paths of virtue: but it is not
so ; for take two, let them have the same ways of
education, the same precepts instilled into them, as
Esau and Jacob had by their father, who were equally
taught ; yet how different were their lives ? Esau's
bad, Jacob's not without flaws. Education had not
the power to root corruption out of either; no, nor out
of any man in the world, without a higher principle.
There is some powerful principle in the soul, which
leads it into by-paths, contrary to those wholesome
rules instilled into it. Hence ariseth a necessity of
some other principle to be put into the heart, to over-
rule this corrupt bias. Man goes astray from the
womb, as it is in Psal. lviii. 3. " The wicked are
estranged from the womb ; they go astray as soon as
they be born." There must be something to rectify
him, and expel this wandering humour. Also,

By the fall of man there was contracted an unfitness to any thing that is good. Man is so immersed
in wrong notions of things, that he cannot judge fully
of what is good ; "to every good work reprobate."
Tit. i. 16. The state of nature, or the old man, is
described, "to be corrupt, according to the deceitful
lusts." Eph. iv. 22. Deceitful, seducing from God,
drawing us into perdition, by representing evil under
the notion of good ; which evidenceth our understandings to be unfit to judge without a new illumination ; inward and spiritual lusts, which are most
deceitful, being accounted brave and generous motions. Lusts or desires, which show the corruption
of the will by ill habits : lust and sin are the mere
composition of corrupted nature ; the whole man is
made up of polluting principles, and vicious appetites.

What was preternatural to man in a state of innocency, became natural to him after his depraved
state. He is carnal, sold under sin. The state being

already out of order, cannot make the motion otherwise than depraved : as when a clock is out of order, it is natural to that present condition of it to give false intelligence of the hour of the day : and it cannot do otherwise, till the wheels and weights be rectified. Our end was actively to glorify God in the service of him, and obedience to him ; but since man is fallen into this universal decay of his faculties, and made unfit to answer this end; there is a necessity he should be made over again, and created upon a better foundation, that some principle should be in him, to oppose this universal depravation, enlighten his understanding, mollify his heart, and reduce his affections to their due order and object.

Not only an unfitness, but unwillingness to that which is good. We have not those affections to virtue, that we have to vice. Are not our lives, for the most part, voluntarily ridiculous? Had we a full use of reason, we should judge them so. We think little of God ; and when we do think of him, it is with reluctance. This cannot be our original state : for surely, God being infinitely good, never let man come out of his hands with this actual unwillingness to acknowledge and serve him; as the apostle saith in the case of the Galatians, " This persuasion cometh not of him that calleth you." Gal. v. 8. This unwillingness comes not from him that created you. How much, therefore, do we need a restoring principle in us! We naturally fulfil the desires of the flesh. There is then a necessity of some other principle in us, to make us fulfil the will of God, since we were created for God, not for the flesh. We can no more be voluntarily serviceable to God, while that serpentine nature, and devilish habit remain in us, than we can suppose the devil can be willing to glorify God, while the nature he contracted by his fall, abides powerful in him. It is as much as to say, that a man can be willing against his will. Nature and will must be changed, or we forever remain in this state.

Man is born a wild ass's colt. No beast more wild and brutish than man in his natural birth; and likely to remain in his wild and wilful nature without grace: a new birth alone can put off the wildness of the first.

Not only unfitness and unwillingness, but inability to good. A strange force there is in a natural man, which hurries him, even against some convictions of his will, to evil.

How early do men discover an affection to vice! Greedily do they embrace it, notwithstanding rebukes from superiors, good exhortations from friends, with the concurrence of the vote of conscience, giving its *Amen* to those dissuasions! and yet carried against all those arguments, deceived by sin, slain by sin, sold under it. This is the miserable state of every son of nature.

Do we not find, that men sometimes wrapt up in retirement, in consideration of the excellency of virtue, are so wrought upon by their solitary meditations, that they think themselves able to withstand the strongest invasion of any temptation? yet we see oftentimes, that when a pleasing temptation offers itself, though there be a conflict between reason and appetite, at length all the considerations and dictates of reason are laid aside; the former idea is laid asleep, and that committed which their own reason told them was base and sordid. So that there is something necessary, beside consideration and resolution, to the full cure of man.

No privation can be removed but by the introduction of another form: as when a man is blind, that blindness, which is a privation of sight, cannot be removed without bringing in a power of seeing again. Original sin is a privation of original righteousness, and an introduction of corrupt principles, which cannot be removed but by some powerful principle contrary to it. Since the inability upon the earth, by reason of the curse, to bring forth its fruits in such a manner as it did, when man was in a state of innocency, the nature of it must be changed to reduce it to its original fruitfulness. So must man, since a general defilement from Adam hath seized upon him, be altered, before he can bring forth fruit to God. We must be united to Christ, ingrafted upon another stock, and partake of the power of his resurrection: without this, we may bring forth fruit, but not fruit to God. There is as utter an impossibility in a man to answer the end of his creation, without righteousness, as for a man to act without life, or act strongly without health and strength. It is a contradiction to think a man can act righteously without righteousness; for without it, he hath not the being of a man; that is, man in such a capacity, for those ends for which his creation intended him.

Well then, since there is an unfitness, unwillingness, inability in a man, to answer his end, there is a necessity of a new life, a new nature, a new righteousness: there is a necessity for his happiness, that he should be brought back to God, live to God, be a son of God; and this cannot be without regeneration: for how can he be brought back to God without a principle of spiritual motion? How can he live to God that hath no spiritual life? How can he be fit to be a son of God who is of a brutish and diabolical nature?

Hence it follows that it is universally necessary. Necessary for all men—our Saviour knows none without this mark: there must be a change in the soul. "Therefore if any man be in Christ, he is a new creature." 2 Cor. v. 17. There must be the habitation of the Spirit. "If any man have not the spirit of Christ, he is none of his." Rom. viii. 9. There must be a crucifixion, not only of the corrupt affections of the flesh, but of the flesh itself. "They that are Christ's have crucified the flesh, with the affections and lusts." Gal. v. 24.

The old nature must be killed, with all its attendants. There is no sonship to God without likeness; no relation of a child of God without a child-like nature. Let a man be of whatsoever quality in the world, never so high, never so low; of whatsoever age, of whatsoever moral endowments; except a man, every man be born again, &c.

And simply necessary. Our Saviour doth not say he is in danger not to see the kingdom of God, or he may come short of it; but he shall not, he cannot. There is no possible way but this for any man; no other door to creep in at but by that of a new birth: salvation cannot be attained without it; and damnation will certainly be the issue of the want of it. As there is no other name under heaven, by which we can be saved, but by the name of Jesus Christ: so there is no other way under heaven, wherein we can be saved, but by the birth of the Spirit.

It is necessary therefore in all places, in all professions. It is not necessary only in Europe, and not in Africa. Let a man be what he will, in any place under heaven, he must have a Jesus to save him, and an Holy Ghost to change him: it is one and the same Spirit acts in all, and produces the same qualities in all :—let men's religion and professions be what they will (men are apt to please themselves with this and that profession and opinion: but) there is no salvation in any profession, or any kind of opinion, but by regeneration. It is not necessary our understandings should be all of one size, that our opinions should all meet in uniformity; but it is necessary we should all have one spiritual nature. It is as necessary to the being of a good man that he should be spiritual, as to the being of a man that he should be rational; though there is a great latitude and variety in the degrees of men in grace as well as their reasons: some are of little faith, some of great faith; some babes in Christ, some strong men. It is not necessary all should be as strong as Abraham; but it is absolutely necessary all should be new born, as Abraham: no age, no time excludes it.

Righteousness was necessary before the fall. The new birth is but the beginning of our restoration to that state we had before the fall. Adam could not have been happy without being innocent. The holiness of God could not create an impure creature. Without it God could take no pleasure in his work.

After the fall it was necessary; continually necessary from the first moment of the fall. This work of regeneration is included in the first promise, "I will put enmity between thee and the woman, between thy seed and her seed." Gen. iii. 15. Naturally we have a mighty friendship to Satan, a friendship to his works, though not to his person. .But if any man have interest in that promise, he must exchange that friendship for an enmity.

If Jesus Christ, who is principally meant by this seed of the woman, had an enmity to Satan, then all Christ's seed must be possessed with the same spirit. For when the seed of the woman was to break the serpent's head, it was necessary that those that would enjoy the fruit of that conquest should be enemies to the nature of the devil and the works of the devil; otherwise they could not join with that interest which overthrows him. It is unreasonable to think the head should have an enmity, and the members an amity: and we cannot have an enmity to that which is the same with our nature, without a change of disposition. It is not a verbal enmity that is here meant : while we pretend to hate him, we may do his pleasure; and Satan is never troubled to be pretendedly hated, and really obeyed. As wicked men do the will of God's purpose, while they oppose the will of his precept ; so they do the Devil's will many times while they think they cross it. There must be a contrary nature to Satan before there can be an enmity. We are never enemies to those that encourage us in what we approve. His nature can never be altered by reason of the curse of God upon him : therefore ours must, if ever the league be broken. In Isa. lxv. 25, it is said, " The wolf and the lamb shall feed together, and the lion shall eat straw like an ox, and dust shall be the ser-

pent's meat." The nature of men may be changed
by the gospel; but dust shall always be the serpent's
meat. The saving some by water in the deluge was
a figure of this inward baptism, which is the answer of
a good conscience towards God, 1 Pet. iii. 20, 21. As
the whole world was so corrupt, that all must be washed
away before it could be restored, so is the little world
of man: the cloud and sea through which the Israelites
passed signified this, as the apostle informs us. Whereupon some think there were some sprinklings of the
water upon them, as they stood like two walls, to
favour their passage.

Necessary in the time of the law. By the moral
law this renewing was implied in the first command,
of not having any other gods before him. We cannot suppose that command only limited to a not
serving an outward image. Is not the setting up self,
our own reasons, our own wills, and bowing down
to them, and serving them, as much a wrong to God,
as the bowing down to a senseless image? nay, worse
than the adoring of an image, since that is senseless;
but our wills are corrupt, and no more fit to be our
God than an image is fit to be a representation of
him. So that in the spiritual part of the command
this must be included, to acknowledge nothing as the
rule of perfection but God; to set ourselves no other
patterns of conformity but God; which the apostle
phraseth a being new created after God.

If all idolatry were forbidden, then that which is
inward, as well as that which is outward. If we
were to have no other gods before him, then we were
to prefer nothing inwardly before him; we were to
make him our pattern, and be conformed to him;
which we cannot without another nature than that we
had by corruption.

Upon this are those scriptures founded which speak
of covetousness to be idolatry; that if any man love
the world, the love of the Father is not in him: he
doth not love God.

Now the preferring self before God, is the essential part of the corrupt nature; therefore all men by the law of nature (which is the same with the moral law,) and the Jews, to whom this law was given, were bound to have another nature than that which was derived from Adam, which essentially consisted in the making ourselves our God. Self-esteem, self-dependence, self-seeking, is denying affection and subjection to God.

By the ceremonial law more plainly. There duty was not terminated in an external observance of the types and shadows under the law; but a heart work God intended to signify to them in all those legal ceremonies. As sacrifices signified a necessity of expiation of sin; so their legal washings represented to them a necessity of regeneration.

Therefore God is said not to require the sacrifices of beasts. "Sacrifice and offering thou didst not desire, (that is, sacrifices of beasts,) burnt offerings and sin offerings hast thou not required;" Psal. xl. 6; viz. as the ultimate object of his pleasure; but as representations of Christ, the *great sacrifice*. So neither did he command circumcision, and other legal purifications, for any thing in themselves, or any thing they could work, further than upon the body; but to signify unto them, an inward work upon the heart. Hence they are said not to be commanded by God, "For I spake not unto your fathers, nor commanded them in the day that I brought them out of the land of Egypt, concerning burnt offerings or sacrifices; but this thing commanded I them, saying, Obey my voice." Jer. vii. 22, 23. That is, God did not principally require these, as the things which did terminate his will and pleasure; but an obedience to him, and walking with him, which cannot be, without an agreement of nature: for how can two walk together, unless they be agreed? Hence God speaks so often to them of the circumcision of the heart; and promises this circumcision of the heart. "And the Lord thy God will circum-

cise thy heart, and the heart of thy seed," &c.
Deut. xxxvi. 6.   And Paul expressly says, that he
was not a Jew, Rom. ii. 28, 29; that is, a spiritual
Jew, one of the spiritual seed of Abraham, who had
the circumcision that was outward in the flesh; but
he that had that of the heart.

So among us, many confide in baptism, which signi-
fieth nothing to men grown up, without an inward renewal, and baptism of the heart, no more than outward
circumcision did to them.

The obligation upon us is still the same. The covenant made with Adam was made perpetually with him
for all his posterity: therefore all his posterity, by that
covenant, were perpetually obliged to a perfect righteousness. If God had made this covenant with Adam,
that he should transfuse this original righteousness to
his posterity only for such a time, then indeed, after
the expiration of the term, the obligation had ceased,
and none had been bound to have it, as a debt required
by God: the fault of wanting it, had been removed,
without any infusion of grace; because the time being
expired, and so the obligation ceasing, it had not been
a fault to want it: neither could Adam's posterity have
been charged with his sin, because the want of righteousness, after the expiration of the time fixed, had not
been a sin: but because there was no time fixed, but
that it was perpetually of force, as to righteousness,
which was the main intent of it, we still remain under
the obligation of having a righteous nature.

Now God seeing the impossibility of answering this
obligation in our own persons, by our own strength,
appoints a way whereby we may answer it in a
second head, not annuling the former covenant as to
the essential part of it, which was a righteous nature;
but mitigating it; as the chancery annuls not the
common law, but sweetens the severity of it.

This latter covenant, is called an *everlasting covenant*. Not that the obligation of the other to righteousness has ceased, but transmitted to another head;

which head cannot possibly fail, as our former did, who hath both a perfect righteousness in himself, and hath undertaken for a perfect righteousness in his people, which he is able to accomplish, and to that purpose begins it here, and perfects it hereafter. To this purpose the Scripture speaks of the eternity of the covenant. " My covenant shall stand fast with him." Psal. lxxxix. 28, that is, with Christ: and if his people sin, as he expresseth it afterwards, " yet my loving kindness will I not utterly take from him." In this respect Christ is called the covenant of the people. "I will give thee for a covenant of the people." Isa. xlii. 6. And the end of placing David, his servant, over his people, is not to give way to unrighteousness, and maintain men in an hostile nature against God ; but that they might " walk in his judgments, and observe his statutes." Ezek. xxxvii. 24. And that *everlasting covenant* of peace he would make with them, is in order to sanctify them, Ezek. xxxvii. 26, 28. When God would make a covenant of peace with them, an everlasting covenant, it was to set his sanctuary among them, and to let the heathen know, that the Lord did sanctify Israel. And the end of the covenant, is to put "his law into the inward parts." Jer. xxxi. 33.

Christ undertook to keep up the honour of God, which was violated by the breach of that covenant, to " make reconciliation for iniquity, and to bring in everlasting righteousness." Dan. ix. 24. This obligation our *second head* entered into for us ; and in him we are complete, even as our head, and as the head of all principality and power, who hath undertaken for our perfect righteousness; of our persons, by his own righteousness; of our nature by inherent righteousness ; as it follows, " In whom ye are circumcised with the circumcision made without hands, in putting off the body of the sins of the flesh," Col. ii. 11. This obligation still remains upon our head, and upon us in him ; and to him we are to have recourse for a full answering of it. And this cannot be answered without a new birth here, which ends in perfection here-after. And Christ by a plain precept, hath made it absolutely necessary now to all under the gospel administration.

So that no age, no time, no administration, excludes it. It was as necessary to Adam, the first man, as to the last that shall be born: for being by nature spiri-tually dead, there must be a restoration to a spiritual life, if ever any be happy. God is not the God of the dead, but the God of the living. What was always necessary, is absolutely necessary, and admits of no exception. And therefore the removal of the diaboli-cal nature is indispensable to him, and to us, since we are all the posterity of Adam, and the inheritors of his corruption. How can any in any age enjoy an infi-nitely holy God, without being changed from their impurity?

Hence it follows, that it is so necessary, that it is not conceivable by any man in his right mind, how God can make any man happy without it. It is not for us, poor shallow creatures, to dispute what God can, and what God cannot do; what God may do by his absolute power: but yet it seems a contradiction, and it is not intelligible by us, how God can make a man happy without regeneration.

What semblance of reason can be given, that any one who is a slave of Satan, a child of wrath by nature, can be made the son and friend of God, with-out an expulsion of that nature which rendered him criminal, and restoring that, in some degree, which renders him innocent.

Without habitual grace, sin is not taken away: and as long as a man remains under sin, how he can be capable of any communion with God, I understand not. For he cannot be at one and the same time under God's greatest wrath, and his highest love. How is it possible, that one can have an enjoyment of eter-nal life, who hath nothing in him, but a relation to eternal death?

God made man's nature fit for his communion; man made himself unfit by guilt and filth. This unfitness must be removed by regeneration, before this privilege man had by creation can be restored. Not that this restored righteousness is the cause of our communion with God in happiness; but a necessary requisite to it. No doubt, but God might have restored this righteousness, without admitting man to a converse with him, if there had been no covenant made to that purpose. That God may give grace without glory, is intelligible; but to admit a man to communion with him in glory, without grace, is not intelligible.

It is not agreeable to God's holiness, to make any an inhabitant of heaven, and converse freely with him, in a way of intimate love, without such a qualification of grace. "The righteous Lord loveth righteousness; his countenance doth behold the upright." Psal. xi. 7. He must therefore hate iniquity, and cannot love an unrighteous nature, because of his love to righteousness; his countenance beholds the upright: he looks upon him with a smiling eye: and therefore he cannot favourably look upon an unrighteous person. So that this necessity is not founded only in the command of God, that we should be renewed, but in the very nature of the thing; because God, in regard of his holiness, cannot converse with an impure creature. God must change his nature, or the sinner's nature must be changed. There can be no friendly communion between two of different natures, without the change of one of them into the likeness of the other. Wolves and sheep, darkness and light, can never agree. God cannot love a sinner, as a sinner because he hates impurity by a necessity of nature, as well as a choice of will. It is as impossible for him to love it, as to cease to be holy.

This change cannot be then on God's part: it must therefore be on man's part. It must therefore be by grace, whereby the sinner may be made fit for converse with God; since God cannot embrace a sinner in his dearest affections, without a quality in the sinner suitable to himself. All converse is founded upon a likeness in nature and disposition. It is by grace only, that the sinner is made capable of converse with God.

It is not agreeable to God's wisdom. Is it congruous to the wisdom of God, to let a man be his child, and the child of the devil at the same time? Is it fit to admit him to the relation of a son of God, who retains the enmity of his nature against God? to make any man happy with the dishonour of his laws, since he is not subject to the law of God, neither will be; one that cannot bear him, but abhors his honour, and the apprehensions of his holiness?

Man naturally hath risings of heart against God; looks upon him under some dreadful notion; hath an utter aversion to him: alienation and enmity are inseparable. "You who were sometime alienated, and enemies in your minds." Col. i. 21. It doth not consist with the wisdom of God, to make any man happy against his will: God therefore first changeth the temper of the will, by his powerful grace, thereby making him willing, and by degrees fitting him for happiness with him.

It is not fit that corruption should inherit incorruption, or impurity be admitted to an undefiled inheritance: and therefore God brings none thither, which are not first begotten by him to a lively hope, by the resurrection of Jesus Christ from the dead. "Which according to his mercy, hath begotten us again to a lively hope, by the resurrection of Jesus Christ from the dead, to an inheritance incorruptible, undefiled, and that fadeth not away, reserved in heaven for you." 1 Pet. i. 3, 4. It cannot be honourable for the wisdom of God, to give a right to eternal life, to one that continues a child of the devil: and bestow his love upon one that resolves to give his own heart to sin and Satan.

This of which I have now discoursed, is founded

upon men's natural notions in their right reason. But if we look into the Scripture, it is certain there is no other way but this; a man without a new birth, can have no right to happiness, by any covenant of God, by any truth of God, by any purchase of Christ. God never promised happiness without it; Christ never purchased it for any one without a new nature. No example is there extant of any person God hath made happy, without this alteration: nor in the strictest inquiries can we conceive any other way possible: therefore if there be any one, that hath hopes to enjoy everlasting happiness without regeneration, he expects that which God never yet bestowed upon any, and which, according to our understanding, God cannot, without wrong to his holiness and wisdom, confer upon any person. I beseech you therefore, let none of you build your hopes upon such vain foundations: you must be holy, or you shall never see God to your comfort.

It is so necessary, that the coming and sufferings of our Lord and Saviour, would seem insignificant without it. That this regeneration was a main end of his coming, is evident by his making this one of the main doctrines, he was as a Prophet, and teacher sent from God, to make known to the world, it being the first he taught Nicodemus. Jesus Christ came to glorify God, and to glorify himself in redeeming a people. And what glory can we conceive God hath; what glory can Christ have, if there be no characteristic difference between his people and the world? And what difference can there be, but in a change of nature and temper, as the foundation whence all other differences do result? Sheep and goats differ in nature.

The righteousness which is given through our Mediator is the same essentially as that we had at first. And his threefold office, of king, priest, and prophet, is in order to it; his priestly, to reconcile and bring us to God; his prophetical, to teach us the way;

and his kingly, to work in us those qualifications, and
bestow that comely garb upon us, that was necessary
to fit us for our former converse. Our second Adam
would not be like the first if he failed in this great
work of conveying his righteousness to us, as Adam
was to convey his original righteousness to his posterity. As that was to be conveyed by carnal generation, so the righteous nature of the second Adam is
to be transmitted to us by spiritual regeneration. In
this respect renewed men are called his seed, and
counted to him for a generation; as, "A seed shall
serve him; it shall be accounted to the Lord for a
generation." Psa. xxii. 30. It shall be accounted as
much the generation of Christ, as the rest are the
generation of Adam; as if they had proceeded out of
his loins, as mankind did out of Adam's. As God
looks upon believers as righteous through the righteousness of Christ, as if it were their own, so he
accounts them as if they were the generation of Jesus
Christ himself.

Christ came to save from sin. Salvation from sin
was more his work than barely salvation from hell;
"He shall save his people from their sins." Matt. i. 21.
From sin, as the cause; from hell, as the consequence.
If from sin, was it only from the guilt of sin, and to
leave the sinful nature unchanged? Was it only to
take off punishment, and not to prepare for glory? It
would have been then but the moiety of redemption,
and not honourable for so great a Saviour. Can you
imagine that the death of Jesus Christ, being necessary
for the recovery of a sinner, was appointed for an
incomplete work, to remit man's sin, and continue the
insolence of his nature against God? It was not his
end, only to save us from wrath to come, but to save
us from the procuring cause of that wrath; not forci-
bly and violently to save us, but in methods congruous
to the honour of God's wisdom and holiness: and
therefore to purify us, " to redeem us from all iniquity,
(all parts of it) by purifying unto himself a peculiar

people, zealous of good works;" Tit. ii. 14, that we might have a holy nature, whereby we might perform holy actions, and be as zealous of good works, and the honour of God, as we had been of bad works, and to bring dishonour to him.

It was also the end of his resurrection, to quicken us to a newness of life, Col. ii. 12, 13. Eph. ii. 5, 6. If any man, without a new nature, could set foot into heaven, one great design of the death and resurrection of Christ would be insignificant.

Christ came to take away sin, the guilt by his death, the filth by his Spirit, given us as the purchase of that death. In taking away sin, he takes away also the sinful nature.

Christ came to destroy the works of the devil. "For this purpose the son of God was manifested, that he might destroy the works of the devil." 1 John iii. 8. These works are two; sin, and the misery consequent upon it. Upon the destruction of sin, necessarily follows the dissolution of the other which was knit with it. If the sinful nature were not taken away, the devil's works would not wholly be destroyed; or if the sinful nature were taken away, and a righteous nature not planted in the stead of it, he would still have his ends against God, in depriving God of the glory he ought to have from the creature; and the creature could not give God the glory he was designed by his creation to return, unless some nature were implanted in him, whereby he might be enabled to do it.

Would it then be for the honour of this great Redeemer, to come short of his end against Satan, to let all the trophies of Satan remain in the errors of the understanding, rebellion of the will, disorder of the affections, and confusion of the whole soul? Or if our Saviour had only removed these, how had the works of the devil been destroyed, if we had lain open to his assaults, and been liable the next moment to be brought into the same condition? which surely would have been, were not a righteous and divine nature bestowed upon the creature.

Christ came to bring us to God. " For Christ also hath once suffered for sins, the just for the unjust, that he might bring us to God." 1 Pet. iii. 18. Was it to bring us to God with all our pollutions, which were the cause of God casting us off? No; but to bring us in such a garb, as that we might be fit to converse with him. Can we be so without a new nature, and a spiritual likeness to God? Would that man who would bring another to a prince to introduce him into favour, bring him into his presence in a slovenly and sordid habit, such a garb as he knew was hateful to the prince? Neither will our Saviour, nor can he bring sinners in such a plight to God; because it is more contrary to the nature of God's holiness to have communion with such, than it is contrary to the nature of light, to have communion with darkness. Can it be thought, that Christ should come to set human nature right with God, without a change of that principle which caused the first revolt from God? Besides, since the coming of Christ was to please God, and to glorify him in all his attributes, as well as to save us; how can God be pleased with the effects of Christ's death, if he brought the creature to him, without any change of nature, but with its former enmity and pollution? Will you say his mercy would be glorified? How can that be, without a wrong to his purity, and a provocation to his justice? Suppose such a dispute were in God, would not holiness, wisdom, justice, joined together, decide against mercy?

But since there can be no such dispute, how can we conceive that mercy, an infinite perfection in God, can desire any thing to the prejudice of the honour of his holiness, justice, and wisdom?

Well then: if we expect happiness without a renewed nature, we would make Christ a minister of sin, as well as of righteousness. As there is a justification by him, so his intent was to plant a living principle in us, whereby we might be enabled to live to him. It is in vain then to think to find any benefit by the death of Christ, without a new nature.

The end of the Spirit's coming, manifests it to be necessary. We are said therefore to be "saved by the washing of regeneration, and renewing of the Holy Ghost." As God by his Spirit, moving upon the face of the waters, created the world; so God by his Spirit, moving upon the face of the soul, new creates all the faculties of it. Can the coming of Christ, and the coming of the Spirit, the most signal favours of God to mankind, be intended for no other end, than to convey to us the mercy of God, with the dishonour of his holiness; to change our misery without changing our nature, and putting us in a capacity both to glorify God, and enjoy him? To what purpose doth the Spirit come, if not to renew? Whatsoever was the office of the Spirit, cannot be supposed to be exercised without this foundation. Can there be any seal of the Spirit, without some impression made upon the soul like to the Spirit, which is the seal whereby we are sealed? Can he witness to us, that we are the children of God, if there be no principle in us suitable to God, as a Father; no child-like frame? Is the Spirit only to bring things to remembrance for a bare speculation, without any operative effect? Is he to help us in prayer? how can that be, without giving us first a sense of what we need, and a praying heart? And how can we have a praying heart, till our natures, so averse to God, and his worship, be changed? He is a quickening Spirit, "the Spirit gives life." 2 Cor. iii. 6. How can that be, while we are under the power of moral death! He is a Spirit of holiness. Can he dwell in a soul that hath an unholy nature? Though he find men so at his first coming, would he not quickly be weary of his house, if it continued so? He comes to change our old nature, not to encourage it. What

fruits of the Spirit could appear, without the change
of the nature of the soil.

From all this it follows, that this new birth is necessary in every part of the soul. There is not a faculty
but is corrupted; and therefore not a faculty but must
be restored. Not a wheel, nor a pin in all this machine,
but is out of frame: not one part wherein sin and
Satan have not left the marks of their feet. "Their
mind and conscience is defiled." Tit. i. 15. It is clear
to a regenerate soul, that it is so, since by the ligh.
of grace he discerns impurity in every faculty. The
more knowledge of God he hath, the more he discovers his ignorance; the more love to God, the more
he finds and is ashamed of his enmity: and though in
our imperfect regeneration here, grace and sin are in
every part of the soul; yet every faculty is in part
renewed: and grace and sin lie not so confounded
together, but that the soul can distinguish them, and
be able to say, this is grace; this is part of the new
Adam; and this is sin, and part of the old Adam in me.

Because there was an universal depravation by the
fall, regeneration must answer it in every faculty,
otherwise it is not the birth of the man, but of one
part only. It is but a new piece, not a new creature.
This or that faculty may be said to be new, not the
soul, not the man. We are all over polluted by sin;
and we must be all over washed by the water of
grace. A whole sanctification is the proper fruit of
reconciliation. "The God of peace sanctify you
wholly." 1 Thess. v. 23. Reconciliation was of the
whole man; so was regeneration. Sin hath rooted
itself in every part; ignorance and error in our understandings; pride, and self-love, and enmity in our
wills; all must be subdued by grace, and the triumphs
of sin spoiled by a new birth.

It is so necessary, that even the dim eye of natural
reason, has been apprehensive of some need of it. And
therefore it is a wonder, that there should be a need

of pressing it upon men under the light of the gospel. Those doctrines that are purely intellectual, and supernatural, are not so easily apprehended by men, as having no footing in reason, whereby reason is rendered more unwilling to consent to them. But those doctrines that tend to the reformation of man, carry a greater conviction, as having some notion of a depravation, which gives them some countenance in the minds of men, though not in their affection. Men cannot conceive any notion of God's greatness, majesty and holiness, but they must also conceive something necessary to an enjoyment of him (wherein their felicity consists,) besides those natural principles which they find in themselves. Natural reason must needs assent to this, that there must be some other complexion of the soul, to fit us for a converse with so pure a majesty. The wiser sort of heathen did see themselves out of frame: the tumult and disorder in their faculties, could not but be sensible to them. They found the flights of their souls too weak for their vast desires: they acknowledged the wings of it to be clipt, and that they never came so out of the hands of God: that therefore there was a necessity of some restorative above the art of man, to complete the work. And I think I have read of one of them that should say, "That there could not be a reformation, unless God would take flesh." They had the work of the law written in their hearts: they knew such works were to be done: they found themselves unable to do them. Whence would follow, that there must be some other principle to enable them, than what they had by nature. To this purpose they invented their purgative virtues; and by those, and other means, hoped to arrive to the likeness of God. As they were sensible of their guilt, and therefore had sacrifices for the expiation of that, so they were sensible of their filth, and had their purifications and washings for the cleansing of that. Hence it was, that they admired those men that acted in a higher sphere of moral virtue and moderation than others. Some of them have acknowledged the malady, but despaired of a remedy, judging it above the power of nature to cure. Certainly that which the wisest heathen, in the darkness of nature, without knowledge either of law or gospel, have counted necessary; and since it is seconded by so plain a declaration of our Saviour, must be indisputably necessary. Plato in several places saith, that there was a certain divine principle in our minds at first: but that it was abolished, and God would again renew and form the soul with a kind of divinity.

How vain then are men, how inexcusably foolish, to neglect both the light of the gospel and that of reason too! that spend not one hour, one minute, in a serious consideration of it, and inquiry after it! that slight their own reason, as well as the express declaration of Jesus Christ! Oh that men were sensible of this, which is of so great importance to them.

CHAPTER II

Regeneration necessary to a gospel state —Contemplated in particular institutions —Incapable of gospel obedience without it. A corrupt nature cannot produce spiritual fruits —A new nature required in order to serve God spiritually, vitally, graciously, voluntarily, joyfully, sincerely, humbly, constantly.

REGENERATION is also necessary to a gospel state.

Nothing can exist in any state of being, without a proper form. That which hath not the form of a thing, is not a thing of the same species. He cannot be a man that wants the rational form of a man, a soul. And how can any man be a Christian without that which doth essentially constitute a Christian? We can no more be Christians, without a Christian nature, than a man can be a man without human nature. Grace only gives being to a Christian, and constitutes him so. " By the grace of God I am what I am : and his grace which was bestowed on me was not in vain, but I laboured more abundantly than they all." 1 Cor. xv. 10. Grace there, is meant of habitual grace, because he speaks of his labour as the fruit of it. In bodily life, brutes go beyond us ; in the vigour of senses, greatness of strength, temperance, natural affection. In reason, and moral virtues, many heathen have excelled us. There is something else then necessary for the constitution of a Christian, and that is Christ's living in him by a new forming of his soul by his Spirit. As the body lives by the soul, which distributes natural, vital, and animal spirits to every part of the body, for the performance of its several functions; so the soul lives by grace, which diffuseth its vigour to every part, the understanding, will, and affections.

There is no suitableness to a gospel state and government without it. In all changes of government in the world, there is a change in the whole state of affairs, in those that are the instruments of government, in the principles of those that submit to the government. After the fall of man, God set up a new mode of government. All judgment was committed to the Son. "For the Father judges no man, but hath committed all judgment to the Son." John v. 22. "And hath given him authority to execute judgment." Ver. 27. The whole administration of affairs is put into his hand ; not excluding the Father, who still gave out his orders in the government; wherefore he saith, " I can of myself do nothing; as I hear, I judge." Ver. 30. There must be therefore some agreement between the frame of this government, and the subjects of it. As there is a new Adam, a new covenant, a new priesthood, a new spirit; so there must be a new heart, new compacts, new offerings, new resolutions. New administrations, and old services, can no more be pieced together, than new cloth and old garments.

The gospel state of the church, is called a new heaven, and a new earth. Man is by the inclinations of his corrupt nature, obedient to the law of sin. There must be a cure and change of those inclinations, to make them tend to an observance of the orders of this new government, and an hearty observation of it. " Old things are passed away, behold all things are become new, and all things are of God," 2 Cor. v. 17, (so they were before,) but now in a new manner and frame ; and this is the reason rendered, why every man in Christ must be a new creature.

All the subjects of this government have been brought in by this way, not one excepted. Though God hath chosen some that he would bless for ever under this evangelical government, yet notwithstanding the purpose of God, they are in as great unfitness for this state, as the worst of men, till God, exerting his power, fashions them to be vessels of honour to himself. It is not God's choice of any man, which puts any man into a gospel state, without the operation of the Spirit, renewing the mind, and fitting him for it. All that were designed by God's eternal purpose, were to be brought in by this way of the new birth ; " God hath from the beginning chosen you to salvation, through sanctification of the Spirit, and belief of the truth." 2 Thess. ii. 13. And by this they were fortified against all those workings of the mystery of iniquity against the government of Christ and the state of the Gospel, which would be damnable and destructive to many : for he had spoken of that before, upon which occasion he brings this in. " A chosen generation, a holy nation, a peculiar people," are joined together. Peculiar they could not be, unless they had something of an intrinsic value in them above others, and a peculiar fitness for special service, and to offer spiritual sacrifices ; therefore called also " a royal priesthood."

The end of the particular institutions, of initiation or admission, under the two different administrations of this government, was to signify this : of circumcision under the law, and baptism under the Gospel. Both signified the corruption and filthiness of nature, and the necessity of the circumcision of the heart, and the purification of nature. Hence baptism is called "the laver of regeneration," Tit. iii. 5, many understanding it of baptism. Not that these did confer this new nature in a physical way, or that it was always conferred in the administration of them; but the necessity of having this, was always signified by them. Therefore one of the Jews, against the opinion of his countrymen, saith absolutely, it is a madness to think that those ceremonies, under their administration, were appointed only for the purification of the body without that of the soul. And in Rom. ii. 29, saith the apostle, "He is a Jew which is one inwardly, and circumcision is that of the heart in the Spirit." So that partaking of baptism, and being intrusted with the oracles of God, make a man no more a Christian, than circumcision, &c. did make a man a Jew. He only is a Christian that hath a Christian nature: the necessity of this nature was evidenced and signified both by the one, and by the other.

In every state there are duties to be performed, and privileges to be enjoyed. So likewise in the gospel state. Without a new birth, we cannot perform the one, or be capable of the other.

There can be no preparation to any service without it. Man's soul at first, could make a spiritual music to God, till the flesh disordered the strings: and no music can be made, till the Spirit puts the instrument in tune again. In Jesus Christ we are created to good works: therefore no preparation can be before the new creation, no more than there was a preparation in the matter, without form and void, to become a world. What evangelical duties can be performed without an evangelical impression, without the forming of Christ, and the doctrine of Christ in the heart; not only in the notion, but the operative and penetrating power of it? The heart must be first moulded, and cast into the frame of the doctrine of the Gospel, before it can obey it : " But ye have obeyed from the heart, that form of doctrine which was delivered unto you;" or, unto which you were delivered. Rom. vi. 17. The mould wherein a thing is cast, makes it fit for the operation for which it is intended. The ship that wants any material thing in its make, cannot sail well, will not obey the direction of the pilot : and he that wants grace, will be carried away with the breath of every sin and temptation. All the motions produced naturally in ways of duty by other principles, cannot make an aptitude to divine services, no more than a thousand times flinging up a stone into the air, can produce any natural fitness in it for such an elevation. Where should we have any preparation? It cannot be from Adam; he died a spiritual death by his sin, and had no natural fitness for any spiritual service ; and therefore cannot convey by nature more to his posterity than what he had by nature. What grace he had afterwards, was bestowed upon his person, not upon the nature which was to be transmitted to his posterity.

Therefore we cannot perform any evangelical service without a new nature. If we have no natural preparation, we can have no natural action. The law must be written in our hearts, before it be formed into the life : " I will put my law in their inward parts, and write it in their hearts." Jer. xxxi. 33, 34. It is then, and then only, that we have a practical and affectionate knowledge of God : " and they shall know me from the least unto the greatest." Restoration to a supernatural life, must be, before there can be supernatural actions; a just nature, before a just walk; as Hosea xiv. 9. " The just shall walk in them ;" that is, in the ways of God. The motion of the creature, is not the cause, but the effect of life : the evangelical service is not the cause of righteousness, but the effect. We cannot walk in one commandment of God, till the law be written in our inward parts. Those that have not a new heart, cannot walk in God's statutes. We can never answer the terms of the covenant, without a new nature. For, no act can transcend the principle of it. There is a certainty in this rule; that the elevation of an inferior nature to the acts of a superior nature, cannot be, without some inward participation of that superior nature. The operation of every thing, follows the nature of the thing. A beast cannot act like a man, without partaking of the nature of a man; nor a man act like an angel, without partaking of the angelical nature. How then can a man act divinely, without a participation of the divine nature? Duties of a supernatural strain, as evangelic duties are, require a supernatural frame of spirit. Nothing can exceed the bounds of its nature; for then it would exceed itself in acting. Whatsoever service therefore doth proceed from mere nature, cannot amount to a gospel service, because it comes not from a gospel principle. We cannot believe without a habit of faith, nor love without a habit of love: for this alone renders us able to perform such acts. Justification is necessary to our state, as well as regeneration: but regeneration seems to be more necessary to our duties than the former; this principally to the performance of them; the other to the acceptance of them.

The nature doth always tincture the fruit of it. Our Saviour, by his interrogation, implies an impossibility, that those that are evil, should speak good things. "O generation of vipers, how can you, being evil, speak good things? for out of the abundance of the heart, the mouth speaketh." Matt. xii. 34. The very hissings of a viper, proceed from the malice of its nature. As the root is, so is all the fruit. From one seed many grains arise, yet all partake of the nature of that seed. Streams partake of the quality of the fountain. If the seed, root, and fountain be good, so is whatsoever springs from them. There is not one righteous man by nature, neither Jew nor Gentile, all

are concluded under sin. " There is none righteous,
no, not one; none that understands and seeks God,"
&c. Rom. iii. 10. He adds "not one," twice; he ex-
empts none: not one righteous by nature; not one
righteous action by nature: none that doth good, no,
not one. He applies it to all mankind. A poisonous
nature can produce nothing but poisonous fruit. Our
actions smell as rank as nature itself. Whatsoever
riseth from thence, though never so specious, and well
coloured, is evil, and unprofitable. If therefore we
would produce good fruit, we must have a new root,
seed and spring. Our sour nature must be changed
into a sweetness and purity. If the vine be empty,
the fruit will be so too. " Ephraim is an empty vine;
he brings forth fruit to himself," or equal to himself.
Hosea x. 1. Unless the tree be good, the fruit can
never be generous. " Neither can a corrupt tree
bring forth good fruit." Matt. vii. 17, 18. We must
have the Spirit, before we can bring forth the fruits
of the Spirit. All good services are related to this,
as effects, to their cause: so that what a man doth by
an act of reason, and natural conscience, and good
education, if his understanding, and conscience, remain wholly under their natural pollution, the service
is not good, because the soul is corrupt: much less
are those services good, which are the fruit only of
humour. How the soul can be habitually sinful, and
yet the acts flowing from it, be good, is not easily
conceivable; it is against the stream of natural observation. It is true indeed, that a man that is habituated
to one kind of sin, may do an action that receives no
tincture from that particular habit, because it doth
not proceed from it: as a drunkard may give alms;
his giving alms hath no infection inherent from that
particular habit of drunkenness; but from the nature,
which is wholly corrupt, it hath: who can bring a
clean thing out of an unclean? not one. Who can
bring a clean service out of an impure heart? Not
one man in the world. We cannot therefore perform

any evangelical service, if those foundations be considered.

Not spiritually, because we are flesh. God must be worshipped in spirit: in a spiritual manner, with spiritual frames. The apostle speaks of walking in the Spirit; and praying in the Holy Ghost. None can act spiritually, but those that are born of the Spirit; and no action is spiritual, but what proceeds from a renewed principle. The most glittering and refined flesh, is but flesh in a higher sphere of flesh: therefore whatsoever springs up from that principle, is fleshly, upon the former foundation, that nothing can rise higher than its nature. You may as well expect to gather grapes of thorns, as spiritual duties from carnal hearts. "Do men gather grapes of thorns, or figs of thistles?" Matt. vii. 16. If a natural man cannot receive, and cannot know the things of God, because they are spiritually discerned, how should he perform the duties belonging to God, since they are spiritually to be performed? We are naturally more averse to motions upon our wills, than to the illuminations of our minds; an appetite for knowledge, and a flight from God, being both the fruits of Adam's fall, who was both curious to know, as God, and fearing to approach to God after his fall. There may be some services in natural men, which may look like spiritual; but in the principle they are not so. Many acts are done by irrational creatures, which look like rational acts. As the order among bees, like the acts of statesmen, regulating a commonwealth; their carrying gravel in their fangs, to poise them in a storm, and hinder them from being carried away by the violence of the wind; yet these are not rational acts, because they proceed not from reason, but from a rational instinct put into them by God, the supreme Governor. So that as no action of an ape, though like the action of a man, can be said to be a human act; so no action of an unregenerate man, though like a spiritual action, can be called spiritual, because it proceeds not from a spiritual principle, but from a contrary one paramount in him. And all actions have their true denomination from the principle whence they flow. They may be fruits of morality, and fruits of conscience, but not spiritual fruits which God requires.

Well then: we must be first built up a spiritual house, we must be a priesthood, before we can offer spiritual sacrifice. We must have the powerful operation of the Holy Ghost in us, before we can have the influence of the Holy Ghost upon our services. In all human acts, we should act as rational creatures: in all religious acts, as spiritual creatures. Now as a man cannot act rationally, without reason; so neither can we act spiritually, without a divine Spirit in us. We are indeed to serve God, and worship him as men: therefore rational acts are due to God, in worship, and we are constituted in the rank of rational beings to that purpose. But since our minds are defiled, they must be purified; since our understandings are darkened, they must be enlightened. There must be a grace infused, a lamp set up, a spiritual awakening, and invigorating our reasons and wills, before we can worship God, as God, in a spiritual manner.

We cannot perform any evangelical service, vitally, because we are dead. Our services must be living services, if in anywise they be suitable to a living God. The apostle wishes us "to present our bodies a living sacrifice." Rom. xii. 1. He doth not mean only our bodies, consisting of flesh and bones, or a natural life; but he names the body, as being the instrument of motion and service, a part for the whole. Present yourselves as a sacrifice consecrated to God, and living to him, and as living by him.

Upon the loss of original righteousness, another form or principle was introduced, called in Scripture, flesh, and a body of death. Hence, by nature we are said to be dead; and all our works before repentance, are dead works. And these works have no true beauty in them, with whatsoever gloss they may appear to a natural eye. A dead body may have something of the features and beauty of a living; but it is but the beauty of a carcass, not of a man. A statue, by the stone-cutter's art, and the painter's skill, may be made very comely; yet it is but a statue still; where is the life? Such services are but the works of art, as flowers painted on a wall, with curious colours; but where is the vegetative principle. Since man therefore is spiritually dead, he cannot perform a living service. As a natural death doth incapacitate for natural actions; so a spiritual death must incapacitate for spiritual actions: otherwise in what sense can it be called a death, if a man in a state of nature were as capable of performing spiritual actions, as one in a state of grace? No vital act can be exercised without a vital principle. As Adam could not stir to perform any action, though his body was framed and perfected, till God breathed into him a living soul; so neither can we stir spiritually, till God breathe into us a living grace. Spiritual motions can no more be without a spiritual life, than bodily motions can be without an enlivening soul. The living, the living, they shall praise thee: and Psa. xxx. 18. "Quicken us and we will call upon thy name." There can be no living praise, nor any living prayer, without a renewed heart. If it be one effect of the blood of Christ, "to purge our consciences from dead works to serve the living God," as Heb. ix. 14; then it is clear, that till our consciences are purged from dead works, we cannot serve the living God: for what suitableness can there be between a living God, and dead services? Is a putrefied carcass a fit present for a king? or a man full of loathsome disease, fit to serve in a prince's chamber? Our best services, without a new nature, though they may appear varnished and glittering to man, yet in the sight of God, have no life, no substance, but are an abomination, because coming from a dead and rotten heart.

Well then, we must be born again: it is not a dead

nature, nor a dead faith, can produce living fruit for God. We may as well read without eyes, walk without legs, act without life, as perform any service to God without a new nature. No, we cannot perform the least: a dead man can no more move his finger, than his whole body.

Not graciously, because we are corrupt. By the same reason that we are to speak with grace, and to sing with grace in our hearts to the Lord; we are to do every other duty with an exercise of grace to God: and without grace our praises are but howlings, our prayers but howlings, as the Scripture terms them; " They have not cried to me with their hearts, when they howled upon their beds." Hosea vii. 14.. How can there be an exercise of that which is not? The skill of the musician cannot discover itself, till the instrument be made tunable. The heart must be strung with grace by the Spirit, before that Spirit can touch the strings, to make harmony to God in a gospel service. Our tempers must be changed, our hearts fitted, before we can make melody to God. The principal beauty and glory of a duty, lie in the internal workings of the heart: and how can that heart work graciously, that hath nothing of God, and his grace in it? It is said, folly is bound up in the heart of a child. So is corruption like poison in the heart of a man. It is entered into the very composition of us. A law of sin is predominant in a natural man, which doth influence all his actions; and all his services are regulated by it: for he hath no other law in his mind, to check the motions of it, and to scent his duties, whereby they may carry a pleasing savour to God. The gift of prophecy, the understanding of mysteries, the depth of knowledge, the removing mountains, bestowing alms, dying for religion, are brave and noble acts; but without charity (love to God,) without which no other grace can work, all these profit nothing. There is a moral goodness in feeding the poor; but no gracious goodness without charity. A little of this, would make those as a diamond doth gold, wherein it is set, more valuable. If all those profit nothing, without this grace of charity, they would profit much with it. How doth grace alter the very nature of services! Those acts which are sensitive in a brute, were he transformed into a man, and endued with reason, would become rational. Those actions which are but moral in a mere man, when changed into a Christian, become evangelical: they would be of another nature, and another value.

Well then, look after the new birth, since it is so necessary. There cannot be gracious practice, without gracious principle. Can any thing fly to heaven without wings? We are to walk as Christ walked: how can we do it without a principle akin to that which Christ had? We are bound to act from a principle of righteousness. Adam was, and his posterity are; and should we not look after that which is so necessary a perfection, requisite for our services? No doubt but the devil could find matter enough for prayer, and from the excellency of his knowledge, frame rare strains (as some word it:) but would it be a service which came from such a nature? As long as we are allied to him in our nature, our services will be of as little value. He transforms himself into an angel of light, but is still a devil; and many men do so in their religious acts, yet still remain unregenerate.

We cannot perform spiritual services freely, and voluntarily, because we are at enmity. A natural man's services are forced, not free. The aversion of our natures to God, is as strong as their inclination to evil. We have no fervent desires to love God; and therefore no desires to do any thing out of affection to him. When sensual habits are planted in the soul, there is an enmity to God in the mind: it will not be subject to the law of God: and whilst that habit sways, it cannot. This inclination to sin, and consequently aversion to good, is incorporated in nature, like blackness in a negro, or spots in a leopard; they are accustomed to sin, and cannot do good. There is no agreeableness between God and man's soul, whilst there is a friendship between the heart and sin: he affects the one, and is disgusted with the other: one is his pleasure, the other his trouble. He hath no will, no heart to come to God in any service; and when he doth, he is rather dragged, than sweetly drawn. The things of God are against the beut of a natural heart: there is nothing so irksome as the most spiritual service. When men engage in them, they row against the stream of nature itself. There must therefore be something of a contrary efficacy to overpower this violent tide; a law of grace to renew the mind, and turn the motions of the will to another channel. Restraining grace may for a while stop the current, but not turn and change the natural course. A carnal mind conceives the things of God, and his spiritnal service to be foolishness; and therefore condemns them. The eye of the mind must be opened, to discern the wisdom of God in them, before he can love them. The heart should be lifted up in the evangelical ways of God. Can mere flesh be thus? Force can never change nature. You may hurl lead up into the air, but it will never ascend of itself, while it is lead, unless it be rarified into air or fire. Keep up iron many years in the air, by the force of a loadstone, it will retain its tendency to fall to the earth, if the obstacle be removed: the natural gravity is suspended, nor altered. Till the nature of the will be altered, it can never move freely to any duty. There must be a power to will, before there is a will to do; as Phil. ii. 18; "It is God which works in you both to will and to do." A supernatural renewing grace must expel corrupt habits from the will, and reduce it to its true object. When faith is planted, it brings love to work by: when the soul is renewed, there is an harmony between God and the heart, between the mind and the word, between the will and the duty: when the appetite, and true taste of the soul, is restored in regeneration, then spring up strong desires to apply itself to every holy service. The sincere milk of the word is frequently desired, after it is spiritually tasted. 1 Peter ii. 2, 3.

Well then, there must be a change in us, or in the law. The law is spiritual, man is carnal; the law can have no friendship for man, nor man any friendship for the law in this state, since their natures are so contrary. What the law commands, is disgustful to the flesh; what the flesh desires, is displeasing to the law. There must then be a change; the law must become carnal, or man become spiritual, before any agreement can be between them. Where do you think this change must take place? It can never be in the law; therefore it must be in man. The wound in our wills must be cured; the tide of nature, that never carries us to God, must be turned, and altered by a stream of grace, to move us to him and his service. Man hath been a slave to his lust by the loss of grace, and is never like to be restored to his liberty in the service of God, till he be re-possessed of that grace, the loss of which brought him into slavery. The Gospel is a law of liberty. A servile spirit doth not suit a free law, neither is it a fit frame for an evangelical service.

We can never perform spiritual services with delight, because we are alienated. This we are to do. Paul delighted in the law of God; and the law was the delight of David: his whole pleasure ran in this channel. Now because of that aversion to God, there is no will and freedom in his service; much less can there be a delight. A corrupt nature can have no divine strains: a diseased man hath no delight in his own acts; his distemper makes his motion unpleasant to him. Things that are not natural, can never be delightful. There is a mighty distance between spiritual duties, and a carnal heart. Things out of their

place can never be at rest.   Sin is as much a natural
man's element, as water to a fish, or air to a bird. If
he be stopped in the ways of the flesh, he is restless
till he return.   He may indeed have some delight
sometimes in a service; not as it respects God as the
object, or God as the end : there is no such friendship
in a natural man's heart to him ; but as there is an
agreement between a service, and some carnal end he
performs it for.   His delight is not terminated in the
service, but in self-love, self-interest, or some external
reward; anchored in it by some hopes of carnal advantage ; not springing from a living love, or a gracious
affection to God.   He hath no knowledge of God ; and
therefore can have no delight in God, or in his service.
It is impossible we can come before him without pleasure and delight, if we know how amiable he is in his
person, and how gracious in his nature : but we naturally think God a hard master.   And man having no
delight in God, can have none in those means which
lead him to God, and as they are appointed to bring
God and his soul together.   He hath wrong notions
of duties, looks upon them as drudgeries, not as advantages : " Ye said, Behold what a weariness it is," &c.
Malachi i. 13.   Without a change of nature, we cannot desire communion with God; and therefore cannot
delight in the means of it.   We can never be in a holy
extasy, without this inward principle, to make the
Gospel services connatural to us.   This alone makes
high impressions upon the soul.   It is the law within
our hearts, which alone makes us delight to do his will,
" Thy law is within my heart." Psalm xl. 8.   He had
a natural affection to it, and then a high delight in it.
It made our Saviour delight to do his work : and it
was the inward man of the heart, wherein the apostle's
delight in the law was placed.   Unless we have a
divine impression of God upon us, we cannot hear his
word with any joy in it; as our Saviour saith, " Ye
therefore hear them not," that is, the words of God,
"because ye are not of God." John viii. 47.   Unless

we have God's light, and his truth, sent forth into us, we can never make God our exceeding joy, or go to his altar with such a frame.

Well then: there is a necessity of the new nature, to have a warm frame of heart in evangelical duties. What is connatural to us, is alone delightful. So much of weariness and bondage we have in any holy service, so much of a legal frame; so much of love and delight, so much we have of a new covenant grace. A spirit of adoption, and regeneration alone can make us delight to come to our Father and to cry Abba, before him.

Without regeneration, we cannot perform evangelical duties sincerely, because we are depraved, and in our best estate vanity. God is a Spirit, and therefore must be worshipped in spirit. God is truth, and therefore must be worshipped in truth. Without a new nature we cannot worship God in truth. The old nature is in itself a lie, a mere falsity, and contrary to that nature God created. It was first introduced by a lie of the devil (ye shall be as gods knowing good and evil;) and thereupon a fancy that God lied in his command. How can we serve God with this nature, which had nothing but a lie for its foundation; a lie of the devil, a lie in our fancy? Therefore our old nature is no better thon a lie. How can we serve God with this nature which is quite another thing from that of his framing? Man in his fall is a liar, "let God be true, and every man a liar;" Rom. iii. 4, a covenant breaker, that kept not his faith with God. God, in respect of truth, and man, in respect of lying, are set in opposition by the apostle there. No man, but would slight and scorn that service from another, which he knew to be a lying service in the very frame of it. There can be no truth in any service which is founded only upon an old nature, and performed by one that is actuated by the father of lies: and so is every unregenerate man, every child of disobedience.

No sincerity can be without a new nature, because

there are no divine motives which should sway the soul. Most services of natural men have such corrupt springs, so unsuitable to that raised temper men should have in dealing with God, that they produce sacrifices not fit to be offered to an earthly governor. "If ye offer the blind for sacrifice, is it not evil, &c. offer it now unto thy governor, will he be pleased with thee?" Mal. i. 8. Had they had divine motives, they had never brought such sickly services. What was not fit for themselves, they thought fit for God. Did but princes know what motives many had in their services, they would with as much scorn reject them, as they do ignorantly receive them with affection. But it is otherwise with God, who knows all the springs and wards in that lock of the heart of his own framing. Do not most services take their rise from custom, or from an outward religious education barely; or at best from natural conscience; which though it be all in a man, which takes God's part, yet it is flesh, and defiled? And what pure vapours can be expected from a lake of Sodom? "To them that are defiled, and unbelieving, nothing is pure; but even their mind and conscience is defiled." Tit. i 15. The mind, which is the repository of natural light; and the conscience, which is the advocate of natural light, and applies it upon particular occasion, are defiled, and that in every unbelieving person. Can the motives which conscience takes from a dark and defiled principle, as the mind is, be divine? It is fear of death, wrath, and judgment, which it mostly applies. These are the motives of defilement. Fear is the natural consequence of pollution: without sin and corruption, we never should have had any fear of hell. That cannot be gracious, which springs naturally from the commission of sin; and can this be divine? Were there no punishment feared, there would be no duty performed. Conscience hath naturally no basis to stand upon, but this. What is the principle of his fear? self. It is not therefore obedience to God, but self preservation, sways a man. Fear is but a servile disposition; and therefore cannot make a service good. All such extrinsic motives which arise not from a new life, are no more divine, than the weights of a clock may be said to have life, because they set the wheels running. The same action may be done by several persons, upon different principles and motives; for which one may be rewarded, the other not, as Matthew x. 41, 42: "He that receives a righteous man, in the name of a righteous man, shall receive a righteous man's reward; and whosoever shall give unto one of these little ones a cup of cold water only, in the name of a disciple, he shall in no wise lose his reward." One may receive a member of Christ, out of respect to Christ, and the relation the person hath to him. Another may receive the same person out of a common principle of humanity. The action is the same; the good redounding to the object, is the same: nay, it may be greater in him that acts from a commiseration of him, as a man, than a cup of cold water from the other, because his ability is greater; but the inward respect to the object is different. One respects him as a man of the same nature with himself in misery; the other respects him as a member of Christ in misery. One respects him as a man, the other as a righteous man. The principle is different; one relieves him out of a natural compassion, common to a heathen with him; the other out of a Christian affection to his Head. The actions are therefore different, because of their motives: one is rewardable, and promised to be rewarded; the other not: one may be from grace, the other from nature. I do not say, it always is, unless there be a constant tenor of such motives in our actions: for a natural man, under the preaching of the Gospel, may do such a thing out of a present and transient respect to Christ, of whom he hears so often and hath some presumption to be saved by him; but it is not his constant frame.

Therefore from hence results a necessity of the

alteration of the frame of our souls, to furnish us with divine and heavenly motives for our actions. A man may do a thing by nature, from a good principle, a principle of common honesty, good in its kind, but not evangelically good, without a renewed affection to God. "If you love me, keep my commandments." John xiv. 15. Keep what I command you, out of affection to me. "Where the imagination of the heart is evil, and only evil, and that continually," Genesis vi. 5, all the service a man in that state performs, riseth from this spring, and hath some infectious imagination in it, highly abominable to God. Either wrong notions of God in it, or wrong notions of the duty, or corrupt motives, something or other of the evil imagination of the heart, mixes itself with it.

Without a renewed nature, as there are no divine motives, so there can be no divine ends. We are bound to refer our natural actions, much more our religious services, to the glory of God. The end is the moral principle of every action. It is that which confers a goodness or badness upon the service: "If the eye be evil, the whole body is full of darkness." Luke xi. 34. This is commonly understood of a man's aim. If the intention be evil, there is nothing but darkness in the whole service. The perfection of every thing consists in answering the end for which it was framed: that which was the first end of our framing, ought to be the end of our acting, viz. the glory of God. But man hath taken himself off from this end, and hath been fond of making himself his chief good, and ultimate end. Men naturally have corrupt ends in good duties. Pride is the cause of some men's virtue: and they are spiritually vicious, in avoiding crimes, because they intrench too much upon their reputation. The Pharisees made their devotion contribute to their ambition, "They pray to be seen of men." Matt. vi. 5. "But all their works they do to be seen of men." Matt. xxiii. 5. There was not one work wherein they had not respect to this.

Their works might well be called the works of the devil, whose main business it was to set up pride and self. All their pretences of devotion to God, were but the adoration of some golden image. Have not many in their splendid actions, the same end with brutes, the satisfaction of the sensitive part, covetousness, pride, emulation, sense of honour, qualities perceivable in the very brutes, as the end of some of their actions? The acting for a sensitive end, is not suitable to a rational, much less can it be the end of a gracious creature. Have not men sinful ends in their religious services, in their prayers to God, in their acknowledgment of God? The devil could intreat our Saviour's leave to go into the herd of swine. Was this a prayer, though directed to Christ, when his end was to destroy, and satisfy his malice in it? At best, a man without grace, is like a picture in a room, which eyes all, and hath no more respect to a prince, than his attendants. A natural man's respect to God, is but equal to a respect to all his other worldly concerns. Indeed it were well if it were so. He parcels out one part for God, one part for himself, and one part for the world; but God hath the least share; or at best, no more than the rest. And truly, as a picture cannot give a greater respect, to fix its eyes more upon a prince than a peasant, because it hath no life; so neither can a natural man, pay a supreme respect to God in his service, without a spiritual life. There is a necessity then of removing those depraved ends, that man may answer the true end of his creation. The principles then upon which such ends do grow, contrary to the will of God, must be rooted out, that the soul may move purely to God in every service. We are come short of the glory of God, "All have sinned, and come short of the glory of God." Romans iii. 23; short of aiming at it, short of his approbation of our acts. Being thus come short, our ends cannot rise higher than the frame of our soul. Grace, grace only can advance our wills to those supernatural ends for which they were first framed. We can never aim at the glory of God, till we have an affection to him; we can never honour him supremely, whom we do not supremely love. An affection to God can never be had, till the nature wherein the aversion is placed, be changed into another frame. We are to glorify God, as God: how can we do this, without the knowledge of him? How can we know him, but by the gospel, wherein he discovers himself? How can we have right conceptions of the gospel, till gospel impressions be made upon us? How can we act for the glory of God, to whom naturally we are enemies? There are none of us born with a spiritual love to God. There must then be an alteration of the end and aim in us; our actions cannot else be good, though ordered by God himself. God employs Satan in some things; as in afflicting Job: but is his performance good? No: because his end is not the same with God's. He acts out of malice, what God commands out of sovereignty, and for gracious designs. Our end without it, is not the same with the end of the action: for moral acts tend to God's glory, though the agent hath no such intention. So the action may be good in itself, but not good in the actor, because he wants a due end.

Well then, those actions only can be said to be evangelical, when the great end of God's glory, which was his end both in creation and redemption, hath a moral influence upon every service; when we have the same end in our redeemed services, as God had in his redeeming love.

We cannot without regeneration perform gospel duties humbly, because of natural stoutness and hardness. Evangelical duties must be performed with humility. Self denial is the chief gospel lesson, and is to run through the veins of every service. Therefore God speaks of giving a heart of flesh, in gospel times, " I will take the stony heart out of their flesh, and give them a heart of flesh, that they may walk in my statutes, and keep my ordinances, and do them."

Ezek. xi. 19. Gospel duties require a pliableness and tenderness of heart. Adam's overvaluing himself, and swelling with designs of being like God, brought an incapacity upon himself of serving his Creator. And man ever since is too aspiring, and has too good an opinion of himself, to perform duties in an evangelical strain, with that contrition in himself, which the gospel requires. Our swelling and admiring thoughts of our own natural righteousness, hinder Christ from saving us, and ourselves from serving him. There must be an humble, and melting, and self-denying frame. The angels are said to cover their faces before God, as having nothing to glory in of their own. And the chief design of the Gospel, is to beat down all glorying in ourselves, " that no flesh should glory in his presence; let him that glorieth, glory in the Lord." 1 Cor. i. 29, 31. And indeed it humbles us no more, than what, upon due consideration, will appear very necessary. Nature then must be changed, before pride be rooted out; old things must pass away, that God may be all in all in the creature. We cannot without a new nature, make a true estimate of ourselves, and lie as vile and base in the presence of God. A stone, with all the hammering cannot be made soft. Beat it into several pieces; you may sever the continuity of its parts, but not master its hardness; every piece of it will retain the hardness nature must be changed, before it be fit for those of its nature. So it is with a heart of stone: the services which require melting, humble and admiring frames. There is a necessity of a residing grace, like fire, to keep the soul in a melting temper.

Without a new nature, we cannot perform gospel services constantly, because of our natural levity. Where the nature is flesh, the heart minds the things of the flesh. The mind thus habituated, will not be long employed about the things of the Spirit. There is a natural levity in man's nature. Do not many seem to begin in the Spirit, and end in the flesh? seem to arise to heaven, and quickly fall down to earth? Do not our very promises vanish with the next wind of temptation; and like sparks, expire as soon as they be born, unless grace be in the heart to keep them alive? The Israelites are accused of not having a heart steadfast with God. " Their heart was not right with him, neither were they steadfast in his covenant." Psa. lxxviii. 37. Are our natures better than theirs? Do we not all lie under the same charge; so uncertain naturally, about divine things, as if there were nothing but wind in our computation? Nothing can be kept up in motion against its nature, but by force. A top hath no inward principle of motion, but is moved by some outward force: when that is removed, the motion languisheth. Any motion that depends only upon outward wires, expires upon the breaking of them. When external motives, which spurred men on to this or that service, cease, the service dies of course, because the spring of the motion fails. If fear of hell, terrors of death, some pressing calamity, be the spring of any duty; when these are removed, there will be no more regard to the duty they engendered. But what is natural, is constant, because the spring always remains. Interest changeth, conscience is various; and therefore the operations arising from thence, will partake of the uncertainty of them. Stony ground may bring forth blades; but for want of root they will quickly wither. A man may mount high in religion, by the mixture of some religious passion, as meteors in the air, which by reason of the gross and earthy parts in them, will not continue in their station. There is no being without, stable, but God, and no principle stable within, but grace. "It is a good thing that the heart be established with grace." Heb. xiii. 9. Whatsoever service is undertaken upon changeable motives, is as changeable as the bottom upon which it stands. If credit, slavish fear of God, worldly interest, inspire us with some seemingly holy resolutions, they will all fly away upon the first removal of those props. There is therefore a necessity of a change of nature and disposition. Where there is no approbation of things that are excellent, there can be no constant operation about them. All action about an object, continues according to the affection to it, and delight in it. We shall then be filled with the fruits of righteousness, to the glory of God, when we have a sincere approbation of the excellency of them; first, " approve things that are excellent;" and then follows, " without offence, till the day of Christ." Phil. i. 10, 11. A stately profession can no more hold out against the floods of temptation, than a beautiful building can stand against the winds without a good foundation under ground. It is the Spirit of the Lord within, as well as without, can alone maintain the standard against temptation.

Well then, upon the whole, there is a necessity of regeneration, for the performance of gospel duties. We cannot else perform them spiritually; because we are flesh; nor vitally, because we are dead; nor graciously, because we are corrupt; nor voluntarily, because we are at enmity; nor delightfully, because we are alienated; nor sincerely, because we are falsity; nor humbly, because of our stoutness; nor constantly, because of our levity: our natures must be changed in all these respects, before we can be fit for any gospel service.

CHAPTER III

Regeneration necessary to friendship and union with God —
Necessary to Justification —To Adoption —To acceptable
services —To communion with God —To the communication
of divine blessings to the soul.

REGENERATION is necessary for the enjoyment of gospel privileges. We are not fit for God's delight, without it. That person who hath his love, must have his image. If ever God could love an old nature, which

he once hated, and delight in that which he once
loathed, he must divest himself of his immutability.
He never hated the person of any of his creatures, but
for unrighteousness. And upon the removal of this
cloud of separation between him and them, the beams
of his love break out in their former vigour. God's
love is not straitened, nor his kindness exhausted, no
more than his hand is shortened, or his ear grown
heavy, that he cannot hear? " But your iniquities have
separated between you, and your God: and your sins
have hid his face from you, that he will not hear."
Isa. lix. 1, 2.

What made the first separation? Was it not sin?
God told Adam before, what the issue would be, upon
his eating the forbidden fruit, " in the day that thou
eatest thereof, thou shalt surely die." Gen. ii. 17. It
is not a temporal death alone that is meant; for he
would then have died that day wherein he fell; the
word surely importing as much. And the punishment of a temporal death was pronounced afterwards,
" Dust thou art, and unto dust shalt thou return."
Gen. iii. 17. Thou shalt surely die; thy integrity and
righteousness will expire that very moment, and thou
shalt die in my just displeasure. It is a spiritual
death that is most properly meant. The punishment
of sin, is death. The chief part of this death is an
alienation from the life of God: that is not to have
God and the righteousness of God's image, living in
him; but to be impure, corrupt, a hater of God, and
servant of sin. Now from this punishment no man
can be freed, but by regeneration; the proper effect
whereof, is to love God, to know his name, to partake
of his holiness, to imitate his virtues. Man forfeited
all God's favour upon his fall, and can challenge
nothing of it.

What then can restore man to God's favour? Can
that which first deprived us of it? The cause of our
destruction can never be the means of our restoration.
Did the loss of Adam's integrity, make him unfit for

paradise, the garden of God, whence he was expelled, as a token of God's displeasure? And can the continuance of that loss, be a means to regain that love which banished us? It was a spiritual death. And is the carcass of a soul fit for God's complacency? There must be not only a satisfaction to his justice for the re-instating man into his favour: but a restoring of his image, by the Holy Ghost. It is as impossible the soul can be beautiful without life, and without holiness, as for a body to be beautiful without a good colour, and proportion of parts. Take away this, beauty must cease, and deformity succeed in the place. It is impossible therefore, that where sin remains in its full vigour, where there is nothing of an original integrity residing, but that the soul must be monstrous, vile, and deformed in the eyes of God. To make it therefore a fit object for God's favour, it is necessary to be beautified with a holy nature, and adorned with its due proportions and vigour. The righteousness of Israel must go forth as brightness; he must be called by a new name; that is a new nature: for what is a name without a nature? And then it should be *Hephzibah*, the Lord delights in thee. "The righteousness thereof shall go forth as brightness, and the glory thereof as a lamp that burneth." Isa. lxii. 1, 2, 3, 4. Righteousness is the glory of a soul, as well as of a church. "Gentiles shall see thy righteousness, and all kings thy glory. Thou shalt be called by a new name;" a new nature wrought by the word of God; "which the mouth of the Lord shall name." Then she should be in favour with God; "a crown of glory in the hand of the Lord, and a royal diadem in the hand of her God." Righteousness is the glory of a soul, and God's delight and complacency is the consequent of a righteous nature.

The elect themselves have no interest in God's favour of delight without it. This follows upon the former. God cannot love the very best of mankind, his own choice, with a love of complacency, without regeneration, without a righteous nature. There is a favour of intention and purpose before it: there is also an executive love in the very infusing the habits of grace, which is a supernatural favour, because there is both a purpose, and then an actual conferring a supernatural good. God is free, and may give his gifts how, and to whom he pleases. But an elect person, whilst he continues in a state of nature, is not simply beloved, though there be a purpose of love; because there is no gracious quality in him, which is the object of God's special favour. It is regeneration only which is the object of God's delight in us.

Hence will follow, that no privileges under heaven, without it, can bring us into God's favour. No, not if any man were related to Christ, according to the flesh. The apostle Paul would not think the better of himself for a fleshly relation to Christ, for being of the same country, descended of the Jewish nation. "Though we have known Christ after the flesh, yet henceforth know we him no more. Therefore if any man be in Christ, he is a new creature." 2 Cor. v. 16. Though it be an honour to be of the same descent with Christ, according to the flesh; to be of the same nation and country; yet this doth not make a man any more beloved of God. Nothing avails in Christ but a new creature. And our Saviour himself pronounceth it so. It was the highest privilege to be the mother of our Saviour, according to the flesh: yet this had been nothing, without her being born again of the Spirit; "Who is my mother, and who are my brethren? Behold my mother and my brethren," pointing to his disciples; "my mother and my brethren are these which hear the word of God, and do it." Luke viii. 21. Those that hear the word, that have the gracious effect of the word wrought in them by the Spirit, are equal to my mother and my brethren, and superior to any of my fleshly relations, if they be without it. There is a necessity of regeneration upon this account.

As there is no favour, so there is no union with God and Christ without it. Man hath some kind of natural union with all things in the world; he hath being with all creatures, rational faculties with angels, sense with animals, vegetation with plants. He wants only that with God, which would beautify all the rest. And this can only be by partaking of the image of God's holiness by a new birth. There must be a capability for this union on man's part. A superior and inferior nature may be united together: but never contrary natures. There must be some proportion between the subjects to be united, which proportion consists in a commensuration of one thing to another. What proportion is there between God and our souls? There can be none without a supernatural grace, infusing a pure nature. As we come out of the quarry of nature, rough and unpolished, we are not fit to be cemented with the corner-stone in the heavenly building; we must be first smoothed and altered by grace.

How can things be united to one another, which are already united to their contraries? Separation from one body must make way for union to another. Naturally we are united to the devil, as the head of the wicked world. We are by nature his members. Our understandings and wills were united with his in Adam, when Adam gave up his understanding and will to him: and ever since he works in the children of disobedience; working, and working in, as a united nature to him, and principle in him. It is necessary this union should be broken, before we can partake of the influence of another head. The diabolical nature and principle therefore, which we have got by sin, must be removed, and another nature, which is divine, must be restored before we can be united to Christ, and enjoy the benefits of union with him.

How can things of a contrary nature be united together? Can fire and water be united, a good angel and an impure devil? Can heaven and hell ever become friendly and compose one body? We are united to the first Adam by a likeness of nature : how can we be united to the second without a likeness to him from a new principle ? We are united to the first by a living soul; we must be united to the other by a quickening Spirit. We have nothing to do with the heavenly Adam, without bearing an heavenly image. We are earthly as in the first Adam; we must be heavenly to be in the second, because his nature is so. If we are his members, we must have the same nature, which was communicated to him by the Spirit of God, which is holiness. This nature must flow from the same principle ; otherwise it is not the same nature. An old nature cannot be joined to a new Adam : there must be one spirit in both; "He that is joined to the Lord is one spirit." 1 Cor. vi. 17. And if it were an union barely of affections, as some would only make it, it is not conceivable how it can be without a change of disposition. But since it is a union by indwelling of the same Spirit in both, it is less intelligible how it can be without an assimilation of our nature to the nature of Christ. " If any man hath not the Spirit of Christ, he is none of his." Rom. viii. 9. It can never be supposed the Spirit should unite a pure head and impure members. Such a union would make our blessed Saviour like Nebuchadnezzar's image; an head of gold, arms of silver, and feet of clay. Shall we loathe to have impure things about us ? and will the holy Jesus endure a loathsome, putrefying soul to be joined to him?

How can any thing be vitally united to another without life ? It is a vital union, by virtue of which believers are called Christ. " As all the members of that one body, being many, are one body, so also is Christ," 1 Cor. xi. 12; and is compared to the union of the members of a natural body, Rom. xii. 4, 5. Members have not only life in their head, but in themselves, because the soul, which is the life of the body, is not only in the head, but in all the parts of

the body, and exerciseth in every part its vital operations. The Spirit, therefore, which is the bond of
this union, communicates life to every member wherein he resides, as well as in the head. What man
would endure a dead body to be joined to him, though
it were the carcass of one he ever so dearly loved?
If a man were united to Christ, without regeneration,
Christ's body would be partly alive, partly dead, if
any one member of it had not a spiritual life. A dead
body and a living head; a member of Christ, with a
nature contrary to him, is an inconceivable paradox.
Did God ever design such a monstrous union for his
Son? Hence results

The necessity of regeneration; for without it there
can be no union with Christ.

There can be no justification without it. We are
not justified by an inherent righteousness; yet we
are not justified without it; we cannot be justified
by it, because it is not commensurate to the law, by
reason of its imperfection: we cannot be justified
without it, for it is not congruous to the wisdom and
holiness of God, to count a person righteous who
hath nothing of righteousness in him, and whose
nature is as corrupt as the worst of men. With what
respect to God's honour can it be expected that God
should pardon that man's sins whose will is not
changed, who still hath the same habit in his will to
commit sin, though he doth not at present exercise it?
It is very congruous in a moral way that the person
offending should retract his sin, and return to his
former affection. There is a distinction between
justification and regeneration, though they are never
asunder. Justification is relative; regeneration inter-
nally real. Union with Christ is the ground of both;
Christ is the meritorious cause of both. The Father
pronounceth the one; the Spirit works the other: it is
the Father's sentence, and the Spirit's work. The
relative and the real change are both at the same
time, "But ye are sanctified; but ye are justified,"

1 Cor. vi. 7: both go together. We are not justified before faith, because we are justified by it. Rom. v. 1. And faith is the vital principle whereby we live. "The life which I now live, I live by the faith of the Son of God." Gal. ii. 20. It is the root-grace, and contains the seeds of all other graces in it: it is habitually and seminally all other graces. So that, unless we be new born, no justification can be expected; no justification can be evidenced. God never pardons sin, but he subdues iniquity. "Who is a God like unto thee, that pardons iniquity? He will subdue our iniquities." Mich. vii. 18, 19. The conquest cannot be made, while the nature, the root of the rebellion remains. When he turns his compassion to us, he will turn away our hearts from iniquity. If a man were justified before he were regenerate, then he were righteous before he was alive: being in Christ, as free from condemnation, is always attended with a walking after the Spirit; and walking is not before living. Pardon would be unprofitable, unless he that were pardoned were made righteous inherently here, and had a right to, and hope of, a perfect righteousness hereafter. If righteousness were not imparted in this manner, it would be an argument a man were still under the law; which saith, "He that doeth them shall live in them;" which is impossible in a man that hath once sinned, though his sins are remitted. But it is clear that righteousness is imparted, since there is no man in the world, whose sins are pardoned, but finds some principle in him, whereby he is enabled to contest with sin more than he was before. Therefore do not deceive yourselves; there is no pardon without a righteous nature, though pardon be not given for it.

There is no adoption without regeneration. We can no more be God's sons, without spiritual regeneration, than we can be the sons and daughters of men without natural generation. Adoption is not a mere relation, without an inward form. The privilege and the image of the sons of God both go together. A state of adoption is never without a separation from defilement, "Come ye out from among them, be ye separate, and I will be a father unto you, and ye shall be my sons and daughters." 2 Cor. vi. 17, 18. The new name in adoption is never given, till the new creature be framed. "As many as are led by the Spirit, they are the sons of God." Rom. viii. 14; that is the signal mark, that they are led by the Spirit, therefore first enlivened by the Spirit. A child-like relation is never without a child-like nature. The same method God observes in declaring the members his sons, as he did in declaring the head his Son, which was "according to the Spirit of holiness, by the resurrection from the dead." So he declares believers to be his sons, by giving them a spirit of holiness, and by a resurrection from sin, and spiritual death. The devils may as well be adopted sons of God, as we, without a change of nature. To be the sons of the living God, was the great promise of the gospel prophesied of, "Ye are the sons of the living God." Hos. i. 10. How will it suit, a living God, and a dead son? God is not the God of the dead, but of the living. Our Saviour's argument for the immortality of the soul will evidence not only a resurrection, but a necessity of a spiritual life. What advantage is there in being the sons of a living God, if we had no more life in us, than his greatest enemies? Regeneration, as a spiritual act, gives us a likeness to God in our nature: adoption, as a legal act, gives us a right to an inheritance; both the great ends of the gospel, accompanying one another. No sonship without a new nature.

There is no acceptance of our services without it. We are not fit to perform any duty without it; and God will never accept any duty from us without it. In the first of Ephesians, election and regeneration are expressed by being holy; adoption and acceptance are linked together, "He hath chosen us that we should be holy, and without blame before him in love having predestinated us to the adoption of children : after follows " grace, wherein he hath made us accepted in the beloved." Ver. 4, 5, 6.   Our acceptance is only upon the account of Christ; but the acceptability is upon the account of grace.   Faith makes our persons and our duties acceptable; and Christ makes them both accepted.   Acceptability ariseth from grace, as damnation ariseth from sin.   God damns none, unless they be damnable : neither doth God accept any in Christ unless they be acceptable.   The papists, that plead for merit, acknowledge nothing of it before grace, but after grace, because then the services have a greater proportion to God, from the dignity of the person, they being acts of God's children, and wrought by his Spirit.   God can love nothing but himself, and what he finds of himself in the creature.   All services, without something of God's image and Spirit in them, are nothing.   As the product of a million of ciphers, though you still add to them, signifies nothing; but add one figure, a unit, the Spirit, grace, it will make the product to be many millions of high account with God.   All the signification depends upon the figure, which if absent, the rest would be nothing.   All moral perfections, without a new nature, are but ciphers in God's account, " Without faith it is impossible to please God." Heb. xi. 6.   Grace is only a good work, " He which hath begun a good work in you, will perform it till the day of Christ." Phil. i. 6; intimating, that their morality, and their natural wisdom, before their regeneration, were not good works in the sight of God.   They were good in their kind ; as a crab, may be said to be a good crab, but not a good pippin.   It is not good, unless it be fruit brought forth in Christ : neither is it ordained as good to the day of Christ, to appear glorious at the time of his triumph.   God looks into our services, whether the Spirit frames them, and Christ presents them : all that we do, must go through their hands, before they can reach God's heart. Acceptance can never be without a renewed nature. The services of the flesh cannot please God, " They that are in the flesh cannot please God," Rom. viii. 8. Their persons cannot, therefore their actions cannot, because they are the products of a nature at variance with him; a nature that is not, nor cannot be subject to his law. So that God must be displeased with his own spiritual law; yea, with his own holy nature, and change his judgment, and change his nature, before he can be pleased with fleshly services; for at the best, they are but empty appearances. The image of the devil, can never be grateful to God. Services flowing from nature, may seem in the outward form of them, to be as acceptable as the duties of a good man: but considering what a sink of impurity the heart is, from whence they proceed, they cannot be so. Good water is sweetest, and bad water most corrupt nearest the spring or fountain: although the streams may lose some of their corruption in their passage. A gracious man's duties are most pleasant to God, nearest the heart; a natural man's services are most distasteful, nearest the spring. When the heart is a good treasure, what comes from it, is regarded as a rich gift, because it comes from a valuable treasure. Hence it is, that a less work, coming from a pure and holy principle in a renewed man, is more acceptable to God, than a greater work, in respect of the external glorification of him in the good of mankind, coming from an impure principle in a natural man. As a cup of cold water given to a disciple, is more valuable than the gift of a prince, from another principle. In the one, God sees a conformity of affection with his holiness: in the other, only a conformity with his providence. One intends God's glory, and the other only acts it, proposing some other end to himself. And we are accustomed to value gifts, rather by the affection of the friend, than the quantity of the gift. Well then, consider it: without a new nature, all our services, though they should

amount to many millions in number, have no intrinsic
value in them with God. For where the nature is
displeasing, the actions flowing from that nature, can
never please him. He that turns away his ear from
hearing the law; that is, from a spiritual obedience to
the law, even his prayer is an abomination. It is
formed by a polluted soul.

There is no communion with God, without a renewed soul. God is incapable on his part, with the
honour of his law and holiness, to have communion
with such a creature. Man is incapable on his part,
because of the aversion rooted in his nature. What
way can there be to bring God and man together,
without this change of nature? What communion
can there be between a living God, and a dead heart?
God loathes sin, man loves it; God loves holiness, man
loathes it. How can these contrary affections meet
together in an amicable friendship? What communion
with so much disagreement in affections? In all
friendship there must be similitude of disposition.
Justification cannot bring us into communion with
God, without regeneration. It may free us from
punishment, discharge our sins; but not prepare us
for a converse wherein our chief happiness lies.
There must be some agreement, before there can be
a communion. Beasts and men agree not in a life of
reason; and therefore cannot converse together. God
and man agree not in a life of holiness; and therefore
can have no communion together. We are by sin,
alienated from the life of God; and therefore from his
fellowship. We must have his life restored to us,
before we can be restored to communion with him.

God can have no pleasure in such communion.
God took a delight in the creation, and rejoiced in his
work. Sin despoiled God of his rest. It can give
God no content, no satisfaction; for to be in the flesh,
is to be in that nature which was derived from Adam;
which brought the displeasure of God upon all mankind. Regeneration by the Spirit, restores the crea-

ture to such a state, wherein God may take pleasure in him; and strips him by degrees of that sin which spoiled his delight in the work of his hands; as it grows, communion is enlarged. God made man at first after his own image, that he might have communion with him. Since the loss of that, what fitness can there be for communion, till the restoration of that which God thought fit for his delight? Suppose that some one work of a natural man, may be good and pleasing to God, it will not argue a communion of God with the person: he may be pleased with the work, but not with the man; for all the goodness he hath, being in the act, and the act being transient, when that is past, his goodness is as the morning dew, vanished. He cannot be the object of God's delight, because he hath no habitual goodness in him. Now God being infinitely holy, can have no communion with that which he abominates: and he cannot have a fixed, and a delightful communion with that which he cannot confide in. It must be, therefore, such a nature as is produced, and preserved by his own Spirit. If the heavens are not clean in his sight, we must have a nature purer and cleaner than the heavens, before God can delightfully behold us, and pleasingly converse with us.

As God can have no pleasure in such communion, so man is contrary to it. Man, as he is by corruption, is at variance with God, and cannot but be at variance with him. An uncircumcised heart will not love God; or, at least, will not pay him such a proportion of love, and love of such a quality, as is due to him. For if the end of the circumcision of the heart, be to love the Lord with all our hearts, "And the Lord thy God will circumcise thy heart, to love the Lord thy God with all thy heart," Deut. xxx. 6; then, it will necessarily infer, that he whose heart is not circumcised, doth not love God with all his heart. Holiness and iniquity are so contrary, that no agreement can be made between them. God must deny his nature before he can deny his hatred of sin; and man must be stripped of his nature, before he can leave his affection to sin. It is equally impossible for wickedness to love holiness, and for purity to love pollution: there can be no fellowship with God, whilst we walk in darkness, and he is light.

Nay, man naturally resists all means of communion with God. It is the Spirit only which is the bond of union, and consequently the cause of communion: the Spirit can alone bring God and us together. Walking in the Spirit hinders us from fulfilling the lusts of the flesh, which makes us incapable of communion. "Walk in the Spirit, and ye shall not fulfil the lusts of the flesh." Gal. v. 16. But every man by nature, as well as the Jews, "resists the Holy Ghost." Acts vii. 51. And while this resistance of the great medium of it remains, this communion can never be: this resistance, therefore, must be removed, and there must be a divine stamp and impression upon our very nature to make it pliable. You see more and more the necessity of regeneration.

As there is no communion with God without it, so no communications of Christ to our souls can be relished and improved without it. All the communications of Christ relish of that fulness of grace which was in his person; and, therefore, cannot be relished by any principle but that of the same nature. Whenever Jesus Christ comes to bless us with the great blessings of his purchase, he "turns away our hearts from iniquity." Acts iii. 26.

CHAPTER IV

The connection of Regeneration with a state of glory—It forms a fitness and aptitude for it—Prepares for the duties of heaven, such as attendance on God, holy contemplation, love and praise—Prepares also for the rewards of heaven, such as perfect likeness to Christ, and fruition of God—Inferences from the discussion.

As regeneration is necessary to a gospel state, so it is to a state of glory. It seems to be typified by the strength and freshness of the Israelites when they entered into Canaan. Not a decrepid and infirm person set foot in the promised land: none of those that came out of Egypt, with an Egyptian nature, and desires for the garlic and onions thereof, with a suffering their old bondage, but dropped their carcasses in the wilderness, only the two spies, who had encouraged them against the seeming difficulties. None that retain only the old man, born in the house of bondage, but only a new regenerate creature, shall enter into the heavenly Canaan. Heaven is the inheritance of the sanctified, not of the unholy. "That they may receive an inheritance among them which are sanctified through faith that is in me." Acts xxvi. 18.

Regeneration is necessary in a way of aptitude and fitness for this state. A fitness in both subjects is necessary to the enjoyment of one another. Since, therefore, our happiness consists in an eternal fruition of God; and that, naturally, we are a mass of corruption; there must be such a change as to make an agreement with that God, whom to enjoy is our happiness. For all aptitude is a certain connection of the two terms, whereby they may touch and receive each other. We cannot enjoy God in his ordinances without an holy nature, much less in heaven. As we are under the condemnation of the law, by reason of our

guilt, so we are under an unfitness for heaven, by reason of our impurity.   We have a remote natural
capacity for it, as we are creatures endued with
rational faculties.   But we have a moral unfitness,
while we want a divine impression to make us suitable
to it.   Justification and adoption give us a right to
the inheritance; but regeneration gives us a "meet-
ness to be partakers of the inheritance of the saints in
light."   We are not meet for it while we are unholy
and while we are darkness, because it is an inheritance of saints, and an inheritance in light.   As the
body cannot be made glorious without a resurrection
from a natural death, so neither can the soul, which
is immortal, be made glorious without resurrection
from a spiritual death.   Our corruptible bodies cannot possess an incorruptible kingdom, unless made
like to the glorious body of Christ; much less our
souls, which are the chief subjects of communion with
him in heaven.   A depraved soul is as much unfit for
a purified heaven as a corruptible body is for an incorruptible glory.   Our Saviour ascended not into
heaven to take possession of his glory, till after his
resurrection from death; neither can we enter into
heaven till a resurrection from sin.   As Jesus Christ
became like unto us, that he might be a merciful and
faithful high priest for us; "it behoved him to be
made like unto his brethren," Heb. ii. 17; so it be-
hoves us to be made like unto him, that we may be
fit offerings in the hand of our high priest, to present
to God, for him to take pleasure in.   The father of
the prodigal forgave him at the first meeting after his
return: but before he admitted him into the pleasure
of his house, he took away his garments, and put
other robes upon him.   God is said, therefore, to work
us to this thing, that we may be fit to be clothed upon
with our heavenly house.   If God be happy in his
nature, man cannot be happy in a nature contrary to
him.   For we can never expect to enjoy a felicity in
such a nature, which if God himself had, he could

never be happy in himself. It is holiness in God which fits him to fill heaven and earth with the beams of his glory: and it is an holy nature in us which makes us fit to receive him. As without holiness God could not be glorious in himself, "Holy, holy, holy is the Lord of hosts; the whole earth is full of his glory," Isa. vi. 3; so, without holiness in our natures, we could not be glorious with God. We are no more fit for heaven in a state of nature, than a vile particle of earth is fit to become a star. In heaven there are duties to be done, and privileges to be enjoyed. The work cannot be done, the reward cannot be received, without a new nature. The glorifying God and enjoying him, is the glory of heaven. How can we do the one, or receive the other, without the change of our affections? Can God have a voluntary glory from his enemy? Or can his enemy delight in the enjoyment of him.

Regeneration and the new nature are necessary to the duty of heaven. Eternity cannot free us from duty. Some duties are essential to the relation of a creature: some result only from this or that state of the creature. The alteration in the state changeth the duty proper to that state: but no place, no state, can exempt a creature from those duties which are essential to him as a creature. It is impossible to conceive any relation, without some new debt, or service. From every change in relations in the world, there doth arise some new duty, which was not incumbent upon a man before. The relation which a regenerate man hath to God here, is the same which it is in heaven: but it is manifest there in a higher degree, and a choicer fruition. Thence therefore will arise, though not any new duty that we can conceive; yet fresher obligations to those services which are proper for that place. Without a change of nature, it is not possible for any man, were he admitted thither, to perform the duties of heaven. Holy work is troublesome to a natural man here; and the more heavenly it is in itself, the more disgustful to corrupt nature. What was in a little measure holy, was a drudgery upon earth: and what was in a greater measure holy, cannot be a satisfaction in heaven to an old frame. There are some natural motives to some duties here; and our indigency takes part with them, as in that of prayer: but those of a more elevated strain, as love, and praise, and admiration of God, our natures are more averse to. What duty can be performed without a will? It is concluded by most, that the happiness of heaven consists as much, if not more, in the frame of the will, than in that of the understanding. If the will be not new framed, what capacity is there to perform the service requisite to that happy state? We must first be made just here, before we can be made perfect above, " Spirits of just men made perfect." Heb. xii. 23. Just by an imputed righteousness, holy by an inherent righteousness, before they were transplanted to a state of perfection. Without a perfect frame, none can perform the choice duties of heaven: and without righteousness here, we cannot be made perfect there.

But what are the duties of heaven, that cannot be performed without a new nature? I answer, attendance on God; some kind of service which we cannot understand, in this state here below. The angels stand before God, and wait his commands; there is a pleasure of God which they do, " Ye ministers of his that do his pleasure." Psa. ciii. 21. There is a will of God done in heaven, as well as upon earth: there are acts of adoration performed by them. They cover their faces: they are commanded to worship the Lord Christ. Their holiness fits them for their attendance; therefore called the holy angels. It is against the nature of devils to perform such acts as those, which the holiness of angels fits them for. Glorified souls shall be as the angels of God in heaven, " But are as the angels of God in heaven." Matt. xxii. 30. Equal to angels in their state, as they are angels in heaven: equal to angels in their work, as they are angels of God, attending on God, and ministering unto him; though what that ministry shall be, is not easily known in the extent of it. Is it usual in this world, to take up a mean person, and bring him to an immediate attendance on a prince, without due preparation? God selects some out for an immediate attendance on him in heaven; but he sends his Spirit to be their tutor, to breed them up, and grace their deformed souls with beautiful features, that they may be meet to stand before him. When God calls any to do him service in a particular station in the world, he gives them another heart; so he did to Saul for the kingdom. Is there not much more necessity of it for an immediate service of God in heaven? A malefactor, by pardon, is in a capacity to come into the presence of a prince, and serve him at his table: but he is not in a fitness, till his noisome garments, be taken off. Can one that is neither pardoned nor purified; one with the guilt of rebellion upon him, and a nature of rebellion in him, be fit to stand before God?

Again, contemplation of God is a work in heaven. There shall be a perfect knowledge, therefore a delightful contemplation. The angels behold his face, and that always. The saints shall see him as he is. It is not a stupid sight, but a gazing upon the face of this sun, with a refined and ravishing delight. For this work, there must be,

A change of judgment. The eye must be restored. It is as possible for a blind eye to behold the sun, or a weak eye to stare in the face of it, as for a blind understanding to behold God. For it is not a being in the place of heaven, but having a faculty disposed, which elevates us to the knowledge of him. Things that are corporeal, cannot know things that are spiritual. We cannot in this sensitive body, view the face of an angel, and understand his nature; much less with a body of total death, see the face of God, which is above all created beings, more than any spiritual creature is above sense. In heaven the saints shall know him, as they are known of him, perfectly, as far as the capacity of a creature may extend. Has God any scales upon his eyes? Does he not know perfectly what he knows? So shall the glorified saints. But if a natural man were admitted into heaven, what prospects could he have with a blind understanding? As men under the gospel administrations, cannot see the kingdom of God, even in the midst of it, without a new birth; so neither could they see the kingdom of God in the midst of heaven itself, without a new frame; if not see it, much less enjoy it.

For the contemplation of God in heaven, there must be a change of will. Men like not to retain God in their knowledge, when he is represented to them in the dark, yet pleasant glass of nature, Rom. i. 28. The apostle there speaks it of the heathen, and the wisest of them, their philosophers, who though pleased with the contemplation of nature, yet were not pleased with the contemplation of God in nature: much less will they like him, when he discovers himself clothed with the light of holiness as a garmnent. That vicious eye, which is too weak to behold, with any delight, the image of the sun in a glass, or a pail of water, will be much too weak, to gaze upon it in its brightness in the firmament. If there be no delight to know God here, what pleasure, what fitness can there be in the same frame, to contemplate him above? Let me ask you; have you any pleasure in the study of God? What is the reason then, that in your retirements, when you have nothing to do, your thoughts are no more upon him? What is the reason, that if any motion doth offer to advise you to fix your thoughts upon him, you so soon shift it off, as a troublesome companion, and some slight jolly thought is admitted with gladness into those embraces which the other courted? Can such a temper be fit for heaven, where nothing but thoughts of God run through the veins of glorified souls? If the discovery of God's glory in the gospel, is accounted no better than folly by natural men; and therefore not received; the manifestation of it above, would meet with no better valuation of it, unless the temper both of judgment and will were changed: they are spiritually to be discerned here, and no less spiritually to be discerned above. The weak and waterish eye must be cured by some powerful medicine, before it can stare upon the light of the sun, or delight itself in its glory.

Love is another duty in Heaven. Love is a grace that shoots the gulf with us, and attends us not only to the suburbs, but into the very heart of heaven, when other graces conduct us only to the gates, and then take their leave of us, as having no business there. " Charity never faileth." And, indeed, it is so essentially our duty in every place, that it is concluded, that God cannot free us from the obligation of it, whilst we remain his creatures; because God, being infinitely good, and, therefore, infinitely amiable, and infinitely gracious to them, it would seem unrighteous and inconsistent with supreme goodness, to forbid the creature an affection to that which is infinitely excellent, and a gratitude to his benefactor, which can be paid only in love. Now, though we are bound to love God in the highest degree, yet every new mercy adds a fresh obligation to return our affection to him. So when we shall have the clearest beams of God's love, darting upon us from heaven, we shall also have higher obligations to love him, both for his excellency, which shall be more visible; and his love, which shall be more sensible. Now, can the heart of a natural man cling about God? Can it forget its father's house, and be wholly taken up with the Creator's excellency? Can he that loved pleasure more than God in the world, love God more than pleasures in heaven, without an alteration of his soul? No: the heart must be first circumcised by God, before we can love God with all our heart. If we will not be subject to the law of God here, how can we be subject to the love of God, which is the law of heaven? How can we cleave to God without love, or relish him without delight? No man in a natural state, could stay in heaven, because he doth not love the person, whose presence alone makes it heaven. How can there be a conformity to God in affection, without a conformity to his holiness? A choiceness of love, with a perverseness of will; a supremacy of delight, without rectitude of heart; a love of God, without a loathing of sin; a fervency of love, with a violence of lust: all these are contradictions. He that hath a hatred of God, cannot perform the main duty of heaven; and, therefore, what should he do there?

Again: praise is a service in heaven. If a pure angel be not sufficient for so elevated a duty, how unfit then is a drowsy soul? What is the angel's note, "holy, holy, holy Lord God," can never be a natural man's: for how can he possibly praise that which he hates? What is the note of glorified saints? It is "alleluiah, salvation, and glory, and honour, and power, unto the Lord our God;" Rev. xix. 1; and again they said, "alleluiah, for the Lord God Omnipotent reigneth," ver. 6. Nothing but alleluiah four times, ver. 1, 3, 4, 6. How can that heart frame an alleluiah, that is filled with jealousies of him? How can he exalt the honour of God, who was always pleased with the violations of it? How can he rejoice at the Lord's reigning, that would not have one lust subdued by his power? How can a natural man, as natural, ever be wound up to a height, fit for such strains, since "out of the abundance of the heart, the mouth speaks?" The tongue can never be framed to praise, while the heart is evil. Our blessed Saviour must be glorified in us, before he can be glorified by us. If a man in a mere natural state, be unfit for this heavenly work, how unfit are then their tongues to sound his praise, which are always filled with reproaches of God? And how can their ears endure to hear it from others which were never offended with the blasphemies of him? They could never rejoice in this heavenly concert, were they admitted. Nay, their enmity to the work would not permit their stay. The smoke of pure incense, is fitter, rather to drive a swine out of the room, than to invite his continuance.

As the new birth is necessary, to the duty, so to the reward of heaven. As the reward is exceedingly glorious the preparation thereto, must be exceedingly gracious. The rewards of heaven are something incorporated with us, inlaid in the very frame of our souls, and cannot be conceived enjoyable, without a change in the nature of the subject. Man was first formed, before he was brought into the garden of Eden, or pleasure: "there he put the man whom he had formed." Man must be new-formed, before he be brought into that place, which is the antitype of Eden, the place of eternal and spiritual pleasure. A natural man can no more relish the rewards of heaven, than a dead carcass can esteem a crown, and a purple robe: or be delighted with the true pleasure of heaven, than a swine that loves to wallow in the mire, can be delighted with a bed of roses. A disorder in nature, is a prohibition to all happiness belonging to that nature. A distempered body, under the fury of a disease, can find no delight in the pleasures of the healthful. A wicked man, with a troubled and foaming sea of sin, and lust in his mind, would find no more rest in heaven, than a man, with disjointed members upon a rack, can in the beauty of a picture. We must be "spiritually minded," before we can have either "life or peace." Righteousness in the soul, is the necessary qualification for the peace and joy in the kingdom of God, "The kingdom of God is not meat and drink, but righteousness and peace, and joy in the Holy Ghost." Rom. xiv. 17. While malice remains in the devil's nature, were he admitted into heaven, he would receive a torment instead of a content. A wicked man would meet with hell in the midst of heaven, as long as he carries his own rack within him, boiling and raging lusts in his heart, which can receive no contentment, without objects suitable to them, let the place be what it will. Heaven indeed, is not only a place, but a nature; and it is a contradiction to think that any can be happy with a nature contrary to the very essence of happiness.

The pleasure and reward of heaven is a perfect likeness to God and Christ. This is the great privilege of heaven, which the apostle, in the midst of his ignorance of other particulars, resolves upon as certain, as that which results from regeneration, and being the sons of God, and is the full preparation for the beatific vision, " Now we are the sons of God, and it doth not yet appear what we shall be; but we know, that when he shall appear, we shall be like him, for we shall see him as he is." 1 John iii. 2. He seems to intimate this, that we can never be like him when he doth appear, unless we be now, while we are here, the sons of God; nor ever be admitted to a sight of him. As Christ presented himself without spot to God, when he laid the foundation of our redemption; so he presents his people without blemish to God, when he lays on the top stone of it in our glorification. Now as we cannot be like to Christ in our walk here, without a new birth; neither can we without it, be like Christ in glory hereafter. It is not the place makes us like to God, but there must be a likeness to God, to make the place pleasant to us. When once the angels had corrupted their nature, the short stay they made in heaven after, neither pleased, nor reformed them. And when Satan appeared before God, among the angels, neither God's presence, nor his speaking to him did any wise better him. He came a devil, and he went away so, without any pleasure in the place, or presence, but by the permission of God to wreak his malice on holy Job. An unlikeness to God, is the misery of the creature. It is therefore impossible, whilst the soul remains in that state, that it can arrive at blessedness, because it is a contradiction, to think a felicity can be enjoyed in a contrariety to, and separation from the fountain of it, " Lo, they that are far from thee, shall perish." Psa. lxxiii. 27. It is by faith beholding the glory of the Lord in the glass of the gospel here, that we must be transformed into his image, before we can be changed into his glory. And we cannot be like God by holy actions only, though we had performed as many of them, as all the holy men in the world ever did, as to the matter of them, abstracted from the principle and end : and the reason is, because God is not only holy in his actions, but holy in his nature; and therefore we must not only have actions materially good, but a holy nature suitable to the holiness of God, otherwise we neither are, nor ever can be like him.

The fruition of God is a privilege of heaven, which necessarily follows this likeness. God is the eternal portion of glorified souls, upon which they live. He is the strength of their hearts : there is none but God in heaven who is the chief object of their love and delight. The presence of God makes the fulness of joy. His favour and the light of his glorious countenance, constitute heaven and happiness; not the place, but the countenance. God's frown kindles hell, and his smile renders any place an heaven. Now an old nature cannot have a good look from God : for since he is infinitely holy, he must hate unholiness ; infinitely true, he must hate falsity. As it is impossible a man can love truth and falsity, righteousness and unrighteousness, as such, at one and the same time, in an intense degree ; therefore an impure nature cannot be happy, unless God be mutable. God cannot smile on the old Adam, unless he hate himself. What satisfaction can such a one possibly have in God's presence ? How can he savour the society of God, that never loved it ? Do we naturally love any warm mention of God ? Have we not a stony deadness to any heavenly motion that falls upon us ? A mighty quickness to receive sinful motions in that which we love? Do not our countenances fall, and our delight take wings to itself, and fly away, at any lively appearance of God. If we have such an enmity to his law, which is but a transcript of his holiness, much greater must our enmity be to the original copy. Hence in Scripture men are said to "refuse his law." Psa. lxxviii. 10, to "forsake his law." Psa. cxix. 53, to be "far from his law." Psa. cxix. 150. Darkness doth not more naturally vanish at the appearance of the sun, than an old nature will fly from the glory and brightness of God. A mass of black darkness, and an immense sphere of light, may as soon be espoused together, as a friendly amity be struck up between God and an unrenewed man. God is light without darkness ; man is darkness itself, as if nothing else entered into the composition of his corrupt nature. If there be therefore a disagreement, contrariety, and unwillingness on both sides, how can any pleasing correspondence be effected? If God should bring a man, with his corrupt nature, into a local heaven, God could not please himself in it, nor such an one delight himself in God, no more than a swine can be pleased with the presence of an angel, or a mole sport itself with the beauty of flowers, or a vitiated eye rejoice at the brightness of light. We must really make God such an one as we shape him in our natural fancy, before we can take any pleasure in converse with him. Our nature therefore must be changed, before we can please him, or be satisfied in him. His presence else will cause fear, while our sinful state remains, an affection inconsistent with happiness.

Inferences.—If regeneration be absolutely necessary to a gospel state, and the enjoyment of eternal glory in heaven ; then it informs us, how much the nature of man is depraved. For otherwise there were no need of his being born again : and no reason could be imagined, why our blessed Saviour should so pressingly urge the necessity of it. If man's nature were according to his original frame, it would please God, because it was of his own creation. But we are flesh by our natural birth; and therefore to be happy, we must be spiritual by a second birth.

If regeneration be so necessary, then how much to be lamented is the ignorance of this doctrine in the world? And strange and sad it is, that it should be so little considered. The common talk is of serving God, and reforming the life; but who of a thousand speaks of the necessity of a new nature? It is a sad case, that when a doctrine is so clear, men should be so stupid, and deludingly damn themselves; that they should be so willfully ignorant of this, who have Bibles in their hands and houses; yet not understand this, which is the great purpose for which God sent the Scripture among the sons of men. It is a shame not to have the knowlege of this great and necessary truth. As the apostle in another case, " Some have not the knowledge of God: I speak this to your shame." 1 Cor. xv. 24. How strange and uncouth doth this doctrine sound in the ears of the carnal world, who wonder at it, as Nicodemus did at our Saviour's proposal; and think all our discourses of it an heap of enthusiastic nonsense? It is as if we would speak parables; as if you should talk of astronomy to the natural fool, or read divinity in Arabic to a man who understands only his native language. How little sensible is the world of the necessity of this work? They expect Christ should change their misery into glory, without changing their hearts, and fitting their spirits for it, which will never be. They think it enough for them that Christ was conceived in the womb of the Virgin, without being formed again in their souls; as the poor Jews at this day expect a Messiah, not to alter the frame of their souls, but the frame of the world; not to subdue their spirits, but to conquer the nations to be their vassals. How should this stupidity of men be a matter of lamentation to us!

If regeneration be so absolutely necessary, how should Christian parents endeavour all they can to have their children regenerated ? There is no necessity they should have great estates, and live ostentatiously in the world: but there is a necessity, a great necessity, they should be new creatures, and live spiritually. In leaving the one to your children, you leave them but earth; in leaving the other, you convey heaven to them. There is an obligation upon you ; their old polluted nature was derived from you by carnal generation; make them amends by endeavouring to secure grace to them by spiritual instruction: you made them children of wrath ; why will you not endeavour to make them children of God and heirs of heaven. Education of itself will not produce this noble work; nor the bare hearing of the word, or any outward means whatsoever, by their own strength ; yet the Spirit doth often bless them, and very much ; and I doubt not but a great number that are regenerated had the first seeds sown in them by a religious education: and I have made the observation in many. Timothy had a religious education, both by his mother and grandmother, though this did not renew him; for Paul, by the preaching of the gospel, was the instrument of that : he calls him his own son in the faith : yet no question his religious instructions from his parents did much facilitate this work. Use all endeavour, therefore, to convince them of the necessity of a new birth ; be earnest with them till you see it produced, that they may not curse you for being the instruments of their beings, but bless you for being the instruments of their spiritual life.

This doctrine acquaints us with the insufficiency of every thing else, without this, to enable us to enter into the kingdom of God.

Great knowledge is not sufficient. All the wisdom of Solomon in a man, though it may enable him to take an exact measure of nature from the highest star, to the meanest insect, doth no more fit him for heaven, than the shining skin of a serpent expels his venomous nature. We have more relics of Adam's nature in knowledge, than we have in righteousness. To be a philosopher, physician, or statesman, is not essential to happiness in this world; much less can it prepare a man for the happiness of another. But grace is as essential to it, as natural heat, and radical moisture are to the life of a man. Jesus Christ came not to make us scholars in natural things, but to endue us with such a knowledge, as is in order to eternal happiness; and with such a renewing principle, as might make us capable of heaven. Knowledge and wisdom are some of the choicest flowers in nature's garden. But it will be a small advantage, to descend to hell with our brains full of wit and sophistry. One saving cry from a new-born infant soul, is of more value than the knowledge of all philosophers. We may possess great knowledge of Revelation, and the doctrines it contains, and be ignorant of God. Nicodemus had a good stock of this; he understood the letter of the Scripture; was well read in all the parts of the law; he was thought fit to be one of the great Sanhedrim; something else was requisite besides this; a new birth was still wanting. What if we understood the mind of the Spirit of God in every verse in the Bible; were able to discourse profoundly of the great mysteries of the gospel; had the gift of prophecy, and knowledge of things to come; had the interpretation of the whole book of the revelation writ in our minds; what will all this avail us? An evangelical head will be but drier fuel for eternal burning, without an evangelical impression upon the heart, and the badge of a new nature. Men may prophesy in Christ's name; in his name cast devils out of bodies, and devils of error out of men's brains; yet not be regarded by Christ: but he says to them, "I never knew you: depart from me, ye that work iniquity." If they had had this mark, and gospel impression, our Lord would have known them. Christ in heaven would have owned himself formed in the heart: he could not have been ignorant of his own nature and offspring.

Well then: a man may have all the learning of Christians and heathen stored up in his head, and not the least stamp of it in his heart. He may be wise in knowledge, and a fool in improvement. A heap and pack of knowledge is not wisdom among men, without an application of that knowledge to particular exigencies and usefulness.

Outward reformation is not sufficient. Regeneration is never without reformation of life: but this may be without that: we may be outward Christians, without an inward principle, though we can never be inward Christians, without an outward holiness. The new birth is properly an internal work, and shows itself externally; as the heat of the heart, and vital parts, will evidence itself in outward motions: "the king's daughter is all glorious within," as well as without, Psa. xlv. 13. What a vanity would it be, to boast of freedom from other diseases, if thou hast the plague upon thee? What a poor comfort is it, to brag of thy being without gross immoralities, whilst the plague of thy nature remains uncured? Outward reformation only (though of excellent use,) is but a new appearance, not a new creature; a change of life, not of the heart: whereas this work we discourse of, is a new birth in the understanding and will; it begins at the spirit, and descends from thence to the body. 1 Thess. v. 23. It is a sanctification in spirit, soul, and then body. Can that which can be no evidence to us in self-examination, be of itself sufficient to waft us to heaven? If you retire to take a view of yourselves, whether you belong to God, will you judge by your outward actions, or inward frame? There is no characteristic difference in any external action, between a true Christian, and an hypocrite; that therefore which is not a sufficient evidence to us, of a right to happiness, cannot be a sufficient preparation of ourselves for it.

Morality is not sufficient. By morality, I mean, not only an outward reformation, but some love to moral virtue, as the heathen had, raised upon the thoughts of the excellency of it. Nicodemus was a moral man: he had some affection to Christ, upon the consideration of his miracles; he had never else ventured to come to him, so much as by night. He had no blot upon his conversation; he had desires to be instructed. This was more than a bare abstinence from sin; yet notwithstanding, besides those moral qualifications, he must have a new birth, before he can see the kingdom of God. Men may do much good, be very useful to others in their generation, yet be in the very bottom of unregeneracy. An healing witch, as well as a hurting one, is the devil's client, and in covenant with him. There is not so great a difference between the highest degree of glory in heaven, and the lowest degree of grace on earth, as there is between the lowest degree of saving grace, and the highest degree of natural excellency; because the difference between these is specific, as between a rational and irrational creature; the difference between the other, is only in degree, as between an infant and a man. It is one thing to have a love to moral virtue, another thing to have a love to God in it; one thing to move for self, and another thing to move for the glory of the Creator; one thing to be animated by reason, and another thing to be inspired by the Holy Ghost. What can a moral honesty profit that man, who values the world's dung above the Creator's glory? What though he be honest, and useful to his neighbours, must his affection to God be measured by his honesty among men? The great business is from what principle it flows. What if he doth good to others, whilst he doth his Creator wrong, by fostering any one thing in his heart above him. Can his goodness to others, make a compensation for his disesteem of God? The greatest man in the whole world, who hath no other descent than from Adam, must have a new quality put into his heart, before he can be happy: for if a new birth be necessary, all endowments below it, are to no purpose for the attainment of that state for which it is intended. Whatsoever is of the old Adam in us, though it be a beautiful flower, must wither and die, " For all flesh is as grass, and the glory of man, as the flower of grass; the grass withers, and the flower thereof fadeth away." 1 Pet. i. 23, 24. The apostle sets in opposition, the incorruptible seed, whereby they were born, and the fairest flowers in nature's garden. The best thing which a man glories in, is a flower, but withering: it is a glory, but the glory of the flesh: it hath no lustre in the sight of God: it is not a flower to be set in heaven: it is only the word of God, and the impressions made on us by that word, which endure for ever. As herbs cannot grow without partaking of the natural influence, and beams of the sun, so nothing stands and flourishes, but what partakes of the nature and Spirit of Christ. Nay, it is so far from being sufficient, that it is a great hindrance of regeneration, without the overpowering grace of God, because it is the glory of a man; that is, that wherein a man glories. Men are apt to rest upon their morals, without reflecting upon their naturals. They see no spots in their lives; and therefore will not believe there are any in their hearts. They are so taken up with the Pharisee, their proud thoughts of their being above others, that they never think how much they have inwardly of the publican, in coming short of the glory of God. Unregenerate morality therefore is not sufficient. The heart must be changed, before moral virtues can commence graces. When this is once done, what were moral before, become divine, as having a new principle to quicken them, and a new end to direct them.

Religious professions are not sufficient. Can you upon a serious consideration conclude, that this only is the import of all those Scriptures which speak of being born of God, raised from a death in sin, quickened and led by the Spirit, created in righteousness and true holiness? Are not these things in the very manner of speaking them, elevated above any mere profession, which may be declared to the world without any such work, which is the evident intention of those Scriptures? It is not the naming the name of Christ, but the departing from iniquity; a departing from it in our nature, as well as in our actions, that is the badge whereby the Lord knows who are his: "The Lord knows who are his: and let every one that names the name of Christ, depart from iniquity." 2 Tim. ii. 19. Religious profession is only but a form, a figure, a shape of godliness: a picture made by art, without life and power and an enlivened faculty, and a divine principle whence it should proceed; it is but a name of life at best under a state of death: "Thou hast a name, that thou livest, and art dead." Rev. iii. 1. Professions without a new nature, are no more the things God requires of us, than sacrifices under the law, without a broken heart: it is not a following our Saviour in profession, but in regeneration which gives the apostles a title to that promise of sitting upon his throne in glory: "Ye that have followed me in the regeneration, ye shall sit upon twelve thrones, judging the twelve tribes of Israel." Matt. xix. 28. Judas had followed Christ till that time, and after, in a profession, but not in the regeneration, not from a regenerated principle.

Multitudes of external religious duties and privileges are not sufficient. Men are very apt to place their security here: it was the great labour of the prophet Isaiah, to bring the Jews in his time off from them: God doth not require attendance on ordinances, as the ultimate end, but as means to the beginning and promoting a new birth: "To what purpose is the multitude of your sacrifices to me? Wash ye, make ye clean." Isa. i. 11, 16. The resting in these is the manifest destruction of men's souls, when thousands of sacrifices to God cannot be acceptable without a new nature. We naturally affect an easy religion; and outward acts of worship, especially under the gospel, have no great difficulty in them. Men would rather be at great expense of sacrificing, than crucify one beloved sin; and bow a thousand times before the cross of Christ, than nail one corruption to it. How easy a work were it, to get to heaven, if nothing else were required but to be a member of the visible Christian church? Circumcision was a privilege, but it availed nothing without a new creature. There was another circumcision made without hands, the work of God, that was required; a new creature, without which, outward circumcision signified nothing. The practice of some duties may stand with an inward hatred of them, as the abstinence from some sins may stand with an inward love to them. Outward worship is but a carcass, when the soul is not conformed to God, the object of worship; and doth not attain an union to, and communion with God, which is the end of worship; what are all acts of worship without a nature suitable to the God we approach unto in them? Judge not therefore of your state, by any external actions; no outward act, but unregenerate persons may do, yea, they may express much zeal in them; they may have their bodies as martyrs consumed by flames, without having their corruption consumed by grace; an impure breath may make as good music to the ear in a pipe, as a sound one: there is something more necessary than a bare performance of duties.

Nay more, convictions are not sufficient. Nicodemus was startled by our Saviour's miracles, believed him to be a prophet sent by God, acknowledged that God was with him, yet still the necessary qualification of a new birth was wanting. Your spirits may be torn in pieces by terror, the heart of stone may be rent asunder, and yet no heart of flesh appear; the ground may be ploughed, yet not sown; sensuality and lust may be kept under by a

spirit of bondage, when it is not cast out by a spirit
of adoption : the sun may scorch you, and not enliven
you : the knowledge of the foulness of sin, and the
fierceness of wrath, is the work of the Spirit in the
law; the new birth is the work of the Spirit in the
gospel; the stone may be cut and hewed by the law,
and yet never polished by the gospel, never brought
into covenant : " I have hewed them by my prophets,
but they like men have transgressed the covenant."
Hos. vi. 5, 7. It is not then great knowledge, fair
coloured fruit, loud professions, glittering services, or
tearing convictions, which are this badge, whereby
Christ knows his own from all the world besides: all
these will be answered, " I know you not." Is it not
then a necessary work, and high time to get that new
nature, whereby God will know thee to belong to him?
Professions may be false, outward reformation may
be but as a painted sepulchre : knowledge only elevates
the understanding, but as our communion lies in the
acts of the will, there must be some work upon that
to fit us for our great happiness. If these things are
not sufficient, then profane men cannot expect heaven
by the way of hell.

If regeneration be so absolutely necessary to salvation, how miserable is the condition of every unregenerate man! What a miserable case is it, that sinners
should dream on in their delusions, till everlasting
burnings confute their fancies, and turn their hopes
into dreadful despair! Oh, how do most men live, as
if this doctrine were a mere falsity; and act as if they
would take heaven by the violence of their lusts, not
by the industry of grace! Know you not that an unrighteous nature shall not inherit the kingdom of God?
" Know ye not that the unrighteous shall not inherit
the kingdom of God? be not deceived," &c. 1 Cor. vi.
9. Is it possible you should be ignorant of that which
stares you in the face, in every page of the Bible? If
you know not this, you know nothing. Be not deceived : nothing is so natural as heart deceit, and pre-

sumptuous confidence; the apostle else would not have spoken of it, with such an emphasis, but that he knew how apt men are to delude themselves with hopes of mercy in a state of sin. Self flattery is one of the strongest branches, which grows upon the pride of nature. How vain is it to fancy to yourselves a fitness for heaven, while there are only preparations for hell? Whence should such imaginations arise? Not from God; it is contrary to all his declarations. Is it from yourselves? What reason have you to believe your fancies in spiritual things, who are so often mistaken in temporal? Is it from the devil? What reason have you to believe your greatest enemy? If this work be wrought, he hath for ever lost you: it is he that cherishes such notions, for he hath no pleasure to undo his kingdom, and lose his subjects, Never did any man use so much diligence to get a new nature, as the devil doth to hinder him.

NATURE OF REGENERATION

CHAPTER I

Difficulty of explaining the nature of Regeneration —How it differs from conversion —How from Justification —How from Adoption —How from Sanctification —It is not a removal of the old faculties, nor a change of the essential acts of the soul, nor an awakening of some hidden, gracious principle of the soul, nor an actual addition to our nature, nor mere Baptism.

I PROCEED now to show the nature of regeneration, the necessity of which I have already insisted upon.

It is difficult to describe exactly the Nature of Regeneration:

Because of the disputes about it; whether it be a quality, or a spiritual substance; whether, if a quality, it be a habit, or a power, or whether it be the Holy Ghost personally. The Scripture discovers it to us, under the terms of the *new creature*, a *new heart*, a *law, put into us*, the *image of God*, a *divine nature;* these, though Scripture terms, are difficult to explain.

It is difficult, because it is visible, not in itself, but in its effects. We know seed doth propagate itself, and produce its like, but the generative part in the seed lies covered with husks and skin, so that it is hard to tell in what atom or point the generative particle doth lie. We know we have a soul, yet it is hard to tell what the soul is, and in what part it doth principally reside. We know there are angels, yet what mortal can give a description of that glorious nature? It is much like the wind, as our Saviour describes it: "The wind bloweth where it listeth, and thou hearest the sound thereof, but canst not tell whence it cometh, nor whither it goeth: so is every one that is born of the Spirit." John iii. 8. The wind we feel, we see the effects of it, yet cannot tell how it ariseth, where it doth repose itself, and how it is allayed: and all the notions of philosophy about it, will not satisfy a curious inquirer: so likewise it is in this business of regenertion; the effects of it are known, there are certain characters whereby to discern it; but to give a description of the nature of it, is not so easy.

It is difficult, because of the natural ignorance which is still in the minds of the best. A man cannot understand all iniquity, for there is a mystery of iniquity; neither can he fully understand this work, for there is a mystery of godliness; not only in the whole scheme of it without, but in the whole frame of it in the heart. It is called the "hidden man of the heart." 1 Pet. iii. 4. Hidden from the world, hidden from reason, hidden from the sight sometimes of them that have it: a man can hardly sometimes see it in his own heart, by reason of the steams of corruption; as a beautiful picture is not visible in a cloud of smoke. The blindness the god of this world hath wrapt us in, that we might not know God, or the things of God, is not wholly taken off. And even what we know of the truths of God, suffers an eclipse by our carnal conceptions of them; for all the notions we frame of them, have a tincture of sense and fancy.

It is hard for those to conceive it, who have no experience of it. If we speak of the motions of natural corruption, as wrath, passion, distrust of God, and enormous sins, men can easily understand this; because we have all sad experience of an inward corruption; but the methods and motions of the Spirit of God in this work, are not comprehended, but by those that have felt the power of them. The motions of sin are more sensible, the motions of the Spirit more secret and inward, and men want as much the experience of the one, as they have too much of the other. Hence it is that many carnal men love to have the nature of sin explained and discovered; partly perhaps, for this reason among others, that they can better understand that, by the daily evidence of it in their own practices; whereas other things, out of the reach of their experience, are out of the grasp of their understanding; and therefore seem to them paradoxes and incredible things: the spiritual man is not judged or discerned by any, but them that are spiritual. It is certainly true, that as a painter can better delineate a stormy and cloudy air, than the serenity of a clear day, and the spectator conceive it with more pleasure: so it is more easy to represent the agitations and affections of natural corruption, than the inward frame of a soul wrought by the Spirit of God. I shall therefore describe it consonantly to the Scripture, thus: Regeneration is a mighty and powerful change, wrought in the soul by the efficacious working of the Holy Spirit, wherein a vital principle, a new habit, the law of God, and a divine nature are put into, and framed in the heart, enabling it to act holy and pleasingly to God, and to grow up therein to eternal glory. This is included in the term of a new creature in the text. There is a change, a creation; that which was not, is brought into a state of being. If a new creature, and in Christ, then surely not a dead but a living creature, having a principle of life; and if a living creature, then possessed of some power to act, and habits to make those actions easy: and if a power to act, and a habit to facilitate that act, then a law in their nature as the rule of their acting; every creature hath so: in this respect the heavens are said to have ordinances; "knowest thou the ordinances of heaven?" and they seem to act in the way of a covenant, according to such articles as God hath pitched upon. And lastly,

as in all creatures thus endued, there is a likeness to
some other things in the rank of beings: so in this new
creature there is a likeness to God, whence it is called
the image of God in holiness and righteousness; and a
divine nature. So that you see the divers expressions
whereby the Scripture declares this work of regeneration, are included in this term of the new creature,
or the new creation, as the word is. It is a certain
spiritual and supernatural principle, or permanent form,
infused by God, whereby it is made partaker of the
divine nature, and enabled to act for God.

Let us therefore see how it differs from other states
of the Christian.

It differs from conversion. Regeneration is a spiritual change, conversion is a spiritual motion. In regeneration there is a power conferred; conversion is
the exercise of this power. In regeneration there is
given us a principle to turn; conversion is our actual
turning; that is the principle whereby we are brought
out of a state of nature, into a state of grace: and conversion the actual fixing on God. Conversion is related to regeneration, as the effect to the cause. Life
precedes motion, and is the cause of motion. In the
covenant, the new heart, the new Spirit, and God's
putting his Spirit into them, are distinguished from
their walking in his statutes, from the first step we
take in the way of God, and is set down as the cause
of our motion: "I will cause you to walk in my
statutes." In renewing us, God gives us a power; in
converting us he excites that power. Men are naturally dead, and have a stone upon them. Regeneration is rolling away the stone from the heart, and a
raising to newness of life; and then conversion is as
natural to a regenerate man, as motion is to a living
body. A principle of activity will produce action.

In regeneration, man is wholly passive: in conversion, he is active; as a child in its first formation in
the womb, contributes nothing to the first infusion of
life; but after it hath life, it is active, and its motion

natural. The first reviving of us is wholly the act of God, without any concurrence of the creature; but after we are revived, we do actively and voluntarily live in his sight; "he will revive us, he will raise us up, and then we shall live in his sight," then we shall walk before him, then shall we "follow on to know the Lord." Hos. vi. 2. Regeneration is the motion of God in the creature; conversion is the motion of the creature to God, by virtue of that first principle; from this principle all the acts of believing, repenting, mortifying, quickening, do spring: in all these a man is active; in the other merely passive; all these are the acts of the will, by the assisting grace of God, after the infusion of the first grace: conversion is a giving ourselves to the Lord: giving our own selves to the Lord is a voluntary act, but the power whereby we are enabled thus to give ourselves, is wholly and purely in every part of it from the Lord himself. A renewed man is said to be "led by the Spirit," Rom. viii. 14, not dragged, not forced: the putting a bias and aptitude in the will, is the work of the Spirit quickening it; but the moving the will to God by the strength of this bias, is voluntary, and the act of the creature. The Spirit leads as a father doth a child by the hand: the father gave him that principle of life, and conducts him, and hands him in his motion; but the child hath a principle of motion in himself, and a will to move. The day of regeneration is solely the day of God's power, wherein he makes men willing to turn to him. So that though in actual conversion the creature be active, it is not from the power of man, though it be from a power in man; not growing up from the impotent root of nature, but settled there by the Spirit of God.

It differs from justification. By justification we are reconciled to God; by regeneration we are assimilated and made like to God. They always go together. As our Saviour's resurrection, which was the justification of him from that guilt which he had taken upon

himself, and a public pronouncing him to be his righteous servant, is called a new begetting him, "God hath
raised up Jesus again, as it is also written in the
second Psalm: thou art my Son, this day have I begotten thee." Acts xiii. 33; because it was a manifestation of him to be the Son of God, who before,
being covered with our infirmities, did not appear so
to the world: so our justification from guilt, and new
begetting us, and manifesting us to the angels, to be
the sons of God, are at one and the same time, and
both are by grace; by grace you are justified, Rom.
v. 1, the quickening and raising us together with
Christ is by grace. The blessing of Abraham, which
is the application of redemption from the curse of the
law, and the receiving the promise of the Spirit by
faith, are both together.

It differs from justification in the nature of the
change.

Justification is a relative change, whereby a man
is brought from a state of guilt to a state of righteousness; from a state of slavery to a state of liberty;
from the obligation of the covenant of works, to the
privilege of the covenant of grace; from being a child
of wrath to be an heir of promise. Regeneration is
a spiritual change, and real, as when a dead man is
raised from death to life; it is a filling the soul with
another nature, "And you hath he quickened, who
were dead in trespasses and sins." Eph. ii. 1. It is
a change of nature, and of that nature whereby we
are children of wrath, not only by the first sin, but by
a conversation according to the course of the world.
And this quickening respects the change of that nature
which was prone to a worldly conversation, and a
fulfilling the desires of the flesh. The first is a change
of a man's condition, this a change in a man's disposition. When a man is made a magistrate, there is a
change in his relation; when a servant or slave is
made a free man, there is an alteration of his condition; but neither the one's magistracy, nor the other's

liberty fills their hearts with new principles, or plants a new frame in their nature.   Relation and nature are two distinct things.   In creation there is a relation of a creature to God, which results from the mere being of the creature; but there is also the nature of the creature in such a rank of being, which is added over and above to its mere being.   The apostle in the verses following the text, speaks of reconciliation, or non-imputation of our trespasses, as distinct from that change wrought in us in the new creation.   In justification we are freed from the guilt of sin, and so have a title to life; in regeneration we are freed from the filth of sin, and have the purity of God's image in part restored to us.

Justification is the immediate fruit of the blood of Christ, "Being justified by his blood;" regeneration is by the immediate operation of the Spirit;" therefore called "the sanctification of the Spirit;" the matter of that is without us, the righteousness of Christ; the matter of the other within us, a gracious habit: the form of the one, is imputing; the form of the other, is infusing or putting into us: they differ in the end; one is from condemnation to absolution; the other from pollution to communion.   In the immediate effect, one gives us a right, the other a fitness.   In their qualities, the righteousness of one is perfect in our Head, and imputed to us.   The righteousness by regeneration is actively in us, and aspires to perfection.

It differs from adoption.   Adoption follows upon justification, as a dignity flowing from union to Christ, and doth suppose reconciliation.   Adoption gives us the privilege of sons, regeneration the nature of sons.   Adoption relates us to God as a father; regeneration engraves upon us the lineaments of a father.   That makes us relatively his sons by conferring a power; this makes us formally his sons by conveying a principle.   By that we are instated in the divine affection; by this we are partakers of the divine nature.   Adoption doth not constitute us the children of God by an intrinsic form, but by an extrinsic acceptation; but this gives us an intrinsic right; or adoption gives us a title, and the Spirit gives us an earnest; grace is the pledge of glory. Redemption being applied in justification, makes way for adoption. Adoption makes way for regeneration, and is the foundation of it. "God sent forth his Son to redeem them that were under the law, that we might receive the adoption of sons. And because ye are sons, God hath sent forth the Spirit of his Son into your hearts, crying, Abba, Father." Gal. iv. 5, 6. Because you are thus adopted, God will make you like his Son, by sending forth the Spirit of his Son, to intimate the likeness it shall produce in the hearts of men to Christ, that you may cry, Abba, Father; behave yourselves like sons, and have recourse to God with a child-like nature. The relation to Christ as brethren is founded upon this new creature, "For both he that sanctifies, and they who are sanctified, are all of one." Heb. ii. 11. They are all of one nature, not the divine nature which Christ had by eternal generation, but that divine nature Christ had by the Spirit's unction. And being of one nature, he is not ashamed, though glorious in heaven, to call them brethren; and being Christ's brethren by a divine nature, thence results also the relation of the sons of God.

It differs from sanctification. Habitual sanctification indeed is the same thing with this new creature; as habitual rectitude with the spiritual life of Adam: but actual sanctification, and the gradual progress of it, grows from this principle as from a root. Faith purifies the heart, "Purifying their hearts by faith." Acts xv. 9. And is the cause of this gradual sanctification; but faith is part of this new creature, and that which is a part cannot be the cause of the whole, for then it would be the cause of itself. We are not regenerated by faith, though we are sanctified by faith; but we are new created by the Spirit of God, infusing faith into us. Faith produceth the acts of grace. but not the habit of grace, because it is of itself a part of this habit; for all graces are but one in the habit or new creature; charity, and likewise every other grace is but the bubbling up of a pure heart and good conscience. Regeneration seems to be the life of this gradual sanctification, the health and liveliness of the soul.

Regeneration is not a removal or taking away of the old substance or faculties of the soul. Some thought that the substance of Adam's soul was corrupted when he sinned, therefore suppose the substance of his soul to be altered when he is renewed. Sin took not away the essence, but the rectitude; the new creation therefore gives not a new faculty, but a new quality. The cure of the leprosy is not a destroying of the fabric of the body, but the disease; yet in regard of the greatness of man's corruption, the soul is so much changed by these new habits, that it is, as it were, a new soul, a new understanding, a new will. It is not the destroying the metal, but the old stamp upon it, to imprint a new: human nature is preserved, but the corruption in it expelled.

The substance of gold is not destroyed in the fire, though the metal and the flame mix together, and fire seems to be incorporated with every part of it; but it is made more pliable to what shape the artist will cast it into, but remains gold still: it is not the breaking the candlestick, but setting up a new light in it; not a destroying the will, but putting a new bias into it. It is a new-stringing the instrument, to make a new harmony. It is an humbling the loftiness, and bowing down the haughtiness of the spirit, to exalt the Lord alone in the soul. The essential nature of man, his reason and understanding, are not taken away, but rectified. As a carver takes not away the knots and grain in the wood, but planes and smoothes it, and carves the image of a man upon it, the substance of the wood remains still; so God pares away the rugged pieces in man's understanding and will, and engraves his own image upon it; but the change is so great, that the soul seems to be of another species and kind, because it is actuated by that grace, which is another species from that principle which actuated it before. New creation is called a resurrection: our Saviour in his resurrection had the same body, but endued with a new quality. As in Christ's transfiguration, neither his deity nor humanity were altered, both natures remained the same. But there was a metamorphosis, and a glorious brightness conferred by the deity upon the humanity, which it did not partake of before. So, though the essence of the soul and faculties remain the same, yet another kind of light is darted in, and other qualities implanted. It was the same Paul when he complied with the body of death, and when he complained of it, but he had not the same disposition. As Adam in a state of corruption had the same faculties for substance, which he had in the state of innocency; but the power, virtue, and form in those faculties, whereby he was acceptable to God, and in a capacity to please him, were wholly abolished. We lose not our substantial form, as Moses's rod did, when it was turned into a serpent; or the water at Cana, when turned into wine. Our nature is ennobled, not destroyed; enriched, not ruined; reformed, not annihilated.

It is not a change of the essential acts of the soul, as acts: the passions and affections are the same, as to the substance and nature of the acts; but the difference lies in the object. And acts, though for substance the same, yet are specifically distinguished by the diversity of objects about which they are conversant. Whatsoever is a commendable quality in nature, and left in man, by the interposition of the Mediator, is not taken away; but the principle, end, and objects of those acts, arising from those restored qualities, are altered. The acts of a renewed man and the acts of a natural man are the same in the nature of acts; as when a man loves God, and fears God, or

loves man, or fears man, it is the same act of love, and
the same act of fear: there are the same motions of
the soul, the same substantial acts simply considered;
the soul stands in the same posture in the one as in
the other; but the difference lies in the objects; the
object of the one is supernatural, the object of the
other natural. As when a man walks to the east or
west, it is the same motion in body and joints, the
same manner of going; yet they are contrary motions,
because the terms to which they tend are contrary one
to the other: or, as when we bless God and bless men,
it is with one and the same tongue that we do both;
yet these are acts specifically different, in regard of
the difference of their objects. The nature of the
affections still remains, though not the corruption of
them, and the objects to which they are directed are
different.

It is not an excitation, or awakening of some gracious principle, which lay hid before in nature, under
the oppression of ill habits: as corn lay hid under the
chaff, but was corn still. Not a beating up something
that lay hid in nature; not an awakening, as of a man
from sleep; but a resurrection, as of a man from death;
a new creation, as of a man from nothing. It is not
a stirring up old principles, and new kindling of them;
as a candle put out lately, may be blown in again by
the fire remaining in the snuff, and burn upon the old
stock; or as the life, which retired into the more secret
parts of the body, in those creatures that seem dead
in winter; which is excited and called out to the exte-
rior parts, by the spring sun. Indeed there are some
sparks of moral virtues in nature, which want blowing
up by a good education; the foundation of these is in
nature, the exciting of them from instruction, the perfection of them from use and exercise. But there is
not in man the seed of one grace, but the seeds of all
sin: " I know, that in me, that is, in my flesh, dwells
no good thing." Rom. vii. 18. Some good thing may
be in me, but it ariseth not from my flesh; it is not

from any seed sown by nature; but it is another principle put into me, which doth seminally contain in it all grace; it is a putting a new seed into the soil, and exciting it to grow; an incorruptible seed. Therefore the Scripture doth not represent men in a trance or sleep, but dead; and so it is not only an awakening, but a quickening, a resurrection. We are just in this work, as our Saviour was when the devil came against him, " The prince of this world cometh, and hath nothing in me." John xiv. 30. He had nothing to work upon in Christ. But he rakes in the ashes of our nature, and finds sparks enough to blow upon : but the Spirit finds nothing in us, but a stump, some confused desires for happiness: he brings all the fire from heaven, wherewith our hearts are kindled. This work therefore is not an awakening of good habits, which lay before oppressed, but a taking off those ill habits, which were so far from oppressing nature, that they were connatural to it, and by incorporation with it, had quite altered it from that original rectitude and simplicity wherein God at first created it.

Nor is it an addition to nature. Christ was not an addition to Adam but a new head by himself, called Adam in regard of the agreement with him in the notion of a head and common person. So neither is the new creature, or Christ formed in the soul, an addition to nature. Grace grows not upon the old stock. It is not a piece of cloth sewed to an old garment, but the one is cast aside, the other wholly taken on; not one garment put upon another, but a taking off one, and a putting on another, " Putting off the old man, putting on the new man." Col. iii. 9, 10. It is a taking away what was before; " old things are passed away," and bestowing something that had no footing before. It is not a new varnish, nor do old things remain under a new paint; not new plaster laid upon old; a new creature, not a mended creature. It is called light, which is not a quality added to darkness, but a quality that expels it : it is a taking away the stony heart and putting an heart of flesh in the room.   The old nature remains, not in its strength with this addition, but is crucified, and taken away in part with its attendants, " They that are Christ's have crucified the flesh, with the affections and lusts."   Gal. v. 24.   As in the cure of a man, health is not added to the disease; or in resurrection, life added to death; but the disease is expelled, death removed, and another form and habit set in the place.   Add what you will, without introducing another form, it will be of no more efficacy, than flowers and perfumes strewed upon a dead carcass, to restore it to life, and remove the rottenness.   It supposeth nothing before, as a subject capable: nothing in a natural man, is a subject morally capable to have grace, without the expulsion of the old corrupt nature.   It is called a new creature, a new man; not an improved creature, or a new dressed man.

It is not external baptism.   Many men take their baptism for regeneration.   The ancients usually give it this term.   One calls our Saviour's baptism his regeneration.   This confers not grace, but engageth to it: outward water cannot convey inward life.   How can water, a material thing, work upon the soul in a spiritual manner?   Neither can it be proved, that ever the Spirit of God is tied by any promise, to apply himself to the soul in a gracious operation, when water is applied to the body.   If it were so, that all that were baptized, were regenerate; then all that were baptized, would be saved; or else the doctrine of perseverance falls to the ground.   Baptism is a mean of conveying this grace, when the Spirit is pleased to operate with it.   But it doth not work as a physical cause upon the soul, as a purge doth upon the humours of the body: for it is the sacrament of regeneration, as the Lord's Supper is of nourishment. As a man cannot be said to be nourished without faith, so he cannot be said to be a new creature without faith.   Put the most delicious meat into the mouth of a dead man, you do not nourish him, because he wants a principle of life to concoct and digest it. Faith alone is the principle of spiritual life, and the principle which draws nourishment from the means of God's appointment. Some indeed say, that regeneration is conferred in baptism upon the elect, and exerts itself afterwards in conversion. But how so active a principle as a spiritual life should lie dead, and asleep so long, even many years which intervene between baptism and conversion, is not easily conceivable.

CHAPTER II

What Regeneration is —It is a real change from nature to grace —It is common to all the children of God —It is the contrary of the former frame.—It is universal as it respects the whole man —It is principally and inward change, a change of principle and a change of end or object, a change of thoughts and comforts —It is also an outward change, in regard to objects and operations.

LET us see what it is positively.

It consists in a real change from nature to grace, as well as by grace. The term of creation is real: the form introduced in the new creature, is as real as the form introduced by creation, into any being. Scripture terms manifest it so. A divine nature, the image of God, a law put into the heart, they are not nominal and notional. It is a reality the soul partakes of; it gives a real denomination, a new man, a new heart, a new spirit, a new creature, something of a real existence; it is called a resurrection. "The hour is coming, and now is, when the dead shall hear the voice of the Son of God, and they that hear shall live." John v. 25. If Christ had said only, that the hour shall come, it had been meant of the last resurrection; but saying, that it was already come, it must be meant of a resurrection in this life. There is as real a resurrection of the soul, by the trumpet of the gospel, accompanied with the vigorous efficacy of the Holy Ghost, as there shall be of bodies by the voice of the Son of God, at the sound of the trumpet of the archangel. All real operations suppose some real form whence they flow; as vision supposeth a power whereby a man sees, and also a nature wherein that power is rooted. The operations of a new creature are real; and therefore suppose a real power to act, and a real habit as the spring of them. It is such a being that enables them to produce real spiritual actions; for the spirit of power is conveyed to them; whereby as when they were out of Christ, they were able to do nothing, so now being in him, they are able to do all things.

It is a change common to all the children of God. If any man be in Christ, he is a new creature: every man in Christ is so. It is peculiar to them, and common to all of them. The new creation gives being to all Christians. It is a new being settled in them, a new impress and signature set upon them, whereby they are distinguished from all men, barely considered in their naturals. As all of the same species have the same nature; as all men have the nature of men, all lions the nature of lions; so all saints agree in one nature: the life of God is communicated to all, whose names are written in the book of life. All believers, those in Africa, as well as those in Europe; those in Europe; those in heaven, as well as those on earth, have the same essential nature and change. As they are all of one family, all actuated by one spirit, the heart of one answers to the heart of another, as face to face in a glass. What is a spirit of adoption in them below, is a spirit of glory in them above; what in the renewed man below, is a spirit crying Abba, Father; that is in them above, a spirit rejoicing in Abba, Father; the impress and change are essentially the same, though not the same in degree.

It is a change quite contrary to the former frame What more contrary to light than darkness? Such a change it is; instead of a black darkness, there is a bright light. As contrary as flesh and spirit; "that which is born of the flesh, is flesh; that which is born of the Spirit, is spirit." John iii. 6. Where both are put in the abstract, one is the composition of flesh, the other of spirit: as contrary as east to west; as the seed of the woman to the seed of the serpent; as the spirit of the world, and the Spirit of God. The frame of the heart before the new creation, and the frame of the heart after, bear as great a distance from one another as heaven from earth. As God and sin are the most contrary to one another; so an affection to God, and an affection to sin, are the most contrary affections. It is quite another bent of heart, as if a man turn from north to south. It is a position quite contrary to what it was; the heart touched by grace, stands full to God, as before to sin; it is stripped of its perverse inclinations to sin, clothed with holy affections to God: he abhors what before he loved, and loves what before he abhorred: he was alienated from the life of God, but now alienated from the life of his lusts: nothing would before serve him but God's departure from him; nothing will now please him, but God's rays upon him. He was before tired with God's service, now tired with his own sin. Before, crucifying the motions of the Spirit, now crucifying the affections and lusts. That which was before, his life and happiness, is now his death and misery; he dislikes his foolish pastimes and sinful pleasures, as much as man does the follies of his childhood; and is as cheerful in loathing them, as before he was jolly in committing them. It is a translation from one kingdom to another; a translation "from the power of darkness, into the kingdom of his dear Son." Colos. i. 13. A word taken from the transplanting of colonies: they are in a contrary soil and climate, they have other works, other laws, other privileges, other natures: as Christ's resurrection was a state quite contrary to the former; at the time of his death he was in a state of guilt by reason of our sin; at his resurrection he is freed from it; he was before made under the law, he is then freed from the curse of it; he was before in a state of death, after his resurrection in a state of life, and lives for ever. God pulls out the heart of stone, that inflexibleness to him and his service; and plants a heart of flesh in the room, a pliableness to him and his will. It is as great a change, as when a wolf is made a lamb, the nature of the wolf is lost, and the lamb-like nature introduced. By corruption man was carnal and brutish; by the new creation he is spiritual and divine; by corruption he hath the image of the devil; by this he is restored to the image of God; by that he had the seeds of all villanies; by this the roots of all graces: that made us fly from God, this makes us return to him; that made us enemies to his authority; this subjects us to his government; that made us contemn his law; this makes us prize and obey it. "Instead of the thorn, there shall come up the fir-tree; instead of the briar, shall come up the myrtle-tree," Isa. lv. 14; and God will preserve it from being cut off, speaking of the time of redemption.

It is a universal change of the whole man. It is a new creature, not only a new power, or new faculty: this, as well as creation, extends to every part, understanding, will, conscience, affections, all were corrupted by sin, all are renewed by grace. Grace sets up its ensigns in all parts of the soul, surveys every corner, and triumphs over every lurking enemy; it is as large in renewing, as sin was in defacing. The whole soul shall be glorified in heaven; therefore the whole soul shall be beautified by grace. The beauty of the church is described in every part, Can. iv. 1, 2, 3, 4, &c.

This new creation bears resemblance to creation and generation. God in creation creates all parts of

the creature entire. When nature forms a child in
the womb, it doth not only fashion one part, leaving
the other imperfect; but labours about all, to form an
entire man: the Spirit is busy about every part in the
formation of the new creature. Generation gives the
whole shape to the child, unless it be monstrous. God
doth not to produce monsters in grace; there is the
whole shape of the new man. You mistake much, if
you rest in a reformation of one part only; God will
say, such a work was none of my creation. He doth
not do things by halves.

It bears proportion to corruption: as sin expelled
the whole frame of original righteousness, so regene-
rating grace expels the whole frame of original corruption. It was not only the head, or only the heart,
only the understanding, or only the will, that was
overcast with the blackness of sin; but every part of
man did lose its original rectitude. Not a faculty
could boast itself, like the Pharisee, and say, it was
not like this or that publican; the waves of sin had
gone over the heads of every one of them. Sin, like
leaven, had infected the whole mass; grace over-
spreads every faculty to drive out the contagion.
Grace is compared to light, and light is more or less
in every part of the air above the horizon, for the
expulsion of darkness when the sun ariseth. The
Spirit is compared to fire, and therefore pierceth
every part with his warmth, as heat diffuseth itself
from the fire to every part of water. The natural
man is denominated from corruption, not an old understanding, or an old will, but the old man. So a regenerate man is not called a new understanding, or a
new will, but a new man.

The proper seat of grace is the substance of the
soul, and therefore it influences every faculty. It is
the form whence the perfection both of understanding and will does flow; it is not, therefore, placed in
either of them, but in the essence of the soul. It is
by this the union is made between God and the soul

but the union is not of one particular faculty, but of the whole soul. He that is joined to the Lord, is one spirit; it is not one particular faculty that is perfected by grace, but the substance of the soul. Besides, that is the seat of grace which is the seat of the Spirit; but this or that particular faculty is not the seat of the Holy Ghost, but the soul itself, whence the Spirit rules every particular faculty by assisting grace, like a monarch in the metropolis sending orders to all parts of his dominions. The Spirit is said to dwell in a man, in the whole man, as the soul doth in the body, in forming every part of it; if it dwelt only in one faculty, there could be no spiritual motion of the other; the principles in the will would contradict those in the understanding; the will would act blindly, if there were no spiritual light in the understanding to guide it: the light of the understanding would be useless, if there were no inclination in the will to follow it; and grace in both these faculties would signify little, if there remained an opposing perversity in the affections. The Spirit, therefore, is in the whole soul, like fire in the whole piece of iron, quickening, warming, mollifying, making flexible, and consuming what is contrary: like Aaron's ointment, poured upon the head, and thence running down to the skirts of the soul.

Therefore there is a gracious harmony in the whole man. As in generation two forms cannot remain in the same subject: for in the same instant wherein the new form is introduced, the old is cast out: so at the first moment of infusing grace, the body of death hath its deadly wound in every faculty, understanding, will, conscience, affection. The rectitude reaches every part; and all the powers of the soul by a strong combination, by one common principle of grace actuating them, conspire together to be subject to the law of God, and advance in the ways of holiness; it is with the whole heart that God is sought. In the understanding there is light instead of darkness, whereby it yields to the wisdom of God, and searches into the will of God; the spirit of the mind is renewed. In the will there is softness instead of hardness, humility instead of pride, whereby it yields to the will of God, and closes with the law of God. In the heart and conscience, there is purity instead of uncleanness, whereby it is purged from dead works, settled against the approbation of sin, and a resolution to be void of offence. In the affections there is love instead of enmity, delight instead of weariness, whereby they yield to the pleasure of God, have flights into the bosom of God: "O, how love I thy law! it is my delight day and night." The memory is a repository for the precepts and promises of God, as the choicest treasure. It is a likeness to Christ; the whole human nature of Christ was holy, every faculty of his soul, every member of his body, his nature holy, his heart holy. If we are not so formed, Christ is not formed in us: look therefore whether the reformation you rest in, be in the whole, and in every part of the soul.

It is principally an inward change. It is as inward as the soul itself. Not only a cleansing the outside of the cup and platter, a painting over the sepulchre, but a casting out the dead bones, and putrefied flesh; of a nature different from a pharisaical and hypocritical change. It is a clean heart David desires; not only clean hands. If it were not so, there could be no outward rectified change. The spring and wheels of the clock must be mended, before the hand of the dial will stand right. It may stand right two hours in the day, when the time of the day comes to it, but not from any motion or rectitude in itself. So a man may seem by one or two actions to be a changed man; but the inward spring being amiss, it is but a deceit. Sometimes there may be a change, not in the heart, but in the things which the heart is set upon, when they are not what they were: as a man whose heart was set upon uncleanness, change of beauty may change his affections; the change is not in the man,

but in the object. But this I change I speak of, is a
change in the mind, when there is none in the object;
as the affection of a child to his trifles changeth with
tne growth of his reason, though the things his heart
was set upon remain in the same condition as before.

It is a change of principle. The principle of a
natural man in his religious actions, is artificial; he
is wound up to such a peg, like the spring of a machine,
by some outward respects which please him: but as
the motion of the machine ceaseth, when the spring is
down, so a natural man's motion holds no longer than
the delight those motions gave him, which first
engaged him in it. But the principle in a good man
is spirit, an internal principle; and the first motion of
this principle is towards God, to act from God, and
to act for God. He fetches his fire from heaven, to
kindle his service: a heat and fervency of spirit
precedes his serving the Lord. There may be a
serving God from an outward heat, conveying a
vigour and activity to a man; but the new creature
serves God from inward and heated affections. Ex-
amine, therefore, by what principles do I hear, and
pray, and live, and walk? For all acts are good or
evil, as they savour of a good or bad root, or principle in the heart. The two principles of the new creature, are faith and love. What is called the new
creature, Gal. vi. 15, is called faith working by love,
Gal. v. 6.

The first principle of the new creature is faith.
Faith is a part of this new creature. This is the first
discovery of all spiritual life within us, and therefore
the immediate principle of all spiritual motion. A
splendid action without faith is but moral; whereas
one less glittering, is spiritual with it. The new
creature being begotten by the seed of the word, and
having thereby an evangelical frame, hath therefore
that which is the prime evangelical grace, upon
which all other graces grow; and consequently all
the acts of the new creature spring from this principle

immediately, viz. faith in the precept, as a rule; faith
in the promise, as an encouragement; faith in the
Mediator, as a ground of acceptance. Therefore if
we have not faith in the precept, though we may do
a service not point-blank against the precept, yet it
is not a service according to a divine rule; if we have
not faith in the promise, we do it not upon divine
motives; if we act not by faith in the Redeemer, we
despise the way of God's ordaining the presentation
of our service to him. All those that you find, Heb.
xi. acting from faith, had sometimes a faith in the
power of God, sometimes in the faithfulness of God;
but they had not only a faith in the particular promise,
or precept, but it was ultimately resolved into the
promise of the Messiah to come: "These all died in
faith, not having received the promises, but having
seen them afar off," &c. ver. 13. The performance
of particular promises, they had received; but not the
performance of this grand promise; but that their
faith respected. They, as new creatures, did all in
observance of God promising the Mediator; and we
are to do all in observance of God sending the Mediator, being persuaded of the agreeableness of our services to him, upon the account of the command; and
of the acceptation of our services by him, upon the
account of the Mediator. This put a difference be-
Paul's prayer, after the infusion of grace into him,
and before; so that our Saviour sets a particular
emphasis upon it, "Behold he prays." Acts ix. 11.
Paul, no doubt, had prayed many times before his
believing, but nothing of that kind was put upon the
file, as a prayer: before, they were prayers of a self-
righteous Pharisee, but these of an evangelical convert; these were praysrs springing from obedience to
Christ, and faith in him; from a "Lord what wilt thou
have me to do?"

There are many principles of action, hope of
heaven, fear of hell, reputation, interest, force of natural conscience, some of those are inward, some out-

ward, which are the bellows that blow up a man to
some fervency in action; but the true fire that contributes an heavenly frame to a service, is the love of
God. The desire of the heart is carried out to God;
his heart draws near to God, because his sole delight
is in God, and his sole desire for him, " Whom have I
in heaven but thee ?" Psa. lxxiii. 25. Then verse 28,
" But it is good for me to draw near to God." This
choice affection in the new creature, inspires his services, makes his soul spring up with a wonderful liveliness. The new creation is the restoration of the
soul to God from its apostasy; a casting down those
rebellious principles which contended with him, and
reducing his affections to the right centre; and when
all the lines meet here in one centre, in God, all the
returns to him flow from this affection. It is but one
thing settled in the soul, as the object of its earnest
desire; and that should be the spring of all its inquiries and actions, the " beholding the beauty of the
Lord." Things may be done out of a common affection; as when a man will raise a child fallen into the
dirt, out of a common tenderness; but a father would
raise him with more natural affection, which is a
sphere above that common compassion. Every affection, therefore, is not the renewed principle, but a
choice affection to God. This is a mighty ingredient
in this change, and doth distinguish the new creature
from all others. One acts out of affection to God, the
other out of affection to self. Man may be offended
with sin, because it disturbs his ease, health, estate,
&c. He may pray, and hear, merely out of a respect
to a natural conscience : but how can these be the
acts of the new creature, when there is no respect to
God in all this ? But a new creature would quench
the fire of corrupt self-love, to burn only with a spiritual and divine flame : he depresseth the one to exalt
the other, and would be disengaged from the burdensome chains of self-love, that he might be moved only
by the spiritual charms of the other purer affection :

It is a death to him to have any steams of self-love rise up to smoke and black a service.

This inward change is a change of end, as well as principle. The glory of God is the end of the new creature, self the end of the old man. Before this new creation, a man's end was to please self; now his end is to please God. A man that delights in knowledge to please his understanding, and for self-improvement, when he becomes a new creature, though his desire for knowledge is not removed, yet his end is changed, and he thirsts after knowledge, not merely to please his inquisitive disposition, but to admire and praise God, and direct himself in ways agreeable to him. As the end of the sensualist is to taste the sweetness in pleasure, so the end of a renewed man is to know more of God, to taste a sweetness in him, and in every religious duty. This is the distinguishing character of the new creature. This design for the glory of God was not to be found among any of the heathen, who were so great admirers of virtue. Most of them intended only an acquiring a reputation among their countrymen; and though some of them might esteem virtue for its native dignity, yet this was to esteem it by the moiety of it, when they referred it not to the honour of God, from whence it flowed to the world. Man was not created for himself, and to be his own end. He therefore that chiefly aims at his own satisfaction in any thing, is not a new creature; he hath his old deformed end into which he sunk by the fall. But grace carries a man higher, and reduceth all to God, and to his well-pleasing. The apostle desires they may be "filled with the knowledge of the will of God, that they may walk worthy of the Lord, unto all well pleasing." Col. i. 9, 10. The very first motion of this new principle is towards God, to act for God. As the first appearance of a living seed in the ground, is towards heaven; thither it casts its look, from whence its life came. What the new creature receives is from God. "They received it as the word of God." 1 Thess. ii. 13. And therefore what he doth is for God.

The principal intent of God in the new creation is for himself, " I will sow her to me ;" Hos. ii. 23, speaking of the church in the time of the gospel : not to sin, not to the world, not for herself, but I will sow her to me. Husbandmen sow the ground for themselves, for their own use, to reap the harvest ; and the corn grows up to the husbandmen that sowed it. What the seed doth naturally, the new creature doth intentionally, grow up for God. Since the new creature is a divine infusion, it must needs carry the soul to please God, and aim at his glory. God would never put a principle into the creature, to drive it from himself, and conduct it to his own dishonour ; this consists not with God's righteousness, this would be a deceiving of the creature. It is impossible, but that which is from God in so peculiar a manner, and with gracious intentions to restore the creature to his happiness, must tend to the advancement of God. Where there are no aims at the divine glory, there is no divine nature, nothing in the soul that can claim kindred with God. Regeneration is a forming the soul for God himself, and to show forth his praise. Hence they are said to be a peculiar people, in respect of their end as well as their state. Certainly that man who makes not God his pattern, and his end, that doth not advance the praise and glory of God, was never new formed by him. What comes from God must naturally tend to him. Is it possible, that the living image of God should disgrace the original ? That a divine impression should be unconcerned in the divine honour ?

The new creation is an evangelical impression, and therefore corresponds in its intention with the gospel. This is the instrument whereby the creature was wrought ; and this was appointed and published for the glory of God ; " Glory to God in the highest." It is to promote holiness in the creature, which is the only way whereby we can honour God: this is the prime lesson the grace or gospel of God teaches, "to live godly," to live to God. What therefore is produced by the efficacy of such an instrument, cannot but aim at the glory of God, which was intended in it: otherwise the gospel would work an effect contrary to itself, which no instrument doth produce, when managed by a wise agent, and contrary to the end of the agent, viz. the Spirit of God, whose end is to glorify Christ, "He shall glorify me," John xvi. 14. The frame and acts of a renewed man, are like the grain, or seed of the word sown in the heart. Nothing the gospel designs more than the laying self low, even as low as dust and death. The first lesson is self-denial. It is in self that the strength and heart of the body of sin and lust lie: and it is the principal end of the gospel, to bring the creature to sacrifice self-love to righteousness, self-interest, self-contentment, wholly to God and his law, and his love, that God may be all in all in the creature. Before the heart was touched with the gospel, it had not the least impulse to bring forth the virtues and excellencies of God into the world; but when it is changed, it is filled to the brim with zealous desires to have his name exalted upon a high throne among men.

A new creation is the bringing forth the soul in a likeness to God. The end therefore of the new creature is the glory of God. As God is the cause, so he is the pattern of the new creature, according to which he doth frame the soul; it is "after God, created in righteousness," &c. Eph. iv. 24. There can be no likeness to God, where the creature dissents from him in the chief end. Without such an agreement, there can be nothing but variance between God and the creature. All the commotions and quarrels upon earth, are founded upon the difference of ends. God aims at his own glory, so doth the new creature: otherwise it were impossible he should walk with God, or follow him, as a dear child. It consists also

in a likeness to Christ; his resurrection is the pattern,
and cause of our regeneration; " Ye are risen with
Christ." What, to contrary ends? Did Christ rise
only to live to himself? No; but to live to God, as
the great end for which he was appointed Mediator.
Did he design to glorify God on earth, and doth he
live to dishonour God in heaven? No, he lives to
the same end there for which he lived and died here.
Our spiritual resurrection is not only a restoring us
to a spiritual life, but to the ends of this life, a living
to God and Christ, and to the ends of his mediation.
Surely the new creature cannot be so brutish, as not
to mind the honour of that nature, to which it is so
nearly allied, the glory of that God unto whom it hath
the honour to bear a resemblance. A new creature
hath a mighty sprightliness, and a height of spirit in
some measure, when any thing in his hands concerns
God, more than when it concerns himself; for his
will being framed according to the will of God, is
filled with an ambition for promoting the excellency
of his name.

The end of the new creation is to advance the soul.
It can never be advanced by an end lower than itself,
or equal to itself. Any interest, lower than God,
would be a degrading of it, a disparagement to its
state, and too sordid for the soul to drive at; for it is
the excellency, or sordidness of the end, which doth
elevate or debase a man's spirit, and his action also;
the one enlargeth, the other shrivels up the soul in its
operation. All things below God are unworthy of
a soul rectified by a new creation. The soul is only
perfected in a tendency to this end, and disgraced and
lost in the impurity of lower aims. That grace that
is most durable, and doth most ennoble the spirit of
a man, has this property, that it seeks not her own,
nor vaunts itself.

It is impossible the soul can have this new creation,
without a change of end. It is not conceivable how
any thing can return to that, which it doth not eye as

its end. The soul, as deriving its original from God, hath an obligation in all its motions to return to him, as its chief end. The new creature hath an higher obligation by grace. Doth that therefore deserve the name of the new creature, that is so far from answering a gracious tie, that it doth not so much as answer a natural one ? That is yet below the sphere of inanimate creatures, who all run back to their fountain, and one way or other, declare the glory of God. He is no new creature therefore, who is devotedly fawning upon himself, caressing himself: he is one that is yet bemired in his old nature, and hath not yet received of the fruit of Christ's purchase, redeeming and renewing grace. Those that are under the efficacious influence of it, and are the temple of the Holy Spirit, do glorify God in their body and spirit too, inwardly as well as outwardly, because they are God's. The understanding and will are both elevated by grace. The more intelligent any creature is, the more noble is his end, or ought to be; and the more he doth intend his end. The aim of a man is higher than that of a child: the aims of men in this or that station, are still more noble than the ends of men in a lower rank. Since the new creation therefore endues man with the most excellent nature he is capable of, it must fix a man upon the most excellent end, which is God and his glory; it were not else a new creature, or worthy of such a title.

This change of end only fits the soul for its proper service. From this end arises a quickness, and an heartiness in every service. When God and his glory are not our end, our hearts flag, and we feel our spirits tired at our entrance into any service for him. When the apostle had made the glory of God his end, in testifying the gospel of the grace of God, then his life was not counted dear to him, that he might finish his course with joy. Where this end sits uppermost in the heart, all allurements to the contrary are mightily despised. What a scornful eye doth the apostle cast upon all other things; and sets no higher value upon them than he would upon dross and dung, when they were not conducing to his main end, which was the knowledge of Christ.

Well then; this is one of the most essential properties of the new creature, and that which is the clearest discovery of this state. A new creature is as earnest in secret, for the glory of God, and as industrious for God, as if the eyes of all the world were upon him; the bent of his heart always stands this way; he glorifies God in his spirit as well as body. When men will be zealous in things that concern God, before men, and negligent in their spirits, and inward part of the soul, then the glory of God was not their end, but themselves. For what is a man's end, sets an edge upon his spirit in private, as well as public. But a new creature is of another frame. When he finds that he hath missed of his full aim, and hath not had that single respect as he ought, he is unsatisfied, and troubled that God hath been no more glorified by him. But he that is not renewed, is well pleased, if any concerns of self have been advanced, though God be not glorified; and his soul is at rest in that act, as it hath lived to himself, and brought in something to increase the treasure of his selfish ends.

As it is an inward change, in respect of principle and end; so it is a change of thoughts. Being new, he is new in the choicest faculty. As when he was after the flesh, he minded the things of the flesh; so now being after the Spirit, he minds the things of the Spirit. As a child hath not the thoughts of a man, so neither hath a natural man the thoughts of a new creature. A principle is placed in his understanding which doth emit other beams different from that smoky light, which was in it before. Though a new creature cannot hinder the first motions, yet he endeavours to suppress their proceeding any further, and excites others in his heart, to make head against them;

and would, as far as he could, hinder the rising of any
wave, the least bubbling against right reason and the
interest of God. When David had an inclination in
his heart to God's statutes, the immediate effect of it
is to hate vain thoughts. " I have inclined my heart
to perform thy statutes:" and it follows, " I hate vain
thoughts," Psa. cxix. 112, 113. The vanity of his
heart was a burden to him, and he loathed all the inward excrescences and buds from that bitter stump
he still bore within him. A new creature is as careful against wickedness in the head or heart, as in the
life. He would be purer in the sight of God, than in
the view of men: he knows none but God can see the
workings of his heart, or the thoughts of his head; yet
he is as careful that they should not rise up, as that
they should not break out. The soul is so changed,
that it is no longer a stranger, and an enemy to the
motions of the Spirit; it will welcome them upon their
entrance, conduct them into the innermost room, converse familiarly with them, and delight in their company; it invites their stay, pursues them when they
seem to depart, holds them fast, and will not let them
go, as the church doth to Christ. He turns much in
upon himself, sets his eye upon his own heart, keeps
that with all diligence, to observe what issues of a
spiritual life are there; as it is directed, " Keep thy
heart with all diligence, for out of it are the issues of
life," Prov. iv. 23. If he perceives any weeds to spring
up there, or mushrooms, as they often will in a night,
he cuts them up. and throws them out. The understanding is more quick and sensible, to discern them
in the first risings, to receive good ones, or check bad
ones, than it was before; the new creature is sensible of any touch contrary to its interest. A corrupt
mind draws to it the vilest things, and unproportion-
able to the true nature of the soul, till by new creation it be set higher, and by a sanctified reason becomes more choice about its objects; and then like
David, the heart is filled as with marrow and fatness,

when he meditates on God in the night-watches. The thoughts of God are an inward spring of pleasure to him, more than the thoughts of sin can be to a deformed and depraved soul.

Change of comforts follows upon this. Since there is a change of nature, there is a change of his complacency. The former nature is his trouble, therefore all his delights which arise from it, are its discontents and burden. Every nature hath a peculiar pleasure belonging to it: the nature of a dove will not acquiesce in that which pleases a swine; nor the new nature in that which pleased the old. The comforts of manhood are of another make than those of a child; and the comforts of a prince more elevated than those of a pleasant, because he hath another spirit. That Spirit who is appointed to renew him, is appointed an officer to comfort him: as therefore he gives him new principles, so he gives him new consolations. He is, as a comforter, to glorify Christ; to receive of his, and show it unto the new creature. They are Christ's own words, " He shall glorify me, for he shall receive of mine, and shall show it unto you," being described before under the title of a comforter. He shall receive of mine, grace from me, suitable to the grace in me, wherewith to beautify; and comforts from me, suitable to those comforts in me, wherewith to refresh you. As they are brought to live the life of God in holiness, so they are brought to live the life of God in joy and comfort. Righteousness, peace, joy, are the trinity which make up the kingdom of God in the heart, " The kingdom of God is not meat and drink, but righteousness, and peace, and joy in the Holy Ghost," Rom. xiv. 17. As the grace of God is their life, so the joy of the Lord is their strength. Strangers to God intermeddle not with it, and have no share in it. There is a joy put into the heart, together with this new creature; " Thou hast put gladness into my heart." A gladness not founded upon any worldly consideration, as the joy of men, not a joy of their own putting in; but the new creature's joy, is a joy of God's putting in. Other mens' comforts are in the creature; the new creature's comforts in the Creator. Others cannot joy, if worldly things be removed, because the foundation of their joy is without them. But these by the loss of worldly things, have their comforts rather increased than impaired, because the foundation of their joy is within them. The comforts of a natural man are derived from broken cisterns. The comforts of a new creature are derived from the full fountain of life, which makes their very sufferings gloriously comfortable to them. The prodigal by his change of mind, had a change of refreshment, robes for rags, and a fatted calf for husks. It is as much his comfort to loathe himself, as derived from Adam, and to love the self implanted by God, as it was before the contrary. He can never look upon the new creature in him, but with delightful views; and a pleasure mingles itself with every cast of his eye upon it. For certainly from making God our end, and doing all things for his glory, flows the highest delight: since God is the only happiness of that soul that is in conjunction with him, as his main end, he must needs have a share in the happiness of God as well as his nature. Felicity and consolation follow it, as the shadow doth the body; and every act of the new creature towards God, is edged with comfort in the very acting.

As it is an inward change, so it is also an outward change. I call it outward, in regard of objects, in regard of operations: though it is principally inward, in regard of the prime seat of it; in regard of the form which causeth the outward. The power of seeing is in the soul, though the vision itself be in the eye. The change our Saviour made in those he cured, was in the organ, when he made the blind to see, the deaf to hear, and the lame to walk, which did necessarily infer a change of objects, and a change of actions. So a man by this new creation sees the things of God, hears the voice of God, walks in the ways of God. All outward changes argue not an inward; but an inward is always attended with an outward.

In regard of objects. The world and sin were before the objects of his inquiries and endeavours: now he seeks the face of God, "his soul follows hard after him." The world and God are so contrary, that the love of the one is enmity to the other. From multitudes of objects which distracted him, he is come to unity, which quiets and settles him. "One thing have I desired of the Lord, that will I seek after, that I may dwell in the house of the Lord all the days of my life, to behold the beauty of the Lord, and to inquire in his temple." Psa. xxvii. 4. It is no lower an object than this that the soul is conversant about, about God himself, to embrace him; about what hath most of God in it, to value and cherish it; about the word of God, to direct him in his ways, and to do his work. The understanding is conversant about the things of God, in the apprehension of them; the will in the election, the affections in complacency in them. Spiritual objects are set up by every faculty, as the delightful things which it heartily embraceth. Before a man had no affection to God, you might as well have persuaded a swine to love the music of a lute, as a natural man supremely to God. All his desires were set upon the dross of the world, the customs, course, corruptions, pleasures of the world: but a truly regenerate man can as little make the world his chief object of desire and affection, as a man used to choice viands can feed upon chaff and husks. The design of the gospel is to set forth God in Christ, as an amiable object, as infinitely glorious. It declaims against the world, to draw men from the affectionate considerations of it. The renewed work then doth consist in fixing upon God in Christ, as the main object of desire and affection. When the heart therefore complies with the gospel, there must be a compliance with the chief subject of the gospel, and in such a manner as may answer the intendment of the gospel. While Paul was in his natural and pharisaical state, Christ and his truth was accounted as dung, trampled upon as dross, fit to be thrown out of the converse of mankind: but when his heart is changed, there is a change in the object of his valuation; Christ is then his treasure, his all; and other things but dross, in comparison of him.

In regard of operations. Old things are passed away, old actions as well as old affections. Operations are never constantly against nature; the heart and the actions do not always contradict one another. According to the abundance of the heart, the mouth speaks. According to the spring of grace in the heart, will the hand of the life stand. It will vent itself more or less, according to the quantity of it. It is an inward baptism with fire, which will quickly break out, and show itself in the members, "By their fruits ye shall know them," Matt. vii. 20. New apprehensions infer new operations. An alteration of judgment cannot be without an alteration of acting. As he hath received Christ Jesus the Lord, so he walks in him. The very design of God in the new creation was this, "Created in Christ Jesus unto good works, which God hath before ordained, that we should walk in them," Ephes. ii. 10. If there be not then new works, there is no new creation, for the chief intention and aim of God cannot be frustrated. Christ formed in a man is not a sleepy and inactive being; actions will scent of him. Fruits bear the image of the root whence they spring, and upon which they flourish. A new root cannot bring forth old fruits: if the nature of a crab tree, be changed into that of a vine, it will bear no longer crabs but grapes. Where holiness is implanted in the nature, holiness will be imprinted in the life. A man that hath reason superior to sense, doth use his sense rationally: a renewed man that hath grace superior to reason, useth his reason graciously. The operations were rational when bare reason held the sceptre; but they are spiritual, when grace ascends the throne. For it cannot be, that that person who is actuated by the Spirit, lives in the Spirit, walks in the Spirit, should do any thing without a spiritual tincture, in that wherein he is actuated by it. For it is impossible, but every action must be dyed of the same colour with the principle whence it flows, and by which it is directed. Actions of sensitive nature are, by reason of grace, directed by a new rule, directed to a new end. He ate and drank to the flesh before, now to God. He degraded his soul to invent ways to pamper his body: now he puts his body in its due posture, to serve the soul, and both to exalt God. Yea, his religious duties are changed, not as to the matter, but the manner. He knew them before, as he did Christ, after the flesh; he now knows them, and performs them after the Spirit. There is zeal instead of coldness, liveliness instead of deadness, brokenness instead of presumption, a spirit of liberty instead of the whip of conscience, confidence in God instead of confidence in duty, melting pleading of promises instead of a pharisaical pleading of works; in a word, grace instead of nature, spirit instead of flesh. Paul of a pharisaical boaster, becomes a Christian suppliant; " behold he prays." This change is outward as well as inward : in a man of an exact morality it is chiefly inward; he walks in his old outward ways with a new heart; in a loose man renewed, it is apparently outward; he hath left both his old ways and his old nature : but a man only outwardly reformed, without any inward change, walks in new ways with an old spirit. " He that lacks these things," saith the apostle, after an enumeration of several graces, " hath forgotten that he was purged from his old sins;" for indeed he never was.

CHAPTER III

Regeneration considered as a vital principle — As a Habit — The renewed nature is disposed to every good work in disposition and activity — It is naturally, voluntarily, fervently, unboundedly, powerfully, easily, pleasantly active. Power of grace in the regenerate renders it difficult for them to sin.

HAVING considered this new creation in the nature of a change,

Let us consider it in the nature of a vital principle. This new creation is a translation from death to life, "We know that we have passed from death to life," 1 John iii. 14. And we have not a spiritual life, till we are in Christ; "he that hath not the Son, hath not life." When our Saviour called Lazarus out of the grave, he gave him a principle of life and motion; the same he doth when he calls men from a spiritual death in sin: whatsoever we had from the first Adam is mortal; whatsoever we have from the second Adam is vital; the one communicates a spiritual life, as the other propagated a spiritual death. The new creature is a vital, powerful principle, naturally moving the soul to the service and obedience of God, and doth animate the faculties in their several motions, as the soul doth quicken the members of the body. It is called the hidden man, the inward man, implying that it hath life and motion. As the life of the body is from the soul, as the effect from the cause, so the life of the soul is from grace; Christ is the meritorious cause of this life in his person; the efficient cause of it by his Spirit; but grace is the formal cause of this life: as God is the cause of our bodily life efficiently, and the soul the cause of it formally. It is not then a gilding, but a quickening; not a carving, but an enlivening. Whatsoever doth proceed from an external cause, is not life or a living motion. A piece of wood may be carved into the shape of a man, but remains wood still, in such a form and figure. But a Christian hath a spiritual life breathed into him, as Adam had a natural. When Adam's body was formed of the earth, it was no more than earth, till a heavenly spark was breathed into him by God, to set him upon his feet, and enable that piece of earth to move. It is distinguished therefore from hypocrisy, which is but the shadow of Christianity; this is a living principle; that a form, this a power; that a piece of art, this a nature. A picture may have the lineaments of a man, but not the life, understanding, and affections of a man.

Let us consider it as a habit, and then see what light the consideration of it, as a vital principle and a habit, gives us into the nature of this new creation. By habit we must not understand, as we do in common speech, a clothing; as when we say, such a one was in such a habit; but by habit we mean an inward frame, enabling a man to act readily and easily; as when an artificer hath the habit of a trade. Since this new creation is not a destruction of the substance of the soul; but that there is the same physical being, and the same faculties in all men, and nothing is changed in its substance, as far as respects the nature of man: it is necessary therefore that this new creation consist in gracious qualities and habits, which beautify and dispose the soul to act righteously and holily. Corruption of nature is the poison, the sickness, and deformity of our nature; grace is the beauty, health, ornament of it, and that which gives it worth and value. When a debauched man is become virtuous, we say, he is another man, a new man, though he hath the same soul and body which he had before, but he hath quitted those evil habits wherewith he was possessed. It is impossible to conceive a new creature without new habits: nothing can be changed from a state of corruption to a state of purity, without them. The making darkness to become light, in the very nature of it, implies the introducing a new quality. This is meant by the seed, "His seed remains in him," 1 John iii. 9; as seed makes the earth capable to bring forth good fruit, which had a nature before to bring forth, not corn, but weeds, till the grain was put into it: and it is expressed by " a fountain of living water springing up into eternal life," John iv. 44.

There is such a habit. God doth provide as much for those that he loves, in order to a supernatural good, as for those creatures that he loves in order to a natural good : but God hath put into all creatures such forms and qualities, whereby they may be inclined of themselves to motions agreeable to their nature, in an easy and natural way. Much more doth God infuse into those that he moves to the obtaining a supernatural good, some spiritual qualities, whereby they may be moved rationally, sweetly, and readily to attain that good: he puts into the soul a spirit of love, a spirit of grace, whereby as their understandings are possessed with a knowledge of the excellency of his ways, so their wills are so seasoned by the power and sweetness of this habit, that they cannot, because they will not, act contrary thereunto. And this habit of grace hath the same spiritual force in a gracious way, as these principles in other creatures in a natural way. As the habit of sin is called flesh, in regard of its nature, and death in regard of its consequence, so the habit of grace is called the new creature and spirit, in regard of its term and consequent life. This habitual grace is the principle of all supernatural acts, as the soul concurs as an immanent principle to all works by this or that faculty. As Christ had a body prepared him, to do the work of a Mediator, so the soul hath a habit prepared it to do the work of a new creature. To this purpose there is a habit of truth or sincerity in the will, and a hidden wisdom in the understanding. As the corrupt nature is a habit of sin, so the new nature is a habit of grace ; God doth not only call us to believe, love, and obey, but brings in the grace of faith, and love, and obedience, bound up together, and plants it in the soil of the heart; to grow up there unto eternal life: he gives a willingness and readiness to believe, love, and obey.

This habit is necessary. The acts of a Christian are supernatural, which cannot be done without a supernatural principle; we can no more do a gracious action without it, than the apostles could do the works of their office, unless endued with power from above, which our Saviour bids them tarry at Jerusalem for. If there were not a gracious habit in the soul, no act could be gracious; or supposing it could, it could not be natural, it would be only a force. New creation is not from the Spirit compelling, but inclining; not like the throwing a stone contrary to its nature, but changing the nature, and planting other habits whereby the actions become natural. As sin was habitual in a man by nature, so grace must be habitual in a new creature, otherwise a man is not brought into a contrary state (though the acts should be contrary) if there be not a contrary habit; for it is necessary the soul should be inclined in the same manner towards God as before it was towards sin; but the inclination to sin was habitual.

This habit is but one. For it is an entire rectitude in all the faculties, and an universal principle of working righteously. As the corrupt nature is called the old Adam, and a body of death; the gracious nature is called the new man, as a man is but one man, a body one body, though consisting of divers members and several parts, all formed by one Spirit, and making up but one habit, so that as all sins are parts of that body of death; so all graces are but branches of this one root; as from that original light, kindled at the first creation by God, were framed the stars and lights of heaven, which have their several appearances and motions, and are distinct from one another, though all arising from the womb of that first light; so all particular graces, though they have their stated seasons of action, and are distinct in themselves, yet all flow from, and are contained in this habit as in a root. They are so many grapes growing upon one stalk, clusters proceeding from one root of the new nature. It is from the participation of the divine nature, that all those graces arise, the exercise of which the apostle exhorts them to, 2 Pet. i. 4, &c. And indeed it being a divine nature, must needs include all the perfections due to it: as the divine essence of God is one, yet contains all perfections immanently; and if there were a deficiency of any, it could not be the divine essence; so the grace infused into the heart contains in it virtually all the perfections wherein it may agree with the nature of God's holiness, otherwise it were not a divine nature; if there were any defect in the nature of the habit, I say in the nature of the habit. And it cannot be otherwise, for though the Spirit may give one gift to one man, another gift to another, yet when he would make a new creature, there must be a nature or habit containing all graces. It could not else be a divine nature, for if the Spirit doth purpose to make a new creature, he cannot but give all grace, which belongs to the essence and constitution of that new creature, otherwise he would either wilfully or weakly cross his own intention.

This habit receives various denominations:

From the subject. It is subjectively in the essence of the soul; but as it shows itself in the understanding, it is called the knowledge of God; as it is in the will, it is a choice of God; as it is in the affections, it is a motion to God; as the body of death is in the understanding, ignorance; in the will, enmity; in the conscience, deadness; in the affections, disorder and forwardness. As diseases receive several names, as they are centered in several parts, yet are but the distemper of the humours.

From the object. As it closes with Christ dying, it is faith; as it rejoiceth in Christ living, it is love; as it lies at the feet of Christ, it is humility; as it observes the will of Christ, it is obedience; as it submits to Christ afflicting, it is patience; as it regards Christ offended, it is grief; yet all arising from one habit and animated by faith; so that it is the love of faith, the joy of faith, the humility of faith, the patience of faith; they all spring from one habit, seated in one soul, conversant about one object, God in Christ; such an unity there is in all these diversities. As the holy oil wherewith the vessels of the tab rnacle were anointed, was but one ointment, though composed of many ingredients; as all the perfections of creatures are immanently in one God; all the evil dispositions of the creatures seminally in man by nature; so all the beauties of grace are immanently included in this habit.

Hence we may take a prospect of the nature of the new creature. It being thus a vital principle, and a habit, therefore the motion to God, and for God, must be

Ready, in respect to disposition. He stands ready and disposed to every good work, upon God's call. As the habit of sin disposeth the soul to every evil work, so the habit of grace prepares it for every good work, and makes it meet for its master's use, " If a man therefore purge himself from these, he shall be a vessel unto honour, sanctified, and meet for the master's use, and prepared unto every good work," 2 Tim. ii. 21. It is just as it was with Isaiah; at the first sight of the vision he complains, "Woe is me! I am a man of unclean lips," chap. vi. 5 ; taken up with self-reflection; no offers to act for God : but when a live coal was taken from the altar, and laid upon his mouth; there is a ready answer to God's question, " Whom shall I send? Here am I, send me," verse 7, 8. No demurs; it was a live coal from the altar had quickened him into a new frame for God. David doth not say, he had performed the statutes of God, but he had inclined his heart to perform them.

That I may not grate upon any troubled spirit; consider, that this readiness is seminally in every renewed person, yet it does not always actually appear. As the old nature contains in it seminally all sins, yet every man is more prone to one than another, according to education, temper of body, or a set of temptations; so the heart of a renewed man hath an habitual disposition to the exercise of all grace because it hath the seeds of all graces in it; yet it doth not act all alike, for want of vigorous occasions. As the attributes of God, though in the highest perfection, yet in their exercise in the world, sometimes one appears more triumphant than another, sometimes more of patience, sometimes mercy, sometimes justice, sometimes wisdom, one is more eminently apparent than another: so the divine nature hath seminally in this habit all grace, and an agreeableness to every duty enjoined; a principle to send forth the fruits of all, when an object is offered, and the grace excited by the Spirit of God; yet sometimes one is more visible than another, according to the call it hath to stand forth and show itself. This habitual disposition may be, when there is not a present actual fitness for some service of a higher strain, by reason of some particular commission of sin, which hath sullied the soul. As a vessel of honour in respect of its formation, may be fit for use; but in respect of some foulness contracted, may not be immediately fit for some noble service, till a new scouring hath passed upon it. A grown Christian who hath his senses exercised in the ways of God, doth not always actually exercise this habit; yet he is ready upon the least motion actually to do it: as a new creature having a change of end, doth habitually mind the glory of God, yet he doth not in every action actually think of it, or will it as his end: but he is ready to bring this habitual aim into exercise upon the least motion, and reaches out his arm to embrace and stand right to that point. David had an habit of repentance in him, while he lay asleep in his sin; and by virtue of this habit, he doth without any resistance comply with the first touch God gave him by Nathan.

His repentance flowed, and never ceased, till it had done its perfect work. It was a sign of a heart of flesh; a heart of stone could not have been so flexible. Job was eminent for patience; but being a new creature, he had a disposition to all the rest, and had acted them with as high a strain, had he had the same occasions.

This readiness to every service doth not actually appear in persons newly regenerate. I think the lowest degree of this habit in one newly regenerate, is a purpose of heart to cleave unto the Lord "When he came, and had seen the grace of God, he was glad, and exhorted them, that with purpose of heart they would cleave unto the Lord." Acts xi. 23. Certainly when there is such a fixed and constant purpose, it is a token of the grace of God: yet to this purpose there may not always be connected an actual readiness to every service: for at the first beginning of the new creature there is a strong resistance; it is in a strange soil; the armies of hell are in array against it; it is like a Daniel in a lion's den, or a Lot in Sodom, only God restrains the force of these enemies. As it is in a child derived from Adam, there is a principle in the natural corruption to exert all kind of wickedness; yet it doth not presently rise to the utmost of its force, till ripened by time and other intervening causes: so though the new creature hath in it a readiness virtually to the most raised action, to be as believing and laborious as Paul, as zealous as Elijah, as patient as Job, yet it mounts not presently to this state; a time must be allowed for growth. There is an infancy in grace, as well as in manhood. And as a child, though his soul be of the same nature with that of a man, yet he cannot exercise those acts of understanding and reason, because of the predominancy of sense, and the indisposition of the organs: so neither can a young Christian: he may have a disposition equal to the best Christians, but not an equal strength; the reluctance of the corrupt habit is more vigorous, not being much mortified; he wants also that additional strength gained by exercise. There may be a greater resistance to one grace, than to another, from the strength of some corruption particularly opposite to that grace; yet " to will is present with him; though he cannot perform that which is good," Rom. vii. 18. The posture of the soul to God, was as natural to him, as the posture of the heart was before to sin. As a young boy first come to school, may have as strong a purpose to get learning, as a man that hath taken all his degrees in the University. The first graces which appear in a renewed soul, are repentance and faith; because regeneration being a rooting up from the old stock, and setting up a new, as it relates to the old stock, it doth necessarily produce repentance upon the sight of his misery, and for being upon the old stock so long; and faith, as a necessary grace for closing with the Redeemer upon a sight of him, and for ingrafting him upon a new stock, And then love, admiration and thankfulness walk the stage, from a reflection upon the greatness of the misery escaped, and the great deliverance attained. Sprouts from a root grow up some faster, some slower; yet all arising from the same root. So some graces appear at the very first setting this habit in the soul, other graces lie hid till new occasions draw them out. This disposition, inclination, will, readiness, purpose, is the first language of a habit.

A second thing wherein you have a prospect of the new creature is this; as it is ready in respect of disposition, so it is in activity of motion. Since it is a life infused by infinite activity; since it is a habit bearing the impression of God, and maintained by a union with him, it is impossible it can be sleepy and dull in a constant way. All life hath motion proper to the principle of it. Rational life is attended with rational actions; sensitive life, with acts proper to sense. It is as impossible then that a spiritual life should be without acts consonant to it, as that the sun should appear in the firmament without darting forth its beams. All life is accompanied with natural heat, which is the band of it, whereby the body is enabled to a vigorous motion. The new creature is not a marble statue, or a transparent piece of crystal, which hath purity, but not life. It is a living spirit, and therefore active; a pure spirit, and therefore purely active, according to the degree of it. It is the same habit in part renewed, which Adam had by creation, which was not a sluggish and unwieldy principle; it must therefore have an activity, it could not else be a proper principle to contest with the contrary principle, which is active like the sea, casting out mire and dirt. Since the old Adam conveyed such a vigorous principle of corruption, the new Adam is not wanting to endue the principle of his conveyance with a suitable activity. Grace abounds in its vigour, as well as sin hath abounded in its kind. Upon Christ's call, Matthew left his receipt of custom, the other apostles their nets; motion presently follows an enlivening call of God. It is first a habit, then an act; first a spirit of grace and supplication, then a " looking upon him whom they have pierced," by an act of their understanding, and a mourning by an act of the will. First a sanctification of the spirit, then a belief of the truth to the obtaining of glory. When any thing ceaseth to act, there is either an oppression, or a death of nature.

This principle of the new creature is naturally active. All vital motions are natural. Sometimes in men there are natural actions without any actual exercise of reason; as when the spirits flow out to any part for the defence of it upon the motion of any passion, as blood starts to the face upon shame, which all the reason of a man cannot hinder. It is as natural to this new habit to produce new actions, as for any thing to engender according to its own likeness and species; as for a living tree to spring out in leaves and fruits. A renewed man, whose seed is within himself, brings forth fruit after his kind, as well as the herbs and the trees. All living creatures move agreeably to their natures, with a willingness and freedom of nature. The bramble doth not more naturally bring forth thorns, than a habit of sin doth steam out sinful actions ; nor a fountain more freely bubble up its water, than a habit of grace springs up in holy actions. For shall the workmanship of God be more unapt to the proper end of it, than the workmanship of the devil, since good works are the end of God's new creating us, that we should walk in them ? Walking is a natural motion, "We are his workmanship, created in Christ Jesus to good works." Eph. ii. 10. A well-dressed vine doth not more naturally bring forth grapes, than a soul rooted in Christ doth the fruits of the Spirit ; neither doth the sun more naturally enlighten the world with its beams, than the new creature shoots forth its desires and affections to God ; for it is impossible but this habit should tend to him, since it is planted by him. The new creature's services are his meat and drink, not his work ; it is as natural to him to do it, as for a creature to desire and take its proper food ; you need not hire a child to suck, by the promises of fine things, it will naturally, without imitation, take the breast. The new creature having a righteous and just nature, cannot but do righteous things ; nothing can act against its nature, while nature is orderly and not disturbed by some disease or frenzy. As God, whose image a regenerate man bears, cannot but do good, because his nature is goodness. "How can you that are dead to sin, live any longer therein ?" Rom. vi. 2. He can no more naturally do it, than a dead man can walk. Not but that there are some mistakes sometimes, which proceed not from nature, but from some obstructing humour. Nature doth not err in its right course, unless hindered by some adversary : the errors renewed men are subject to, proceed not from the regenerate principle in them, but from that remainder of corruption, which by degrees is weakened by the other, and at last wholly put off.

It is voluntarily active. There is a kind of natural necessity of motion, from life and habit, yet also a voluntary choice; it is a power which constrains and inclines the will. The Apostle tells us, there was a necessity laid upon him to preach the gospel, yet it was not a compulsion, but a voluntary act, after his will was changed. The new creature is not constrained from without, but flows freely, is not forced; the chief work is upon the will; the proper effect of any work upon the will is voluntariness; the Spirit works to make it willing, its motion then is not by compulsion: there is a sweet necessity of the new nature, and a gracious choice of will, which meet together, and kiss each other. How freely doth the soul, winged with grace, move to and for God, as a bird in the air! With what a free and ready spirit doth the new creature go to prayer, reading and hearing! How freely doth it breathe in the air of heaven! Not spurred by outward interest, or dragged by the threatenings of the law, nor chid to it by the clamours of conscience, but gently moved to it, and upheld in it, by a soft and dovelike and free spirit. How great is the difference between the flowing of a fountain, and the dropping of a sponge! One is free, the other squeezed. Between a statue drawn upon wheels and a living motion; one moves, the other is moved. Our Saviour by washing us from our sins in his own blood, "hath made us kings and priests unto God." First, kings, putting into the creature a royal and magnanimous frame, as he did into Saul, when he advanced him to the kingdom; and then priests to offer sacrifices to God with this royal and generous spirit: so that it is as troublesome to a soul, having this royal spirit, to omit things proper to this frame, as it is for a legalist to do them. Therefore where there are frequent omissions of duty, or a constant dulness in it, it shows the want of this kingly

frame, and, consequently, that we are not washed from
our sins in the blood of Christ.   There is both such a
nature and such a choice that as the apostle saith,
" We can do nothing against the truth, but for the
truth," 2 Cor. xiii. 8. So the new creature cannot but
do the things which are holy, just, and good, so far as
he is regenerate, were there no rule without to guide
him, because he hath a habit of holiness within him, a
will set to the right point.   His former state made him
have an aversion from holy services ; this makes all
spiritual duties connatural to him : so that it is as irksome for him to live without God in the world, as
before it was to live with him : he can as soon strip
himself of his own soul as act from a renewed principle contrary to God and righteousness.

It is fervently active.   The nobler the being of any
thing is, the greater degree of activity it is attended
with; the more spiritual the quality, the more vigorous
the effect.   Both the spirituality of the principle, excellency of the object, and affection to the end, conspire together to increase this activity.   The principle
is spiritually vital; the operation therefore is vigorous:
the object is God as amiable, the warmer therefore the
zeal : the acts are, loving God, trusting in God, de-
pending on God, promoting his kingdom in the heart,
acts delightful in themselves, delightful in their issue,
the motion in them more quick : the end is the glory
of God, the happiness of the creature ; the higher the
end, the more elevated the soul.   There is an innate
principle in every thing to preserve its happiness, it is
as natural as life itself.   Inanimate creatures are endued with this nature ; the flame aspires to heaven,
and waves on this and that side greedily, to catch
what may supply a fuel : much more will other creatures act vehemently for that which preserves their
beings ; the toad to its plantain, the swallow to its
celendine, the babe to the breast, and the Christian to
the word.   There is in the new creature an impetus
and force, settled in the soul to do good.   In this re-

spect it is likened to creatures of the greatest activity;
fire, wind, a spring of living water. What more active,
in the rank of corporeal beings, than fire and wind,
either above, or in the bowels of the earth? Witness
the many stately buildings speedily consumed by the
one, or overthrown by the other. The new principle
in the creature fills every part, dissolves the hard
heart, and makes it movable in the ways of God with
a glowing heat. But above this, there is a higher
denomination. The new creature is called spirit, "that
which is born of the Spirit, is spirit;" John iii. 6, that
is a spiritual creature. The activity of a spirit doth
inconceivably surmount that of a body. What vast
strides can a spirit take in a moment, from heaven to
earth! The habit of sin, in respect of its vehemence
to evil, is called a spirit, a spirit of whoredom; as well
as the habit of grace, in respect of its vehemence to
good, "a spirit of love," 2 Tim. i. 7. How active is
the new creature in its motion to God! It can fly in
a thought from earth to heaven, enter the bosom of
God, clasp about him, hold him fast, even till the
Almighty says, Let me alone. Where there are rivers
of living waters in the soul they will flow; where there
is a divine habit, the soul will have a paroxysm of
divine heat for the glory of God. Acts xvii. 16.
Paul's spirit was stirred in him upon the sight of the
Athenians' idolatry. If created to good works, then
not to a dull and sluggish motion in them; this was
not the design of the Creator, and therefore not the
disposition of the creature.

It is unboundedly active. This new creature's desires are as large as his nature; he cannot be bound
up in the narrow and contracted motions of his former
disposition. The natural activity of the soul over-
flows, like a swelled river, all natural bounds, since
it is possessed by a spiritual habit. A man without
a habit in an art, doth but bungle at his work, is
quickly tired, desponds of attaining what he would;
but he that hath a habit, suppose of mathematical

knowledge, finds one proposition following upon another, one deduction rising up from another, that he hath a largeness he knows not where to end: so the new creature finds one affection coming upon the neck of another, many times in transports and outgoings to God, which know no limits. It is unboundedly active,

In affections to God. The new creature would be as unlimited in its affections to God, as God is in his affections to him. It will not fix lower than the object it hath pitched upon in heaven; all its operations tend thither; nothing below can give them a cessation, though they may suffer an interruption; it flies up, and is pulled back; it mounts again and again, follows hard on after the Lord. His affections are larger than his ability. " Whom have I in heaven but thee? and there is none in earth that I desire besides thee." Psa. lxxiii. 25. He seems to scorn every thing else in comparison of God, though it were an angel. Like a man that makes haste to some mark, turns the impediments on this side and that side; the new creature puts by the temptations of the flesh and the world, to make its way into the bosom of God, the centre of its rest, and the boundless limit of its soul. The sun, so many thousand miles distant from us, sends its rays as far as the lowest valley of the earth; and the new creature, the dartings of his soul to the highest heavens. " Where the Spirit of the Lord is, there is liberty;" the veil is taken away, it " beholds, as in a glass, the glory of the Lord;" like an eagle, mounts up as near as it can to the sun, gazes upon it till its eyes be dazzled with its brightness: he is never glutted with the views of him; his desires for him are never bounded but by him; one breathing after another, that he may fill God, as it were, with his affections, as he is filled by him, with his Spirit. In his obedience too, he would have his heart enlarged, that he may run, not creep, in the ways of God's commandments; it is his grief that he cannot keep pace with God's commandments: it is his joy that God flies upon the wings of the wind to him, and his sorrow that he cannot fly upon the wings of the wind to God. He groans under his dulness, and his pleasure consists much in a liberty in God's service.

The principle of the new creature is active in disaffection to sin. He hates that body of death which hinders the accomplishment of the desires of his soul; and regards it at no other rate, than his fetter, disease, and torture. He is discomposed when he meets with any check in his religious course; it is a violence to his new nature, and he cannot bear it without regret. His anger and impatience rise with as much force against any obstacle to a free converse with God, as it did before against any impediment in the way of his lust. Nature is restless till it hath got the conquest of the disease and corrupt humours of the body. Neither can a new creature be at quiet, till all that is against the interest of the new nature be purged out; and to that purpose he daily knocks at heaven's gate for new strength and recruits of power against sin in the spiritual conflict. It is a trouble to him that he hath not as full a sense of his own corruptions as he would, and therefore he goes frequently to God to beg new discoveries of sin, that he may fetch his enemy out of his holds, and beat it to death; for by this habit the understanding is more quick in discerning the first rising of any sinful motion, and sensible of the least touch contrary to the new interest of it.

The new nature is powerfully active. There is not only an unbounded affection, but there is a power inherent in this habit to enable the soul to act; all habits add strength to the faculty. It is therefore called "might in the inner man;" "and a spirit of power." It is put as a stock into the heart, to maintain the acts of holiness; as there is a stock of sap in the root to produce branches and fruit; a power of acting is always united with a form, and rooted in it. In regard the new nature is implanted by a higher cause than any moral habits, even by the Spirit of God, it must be able to do more than any moral nature can; and being more excellent than moral nature, must produce more excellent operations, otherwise it were not of a more excellent kind, if it had not a more excellent power. Jesus Christ was appointed to be a quickening Spirit, to convey a powerful life, to enable us to live to God. The kingdom of God in the heart, as well as that in the world, is not in word but in power. Move steel as often as you will, you can never make it of itself move towards the north; but by the impression made on it by the loadstone, there is a power derived to turn, and stand that way of its own accord. By nature we are without strength, because without life. But in the renewing there is strength conveyed together with life; an ability to walk in God's statutes, conveyed with the new heart: out of weakness the soul is made strong; and the grace within, in concurrence with the supplies of the Spirit, is sufficient for it. It is not only an outward strength, as is a staff in a sick man's hand; but an inward might. But beside this inherent strength, there is an adherent ability; for Christ, who is his life, is also his strength; "I can do all things through Christ which strengtheneth me," Phil. iv. 13. So that whatsoever active power is wanting in itself, can be supplied by the head. And therefore the new creature hath a kind of almighty power of activity, by the communication of another, which is called a greatness of power, and a mighty power which works towards them, or in them that believe. This power doth reside in the heart, and this adherent power is ready for it; but neither of them is always perceptible, but upon some emergency; as a sound man hath a greater power to act than he puts forth upon all occasions.

It is easily active. Since that motion to God, and for God, is connatural and voluntary, and a power and ability also in the new creature, it must follow, that the motion is very easy. Habits are to strengthen the faculty and facilitate the acting of it. Bubbling is no pain to a fountain: rivers of water flow out of their sources easily, because naturally. The motion of this habit is as easy as the motion of the lungs, or the pulse of the artery; though constant, yet not troublesome or painful in itself; but by reason of some imparted humour settled in them. This stock of grace is called the unction. "But ye have an unction from the holy One;" 1 John ii. 20; the inward oiling the soul, as oil communicates agility to the body. This unction some understand of habitual grace, conveyed from the holy One by the Spirit. As this unction upon our Saviour was the cause of his activity for God in doing good; "God anointed Jesus of Nazareth with the Holy Ghost, and with power, who went about doing good;" Acts x. 38; so it being the same in the new creature, will have the like effect upon him. Supernatural motions are as easy by the strength of a supernatural habit, as natural motions are by the strength of natural habits. A bird flies with as much ease upward, as a beast walks upon the ground; and the seed doth with as much ease spring up, and put its ear out of the ground, as a bitter root doth its unwholesome fruits and flowers. So when the soul is filled with this new habit, the walks in the ways of God are as easy by virtue of it, as a course of sin and folly was before. The yoke of itself is easy, and the motion under a light yoke cannot be grievous: the very yoke is not a shackle and burden, but a privilege. There is indeed some reluctance sometimes, which ariseth not from the will, as renewed, but from some evil habits resident in the soul, not yet fully conquered by renewing grace. You know how the apostle Paul doth distinguish between the posture of his will, and the interruptions by that sin which dwelt in him.

It is pleasantly active. As all actions which flow

from life are pleasant, so those which flow from a
divine life in the soul.   It is a joy to a just man to
" do judgment."   That is, the entire inclination of the
soul, stands right to such actions : and it is as much a
joy to him to do judgment, when enabled thereunto
by a gracious habit, as it is to a sinful man under the
bonds of iniquity, to commit evil.   His soul leaps as
much at an opportunity of pleasing God as John the
Baptist did in his mother's womb at the appearance
of Christ ; as much as his heart sprung up before at
the proposal of a sinful object.   Never did the sun
naturally rejoice so much " like a strong man, to run
its race" in the heavens, as the new man doth spiritually rejoice to run his race to heaven.   It is a mighty
pleasure to have our spiritual enemies under our feet,
to be estranged from them : it is the purest delight to
comply with God, and be embosomed in him.

From all these things there appears,

A predominance of grace in the new creature.   As
a state of nature consists in the prevalence of the corrupt habit, which leavens the whole man ; so the state
of grace, in a predominance of the gracious habit,
which spreads itself over the whole soul, striving with
the powerful opposite, which in part resides there still.
It is a habit put into man, and destroys that habit of
sin which was there before ; the soul by it is made
alive from the dead, " Yield yourselves to God, as
those that are alive from the dead," Rom. vi. 13.
Life triumphs over death ; grace over nature, whereby the members become instruments of righteousness unto God, instead of being instruments of unrighteousness unto sin.   It is put in to guide reason and
will, and therefore is invested with the sovereign power.
As sense was first in man, but that veiled when reason
stept into the throne, as being a more excellent principle than sense ; so must reason descend and give
place to grace when that comes in, as being a more
excellent principle than reason.   It is reason it should
have the sovereignty, for it doth but regain its own

right, and take possession, which by the law of creation it ought to have kept till violently ejected by man.
He that hath this habit hath a spirit of might, as well
as of the fear of the Lord, the same Spirit which was
in Christ, which is a spirit of might. "They that are
Christ's have crucified the flesh with the affections
and lusts;" have, not shall: as soon as ever they are
Christ's, which they are by this principle, a deadly
wound is given to sin. Such a one scorns to have any
thing more to do with idols; he overcomes the world,
"Whatsoever is born of God overcomes the world,"
1 John v. 4; he can do all things, enter the lists with
the strongest Goliah; repel the sharpest temptations,
through Christ which strengthens him.

There follows from hence a difficulty to sin. No
creature can easily act against a rooted habit. How
hard is it to make a beast do that which is different
from, and contrary to his nature? To act contrary
to nature is burdensome and intolerable. What creature would willingly change its element? Will a bird
sink of its own accord into the water, or a fish delight
to leap upon the land, whose only element is the water?
What creature would court the destruction of its life?
What man would willingly deform and gash his own
body? Men never do so by nature, but when phrenzy
hath dispossessed them of their reason. Sin must dispossess a Christian of his grace, before it can be easy
for him to run into ways destructive to his nature and
blessedness. That principle which is in all natures,
must be more eminently in the highest nature, and
proportionably in every nature that is of nearest approach to it. Righteousness and holiness are the very
constitution of the new creature, "The new man
which after God is created in righteousness and true
holiness," Ephes. iv. 24. It is as impossible for
the new creature to sin by the influence of habit, as for
fire to moisten by the quality of heat, or water to burn
by the quality of cold. It is as impossible for that
habit to bring forth the fruits of sin, as for the sun to

be the cause of darkness; or a sweet fig-tree to bring forth sour fruit. Yet as there is darkness in the air, though the sun be up, by the interposition of thick clouds, so is there darkness in the new creature from the habit of sin in the soul, which is not only a lodger, but an unwelcome inhabitant; Rom. vii. 20. Sin that dwells in me still, and acts according to its nature, though much overpowered and weakened by degrees by the habit of grace. Therefore it is a hard thing for him to sin, "he cannot sin," 1 John iii. 9. It is as hard for him to contradict the new nature, as before to cross the old. I cannot do this wickedness, said Joseph; it is against the frame and disposition of my soul.

It must be difficult to sin against purpose of heart, which is the lowest step of the new nature though it be not hard to sin against a flashy resolve.

It is hard for a man to sin who hath cordially chosen God for his portion, which every new nature doth, with a fixed resolution to keep his word, "Thou art my portion, O Lord: I have said, that I would keep thy words," Psa. cxix. 57. When it is carried out with a free motion to God, it cannot easily be diverted from that charming object: he cannot but value any diversion at no better a rate than that of punishment.

It is difficult for him to contradict the new habit, wherewith he is so highly pleased, and which he is assured hath nothing but happiness in the womb of it. It must be difficult for him to act that, which by virtue of this habit he is daily in the mortification of. It is difficult for the habit of sin in him, to do the same acts, after it hath received a deadly wound, as for a wounded man to do that which he could when he was sound.

This nature cannot be in a man without an universal enmity to sin, though it may without an universal victory; this belongs to the perfection of it; but enmity to the very constitution of it; I will put enmity between the seed of the woman, and the seed of the serpent. He can at the best but half sin, and scarcely that: he could not commit sin very freely before, because of the reluctance of natural conscience; he can less freely do it now, since there is a habit of grace in him, which doth more powerfully fly in the face of sin when it appears; therefore there can be but a partial will to it, or delight in it. The new man in the heart can never do it; the old man remaining cannot fully do it, because of the contradiction it receives from the new habit. If he doth at any time sin, this new nature can be no more pleased with it, than the nature of a man is with the poison which he hath wilfully taken, which will contest with it, and endeavour to expel it, whether a man will or no: so that if a new creature be overcome at a disadvantage, and be defiled by the remaining habit of sin in the heart, his spirit is wounded, his soul bleeds, his conscience upbraids him, he is displeased with himself, and with his sin, runs to God, searcheth into himself, calls heaven and earth to his assistance, sharpens his spiritual weapons, and by virtue of this habit in him is dissatisfied, and in little ease, till he hath overcome this rebellion of lust, dispossessed it, removed the guilt, and cast out the filth.

CHAPTER IV

Regeneration considered as a law put into the heart —It is the law of grace restored in the heart —It does not make the outward law useless —It consists in inward knowledge of the law, conformity of the heart to it, affection for it, ability to obey it —There is a likeness to God in the regenerate, not in essence but by participation —Likeness to Christ and the Holy Spirit —This likeness consists in affections, in actions, in holiness — The inferences deducible from the doctrine.

As we have considered this work as a change, a vital principle, a habit, so we will consider it as a law put into the heart. Every creature hath a law belonging to its nature, so hath the new creature. Man hath a law of reason; beasts a law of sense and instinct; plants a law of vegetation; inanimate creatures a law of motion. A new creature hath a law put into his heart. "I will put my law in their inward parts, and write it in their hearts," Jer. xxxi. 23: cited by the apostle, Heb. viii. 10. It is called, the law of the mind, Rom. vii. 23; its first beginning is in the illumination of that faculty; as sin began first in a false judgment made of the precept of God, "ye shall be as Gods knowing good and evil."

This law of the mind, or law written in the heart, is not wholly the same with the law of nature. Some indeed tell us, that it is nothing but the law of right reason. But certainly they are mistaken, it is a law of grace. The law of nature was the law of a covenant of works; this law of the mind is the law of the covenant of grace. The law of nature is in all men; this law of grace only in some: the law of nature was in Paul before his conversion, this law of the mind was in him upon his conversion. The law of nature consists not of faith in a Mediator; but faith is a main part of the law of grace. The law of nature acquaints not a man with the knowledge of all sins, not with unbelief; this law of grace doth, for the conviction of this is a work of the Spirit. "Of sin, because they believe not in me," John xvi. 8, 9. The law of nature is the general work of the Mediator in all men, who enlightens every man that comes into the world. This is the peculiar work of the Mediator by his Spirit, in the hearts of those that believe: the law of nature doth not oppose sin as sin, this law of grace doth: the law of nature is no part of sanctification, for this is in men that are born of the flesh; but the law of the mind is a part of sanctification, and wars against the law of the members: there is indeed a war and a contest from the law of nature against some gross sins, but not against the law of sin in the members. As sin wars against the law of the mind, as a law of direction; so the law of the mind, or the law of grace, wars against sin, as it is a law which pretends to guide and order the ways of a man.

Yet it is the restoring of that law, which was the law of nature originally. It is a renewing in the heart that law, which was written in the heart of Adam, "That new man which after God is created in righteousness and true holiness," Eph. iv. 24; alluding to that righteousness wherein Adam was created, lost by him, and restored by Christ: this righteousness which Adam had, was the first righteousness of the law. This was the law written in the heart originally, which was defaced by the fall; and whatsoever relics there were of this law in man, were only upon the account of the mediation of Christ; it is this law which is new engraven in the soul by regeneration. God doth not say, I will write another law in their hearts, but my law; that which was my standing law, my law to Adam, and to your fathers. The law written in the heart is not substantially distinct from that in the nature of Adam. Man by his fall did blot this law, lost his righteousness, had an enmity in his heart to it, and to the very relics of it. He is not naturally subject to the law, nor can be, as it is the law of God, because of his enmity to God; the law of sin had taken the place of it. Regeneration is a taking down the law of sin, and fixing the law of God in its due place and posture.

This law is written in the heart wholly. The whole law; every command which hath the print of God upon it, is written there. As God writ his whole law in tables of stone, so he writes the whole law in the fleshly tables of the heart. It is true holiness and righteousness; true, as to its essential and integral parts. God doth not write one part of the law upon the heart, and leave out another; it is not a moiety of it, the impression of one command, and the defect of another. If it were not the whole law, something belonging to the essence of a new creature would be wanting; it would not be a new creature, because it would be a monster, wanting something necessarily requisite to the constitution of it; and would not be a new creature according to the original copy. Where there is an agreeableness in one nature to another, it is to the whole nature, the nature of the soul to the nature of the law.

This law written in the heart doth not make the outward law useless: for that is still a rule. This inward law written in the heart, is a conformity to the outward rule; and therefore is not a rule itself. The law in the heart is imprinted by the external word in the hand of the Spirit; and therefore to try the truth of the law within, we must have recourse to the law written. If a man hath notions of any human law, he must consult the law written, to know whether his notions of it be right, and whether his actions be according to the letter and reason of the law, or no: as the law of sin within a man is not the rule of judging of sin, but the law of God; so neither is the law of grace within the rule of judging good, but the word of God. The law within, though it be commensurate to the law in its essential parts, yet is imperfect as yet; but a rule ought to be perfect, and so the written law is. It is this law written in the word, that we are to take heed to, for the cleansing of our ways. " Thy word have I hid in my heart, that I might not sin against thee." When this writing of the law in the heart was promised, there was also an inward teaching promised. " And they shall teach no more every man his neighbour, saying, Know the Lord:" Jer. xxxi. 32; which is spoken in regard of the abundance of the knowledge which should be in the time of gospel light, above what was in the twilight of Jewish ceremonies; so that the weakest Christian under the gospel knows more of God and his attributes in Christ, than the greatest Jewish doctor did before the coming of Christ, This was not so understood by Christ, as if teaching others were utterly useless; for then why should he institute Apostles, Pastors, Teachers, &c., and promise to be with them to the end of the world, if this promise of inward teaching made outward teaching useless? In like manner, neither doth the writing the law in the heart, make the outward written law useless, but rather it doth establish and advance it, and the esteem of it. The outward law is the rule; as the model of a house is the rule by which a carpenter is to make a building, and to which he is to conform that idea he hath in his mind of it; but that idea or figure of it which he hath in his mind, is to be suited to that rule which is prescribed to him in the outward pattern; and therefore that pattern is to be consulted. The law of God is of eternal duration; and as it is a law of holiness and love of God, doth oblige every reasonable creature, in what condition soever he be, whether of nature, grace or glory.

Wherein doth this writing of the law in the heart consist? I answer;

In an inward knowledge of the law, and approbation of it in the understanding. The knowledge of righteousness, and the being of the law in the heart, are put together as the proper character of the people of God. " Hearken to me ye that know righteousness, the people in whose heart is my law." Isa. li. 5. Lest they should think a knowledge were enough, he adds, in whose heart is my law; not in the head, but in the heart. There is in a renewed understanding, a principle teaching how to make use of the law. It is like the inward skill of a pilot, who guides the ship by the compass and rudder. The outward law is the compass by which we must steer; the inward law is the practical knowledge of this; an inward skill to make application of it to particular occasions. The word of God being a seed, doth, as every seed, produce a being like itself, and like that plant whose seed it is; from the seed of corn ariseth a grain of the same nature. This seed being sown first in the understanding, is there cherished, and grows up in principles and

thoughts agreeable to itself, whereby the mind becomes
the epistle of Christ, and an ark to preserve the tables
of the law; whence David speaks of his soul keeping
God's testimonies, and not forgetting them.   The new
creature by its new light sees an amiableness in the
law, a holiness in the precepts, and a filthiness in himself thereby.

It consists in an inward conformity of the heart to
the law.   The soul hath a likeness to the word and
doctrine of the gospel within it; it is delivered into
that mould.   " Ye have obeyed from the heart that
form of doctrine, into which ye were delivered."
Rom. vi. 17.   He considers the gospel as a mould,
and the Romans as a metal poured into it, and putting
on the form of it.   As melted metal poured into a
mould, loses its former form, and puts on a new shape,
the same figure with the mould into which it is poured;
the soul which before was a servant of sin, and had
the image of the law of sin, being melted by the Spirit,
is cast into the figure and form of the law.   As when
a seal hath made its impression upon wax, the stamp
in the one answers exactly to the stamp on the other;
put the seal on again, and they both will meet as close
as if they were one body, the wax will fill every cavity
in the seal; but put this seal to any impression made
by another seal, there will be an inequality, the stamp
on the seal and that on the wax will not close.   The
law of sin and the law of God being contrary impressions, cannot close together; but the law of grace in
the heart, and the law of God, close, they being but
one and the same stamp.   So that when any command
of God appears, a new creature finds something
within it of kin to it; as a natural man finds something
ready to close with sin upon the appearance of it.
The heart answers to the law as a lock to a key,
ward for ward; sometimes it may not answer, but
resist, as a lock doth, because of some rust or some
filth got into it; but then it needs not a new making
but a new cleansing, to answer exactly to the key of

the law: so that as the "Gentiles having not the law, are a law to themselves," having it written upon their minds in those notions common to mankind; so the new creature, if he had not the written law, would be a law to himself. So natural is this conformity, that were there no law without, the renewed soul would naturally be carried out in the ways of holiness. The law, saith the apostle, is not made for a righteous man: it is not chiefly intended for the righteous, but for the unrighteous, who would not stir one step in any good action without it, and will hardly stir with it. There would be no need of any written law in a commonwealth, if all men had an exact justice and righteousness in their own minds, and did jointly conspire to the good of the community. But when disturbers of the peace and common welfare start up, there is need then of public laws to restrain them. But there is no need of a public enacting of a law for them that are good, because what the law enjoins, they do by their own judgment and inclination. So that what a new creature doth in observance of the law, is from natural freedom, choice and judgment, and not by the force of any threatenings annexed to it.

It consists in a strong propensity to the obedience of it. As there was a strong impetus in the old nature, inclining it to sin; so there is a strong impulse in the new nature, biassing it to observe the commands of the law. In this respect it is chiefly called a law written in the heart, in regard of the efficacious virtue of this new nature, sweetly constraining, and directly conducting to the performance of it. The law without us commands us: the law within constrains us: that enjoins a thing to be done; this inclines us to the doing of it. The first law is written in the Scripture, or in the conscience, whereby we judge those commands to be kept; the other consists in the propension of love, or faith working by love. As the impulse of concupiscence is called the law of sin, so the impulse of grace is called the law in the heart; not as a thing distinct from the law without, but only a counterpart of it, and indenture answering to the other. They are but two parts united between themselves, and compose one perfect law: one as the direction, the other as the practice: that lays the injunction, this embraceth it; and as naturally from the disposition of the new nature, as he did embrace the law of sin, from the disposition of the old. It is a powerful, operative law of the Spirit of life, which sets us free from the law of sin and death; not a dead letter, but an active principle, quickening the heart to close with the law, and delivering it from that which was the great hinderance to it. As the devil doth act in men's hearts, not personally, but by a principle in the heart, the law of sin; so doth the Spirit of life, by the law of grace: for being written by a living Spirit, it is a living law. This is the chief intent of the whole new creation, to cause us to walk in God's statutes. "The law of God is in his heart, none of his steps shall slide." Psa. xxxvii. 31. The soul being thus evangelized, and spiritualized, may be said to do by nature the things contained in the gospel, as the Gentiles are said to do by nature the things contained in the law, because there was a law of nature engraven in them.

It consists in a mighty affection to the law. What is in the word a law of precept, is in the heart a law of love: what is in the one a law of command, is in the other a law of liberty. "Love is the fulfilling of the law:" the law of love in the heart, is the fulfilling the law of God in the spirit. It may well be said to be written in the heart, when a man doth love it; as we say, a beloved thing is in our hearts, not physically, but morally. It is a love that is inexpressible. David delights to mention it in two verses together, " I will delight myself in thy commandments, which I have loved: my hands will I lift up to thy commandments, which I have loved," Psa. cxix. 47, 48 ; and often in that Psalm resumes the assertion. Before the new creation, there was no affection to the law; it was not only a dead letter, but a devilish letter in the esteem of man: he wished it razed out of the world, and another, more pleasing to the flesh, enacted: he would be a law to himself. But when this is written within him, he is so pleased with the inscription, that he would not for all the world be without that law, and the love of it: whereas what obedience he paid to it before, was out of fear, now out of affection; not only because of the authority of the lawgiver, but of the purity of the law itself. He would maintain it with all his might against the power of sin within, and the powers of darkness without him. He loves to view this law; regards every lineament of it, and dwells upon every feature with delightful ravishments. If his eye be off, or his foot go away, how doth he dissolve in tears, mourn and groan, till his former affection hath recovered breath, and stands upon its feet! If he finds not his heart answering the law, he longs after the precepts, as the prophet saith, " I have longed after thy precepts, quicken me in thy righteousness," Psa. cxix. 40. He longs to join hands again with the holiness of them. As his heart is inclined to obey it, so it is wounded upon any neglect of it, and never at ease, till he be reduced to his former delight in it. He hath no mind ever to part with it, because of its intrinsic goodness, as well as conveniency for him. It is his pleasure, not his confinement; his ornament, not his fetter: he hates every thing that is contrary to it. How did Paul grieve, and groan under the body of death, when he considered what opposition the law in his members made against the law of his mind? The law in his members brought him into captivity to the law of sin: then, O wretched man that I am! though he knew he was in part delivered from it: how doth he long for a perfect redemption from his shackles, which hindered him from following the law of his delight. And he that never murmured at his sufferings, but could glory in persecutions and death for

Christ, seems to be impatient, till he could hear the last expiring groan of this enemy : all which was the effect of his delight in the law of God after the inward man. And that this writing the law, doth principally consist in this affection, those two expressions, "putting the law into the inward parts," and "writing it in the heart," intimate. The nature of man being enmity against the law of God, the writing it argues, not a change of the law, but a change of the frame of the heart to the law, that should be so fashioned, that the law should reign there, and all his affections subscribe to it. As the writing the law in the heart of Christ, was nothing else but the agreeableness of the mediatory law to him, and his delight in it; so it is with a new creature.

It consists in an actual ability to obey. Writing the law in the heart, implies a putting a power and strength into the soul, enabling it to run the ways of God's commandments, as well as to incline the heart and affections to them; the promise is made to the latter times : not but that the ancient patriarchs were regenerate, but not by the law; not by any covenant of works : this ability did not reside in the law, but was transferred to them from the gospel. In this respect it is called a letter, because it did only instruct the eye or ear, when read or heard; this teaches the heart; that a killing letter, this a quickening spirit; that exacted the observance of its precepts, but wrote nothing in the heart to answer it, but condemned upon neglect; this commands the observance of the law, and gives an ability evangelically to perform it. That was a ministration of condemnation, this of righteousness; that could do no other but condemn, because it gave no intrinsic power to observe it. It is through Jesus Christ that we are enabled by virtue of this inward writing to serve with our minds the law of God, though in our flesh we be captivated by the law of sin. As an unregenerate man is dragged to any good, but is willingly obedient to the motions of sin; so a regenerate man is sometimes under the tyranny of sin, but is willingly obedient to the motions of grace. So that the law is written in the heart, in respect of the assent of the understanding, consent of the will, pleasure of the the affections: in the understanding, by the clearness of the light of faith; in the will, by the heat of the fire of love. In the understanding there is a judicious approbation of it; in the will, a motion to it, closing with it, and an affection to keep it; and according to its ability, an endeavour to keep pace with it.

As there is a vital principle, an habit, a law written in the heart, so there is a likeness to God in the new creature. Every creature hath a likeness to something or other in the rank of beings; the new creature is framed according to the most exact pattern, even God himself. In this the form of regeneration doth consist. The new creature is begotten; begotten then in the likeness of the begetter, which is God. As sin is the impression of Satan's image, which was drawn over all by the fall, so renewing grace is the impression of the image of God; for it is a quite contrary thing to corruption. This likeness to God was man's original happiness in creation, and is his restored happiness in redemption, " renewed in knowledge after the image of him that created him," Col. ii. 10. His misery consisted in losing it; our felicity therefore doth consist in recovering it. Hence it is called a divine nature. Every thing receives its denomination from the better part. A man is denominated rational, though he hath both a sensitive principle common with beasts, and a vegetative, or growing principle, common with plants: so a new creature is denominated divine, because grace, a divine principle is superior to the soul. Every perfection in the creature is supposed to be essentially somewhere. Every impression supposeth a seal that stamped it; every stream a fountain from whence it sprung; every beam a sun from whence it is shot. Grace being the highest perfection of the creature, must be somewhere essentially: where can that be but in God? It must then have a resemblance to him as a child to the father, the copy to the original. We are said to be born of God. Now to be born of any thing, is to receive a form like that, which the generating person hath. But,

It is not a likeness to God in essence. It is no participation of the essence of God. It is a nature, not the essence; a likeness in an inward disposition, not in the infinite substance, which is communicated by generation only to the Son, and by procession to the Holy Ghost. The divine essence is incommunicable to any creature. Infiniteness cannot be represented, much less communicated. Man is no more renewed according to God's image, than he was at first created according to it; which was not a communication of the divine essence, but of a righteousness resembling the righteousness of God, according to the capacity of Adam's nature; which image of God in Adam, is by the apostle restrained to that of "righteousness and true holiness." The likeness in a state of glory, is founded upon a sight of God as he is; which may more properly be meant of the seeing of Christ, as he is in glory; for the apostle goes on in the discourse, without naming of Christ; but without question, means him, when he says, that "he was manifested to take away our sins." We shall be like him as we shall see him; therefore not in essence. His essence is concluded by most to be invisible, even in glory. How can finite creatures behold an infinite being? He must be God that knows God's essence. We shall understand him in his affections, as a father; in his wise acts, as a governor; in his judicial acts, as a justifier; in his merciful acts, as a reconciler: we shall see him in all his relations to us. Such a vision we shall have, whatsoever it is, which shall transform us into as high a likeness to him as a finite creature is capable of. There can be no participation of the substantial perfections of God, which are incommunicable: for then it would not be a participation, but an identity, oneness, or equality. God put in one letter, and the chiefest of his name, Jehovah, which is twice repeated in it, into the names of Abraham and Sarai, reckoned Nehem. ix. 7, as one of his favours to Abraham; but not the whole name; that is incommunicable; and Jacob's name is changed to that of Israel, putting in a communicable name of God.

Yet it is a real participation. It is not a picture, but a nature; it is divine. God doth not busy himself about apparitions. It is a likeness, not only in actions, but in nature. If God communicates to the creature, a singular participation of the divine vision, and divine love, why may he not also give some excellent participation of his nature? There is a nature, for there is something whereby we are constituted the children of God: a bare affection to God doth not seem to do this. Love constitutes a man a friend, not a son and heir by generation. The apostle argues, "If children, then heirs." He could not argue in a natural way, if friends, then heirs. And the scripture speaks of believers being the children of God, by a spiritual generation, as well as by adoption. So that grace, which doth constitute one a child of God, is another form whereby a divine nature is communicated. Generation is the production of one living thing by another, in the likeness of its nature, not only in the likeness of love; so is regeneration. Were not a real likeness attainable, why should those exhortations be, of being holy as God is holy, pure as he is pure? The new creature receives the image of God; not as a glass receives the image of a man, which is only an appearance, no real existence, and though it be like the person, yet hath no communion with its nature: but as wax receives the image of the seal, which though it receives nothing of its substance, yet receives exactly the stamp, and answers it in every part: so the scripture represents it, "Ye were sealed with that holy Spirit of promise." Eph. i. 13. Something of God's perfections are in the new creature by way

of quality, which are in God by way of essence.   In
a word, it is as real a likeness to God as the creature
is capable of, laid in the first draughts of it in regeneration, and completed in the highest measures in
glory.

It is the whole image of God, which is drawn in the
new creature.   It is the image of God, not a part: a
foot, or a finger, is but the image of those parts, not
of a man.   The members in a child answer to those
in a parent, that is but a chip from the body of his
father, though not in so great a proportion. The image
of a man hath not only the face, or eyes, but the other
members.   Though a Christian may have one or two
parts of this image, more beautiful than the rest; as a
man may have a sparkling eye, that hath not a pro-
portionable lip: yet he hath all the members of a man.
The painter's skill appears in some lineaments more
than in others.   So the Spirit's wisdom appears in
making some eminent in one grace, some in another,
according to his good pleasure; yet the whole image
of God is imprinted there; it would be else not a likeness, but a monstrous birth in defect.   " The fruit of
the Spirit is in all goodness, righteousness, and truth:"
and therefore the immediate effect of the Spirit in the
soul is the engraving all goodness, righteousness, and
truth in the essential parts of it.   As God's nature is
holy, his perfections holy, his actions holy, so holiness
beautifies the nature, inspirits the actions, and is
written upon all the endowments of a renewed man.
There is an impression of the wisdom of God in the
understanding, and of the holiness of God in the will.

It is more peculiarly a likeness to Christ, wherein
we partake of his nature.   He that doth righteousness
is righteous, as Christ is righteous.   There is a real
likeness to Christ in righteousness, though not an equal
perfection.   The new nature is a draught of Christ;
something of Christ put into the soul; such a likeness
to Christ, that it seems to be, as another Christ; as the
image of the sun seems to be another sun, in a pail of

water; therefore called a "forming of Christ in us."
Not by any communication of his substance, either of
the divine or human nature; but by conveying such
affections into us, which bear a likeness to the affections of Christ. Hence we are exhorted to have the
same mind which Christ had, and to arm ourselves
with the same mind; which supposes such a mind put
into the new creature, which he is to excite, and put
into actual exercise. And the apostle speaks of a
conformity to Christ in his death and resurrection.
And God did predestinate all his own to be conformed
to the image of his Son. Jesus Christ conformed himself to us, by assuming the human nature; and God
conforms us to Christ by bestowing upon us a divine.
Hence we are said to be the seed of Christ. Not a
carnal seed, as the Jews say; and therefore deny
Christ to be the Messiah, because he left no posterity.
Whereas seed is spiritually understood; as in the first
promise, the seed of the serpent or the devil. Devils
do not beget, but metaphorically, as they instil their
cursed principles into men. So Christ sows his principles in us, whereby we become his seed. Hence also
renewed men are called his fellows. If fellows with
him in the covenant, and fellows with him in glory,
fellows also with him in his disposition of loving
righteousness, and hating iniquity. This disposition
was the inward motive of his death, and the foundation of his advancement. Without this disposition we
cannot be conformable to him in his death, and consequently not his fellows in his advancement. The new
creature is a likeness to Christ; therefore called the
new man; as the natural man is like to Adam, therefore called the old man. The new man and old man
are titles of Christ and Adam, and transferred to
others by a figure. These are the heads and roots of
the two distinct bodies of men in the world. All are
in the old Adam by nature, and so partake of the old
man. All believers are in the new Adam by faith,
and so partake of the nature of the new man: as we

did partake of Adam's nature by our natural birth, so we partake of the nature of Christ by our spiritual; by the one we have the image of the earthly, by the other the new creature has the image of the heavenly; the one derives sin, the other righteousness: they both imprint their image according to the quality of their extraction. Christ is full of purity, righteousness, charity, patience, humility, truth, and in a word, all the parts of holiness; then the form and image of Christ in the new creature can be no other than a lively representation of those divine qualities: a soul glittering with goodness, humility, &c., which the apostle comprehends in two words, righteousness and true holiness. Therefore if there be not a likeness to Christ in the frame and qualities of our souls, we are not born of him. No man will say an ox, or a sheep, or a dog, descends from Adam, because they have not the likeness, shape, and qualities of Adam; neither can any man without such a likeness to Christ in faith, humility, patience, love, obedience, and minding the glory of God, number himself in the spiritual seed of Christ. He retains the nature poisoned by the serpent, creeping upon the earth, feeding upon the dust, not the nature formed by the eternal Spirit.

It is a likeness to the Spirit, which is the immediate cause of it. Therefore the new creature is called spirit in the abstract, as a natural man is called flesh in the abstract. " That which is born of the flesh is flesh; and that which is born of the Spirit is spirit." John iii. 6. As that which is born of the flesh, is like to flesh in its nature; so that which is born of the Spirit is like to the Spirit in its nature; as light in the air, being the natural effect flowing from the sun, is like to that light which is in the sun: its relishes, delights, breathings, are according to its spiritual original, Its motions, purposes, dispositions, are like those of the Holy Ghost, of whom it is born. The principles and impressions in the nature must be agreeable to those the Spirit hath. The Spirit is a

Spirit of holiness, grace, love, and zeal for the glory of God; his office is to exalt and glorify Christ. If we are renewed, then we shall have the same draught in our hearts, the same design, the fleshly principle will be changed into spiritual. They will be habitual too, as the frame of the Holy Spirit is; a natural man may do some acts that look like spiritual, by fits and starts; but there is no settled principle. Whereas the Spirit in a new creature is a spirit of meekness, and curbs the passions; a spirit of humility, and overthrows pride; a spirit of zeal, and fires the heart; a spirit of power, and arms the soul against sin; a holy spirit, and therefore cleanseth it; an heavenly spirit, and therefore elevates it.

Wherein doth this likeness to God chiefly consist?

In a likeness of affections. God has no bodily shape; we cannot be like him in our bodies, but in our souls as they are spirits; but if there be a dissimilitude of affection and disposition, the unlikeness to God is greater than a likeness to him in point of the natural being. There is no draught of this image in us, unless we have a conformity of affections to God; it is then chiefly evidenced by a delighting in him, by faith and love, wherein we bear a resemblance to him in his affection to himself; by delighting in his image in others, wherein we imitate his affection to his creatures. He that loves not that image of God which is visible, cannot love the invisible original, 1 John iv. 12, 20, and so having no likeness to God in his affection, can have no likeness to him in his nature. And the apostle positively affirms, that "he that loves is born of God," 1 John iv. 7. The new creature extends its arms to every thing which hath a resemblance of that whose image it bears. The divine nature is chiefly seen in the objects of the affections; when they are set upon the same objects, and in a like manner as God's and Christ's are. When we grieve most for sin, for this grieves the Spirit; when we desire most an inward holiness, this God most longs

for ; O that there were such an heart in them ! When
we hate sin as God hates it, because of the inward
filthiness; when we love grace as God loves it, because of its native beauty; when we can love God
and Christ above all the world, and other things in
order to him and his glory; when we can trust Christ
with all our concerns, as God doth trust him with his
glory; then, and not till then, there is an image of God
in us, which God values above all the world. When
the soul is thus touched and quickened by grace, she
can no more strip herself of the object and manner
of her affections, than she can of the affections themselves. And when she doth reach out herself to all
that is good, and hath a complacency in it, it is her
happiness, because it is the great likeness to the spring
of happiness. When we have the like affections with
God, we have in our measure a like happiness and
blessedness with God.

In a likeness of actions. Men by sin are alienated
from the life of God, by restoring grace then they are
brought to have communion with God in his life, to
live as God lives. By nature men live the life of beasts
and devils; by grace they come to live the life of
Christ. If he live then the life of God, he must be
conformable in his actions to the acts of God. No
nature is stripped of affections and actions proper to
it ; it would be else a picture without breath, a body
without motion, a lifeless colour. The divine image
is not a painted statue, but an active being. The
nearer any thing approacheth in its nature to the
fountain of life, the more of liveliness and activity it
must needs partake of. The communicable perfections of God are instamped upon the soul as a pattern
to imitate, and as a principle to quicken. A new
creature acts like God ; as melted and inflamed gold
will act after the nature of fire, by the assistance of
that quality communicated by the fire to it; so doth
the soul by that divine quality it partakes of. It is as
impossible that this image of God can produce any

thing but divine acts, as that the image of the sun in a burning glass should produce a darkness and coldness in the air. There will be the manifestation of the life of Christ in the motions of our soul, as the apostle speaks in case of sufferings for him there will be in our bodies. Natural men are called the devil's children, because they resemble him in nature and works, driving on to sin, and delighting themselves in their own and others' iniquities: so renewed men are God's children, because they live the life of God, and abound in the works of God. As there is the same nature, and the same Spirit which Christ had, there will be a following of him in his works: all creatures of the same species have the same instinct, the same nature, the same acts that the first creature of that kind had originally in its creation. Grace being a new excellency advancing the soul to a higher state, endues it with a more noble kind of operation. Nothing is lifted up to a more perfect state of being, but in order to a more perfect manner of acting: if a beast should be elevated to the nature of man, would you then expect from him the actions of a beast still? And can any have the implantation of the divine nature, who hath only the actions of a man, which bear no resemblance to God?

This likeness to God consists principally in a likeness to him in holiness. It is only he that does righteousness, that is born of him. "If ye know that he is righteous, ye know that every one that doeth righteousness, is born of him." 1 John ii. 29. It is by this the children of God are manifest from the children of the devil, 1 John iii. 10, in doing righteousness. If we are unlike to God in this, we are like him in nothing; God hath not a pretence of holiness, but a real purity. He that hath not escaped the corruption that is in the world through lust, is no partaker of the divine nature; the apostle puts that as a necessary qualification, 2 Pet. i. 4. If by afflictions good men are partakers of God's holiness, much more by regeneration. " He chasteneth us for our profit, that we might be partakers of his holiness." Heb. xii. 10 If God aim in his corrections at the bringing his people to partake with him in holiness, as a father does at the reformation of his child, that he may be a follower of his virtues; much more does God aim at it in regeneration, when a spirit of holiness is infused into the soul. The new creation is a drawing this excellency of God in the soul: if any attribute lift up his head above another, it is this; in this we chiefly are to imitate him; this is the greatest evidence of the divine nature. By sin we come short of that which is the glory of God; by the renewing of the soul we attain the glory of God; that is, attain a state of holiness, and at last a perfection of it, a communion with him in holiness here, and a full enjoyment of it hereafter. Whatsoever our fancies, our hopes, our presumptions are, if this be not drawn in our soul, if we have not an internal holiness, we are not new creatures, and therefore not in Christ.

If regeneration be such an inward change, a vital principle, a law put into the heart, the image of God and Christ in the soul; then,

How few in the world are truly new creatures! Is the law transcribed in many men's lives? Nay, can we all read it copied in our own hearts? Cannot many see the image of the devil sooner than the image of God in their own souls? Is not the law of sin written in capital letters, and with many flourishes; when the law of God is written in characters hardly legible, and crowded into a narrow room? How many are changed from childhood to youth, from youth to manhood, from manhood to age, and the old nature still remaining in its full strength, and the body of death more vigorous than twenty or thirty years ago! Changed years, and unchanged hearts, are a very sad spectacle.

Profane men are numerous. None will offer to rank these in the number of new creatures. Such filthy souls are no branches of Christ, nor habitations for him; we read of the devil in swine, but never of our Saviour in swinish souls; are such regenerate? Can brambles be ever accounted vines, or thistles fig-trees? These rather look like hellish than divine creatures; diabolical, not god-like natures. A devotedness to the sins of the flesh is inconsistent with the circumcision made by Christ. "Putting off the body of the sins of the flesh, by the circumcision of Christ," Colos. ii. 11, that is, the body of sins which exert themselves in the flesh or natural body; whereas such have the body of sin, with an activity in every member of it. Is the image of Christ in such men? Is not he meek as a lamb? Are not they fierce as lions? Is not he holy, and they defiled with intemperance? Did not he labour for nothing but the glory of his Father, and the salvation of souls? And they mind nothing but the dishonour of God, and the destruction of themselves and others. Did not he do good to his enemies, and they scarcely spare their friends? Alas, with this contrariety, how can they pretend the image of Christ, when they have nothing but what looks like the image of his enemy, the devil? Is not the gospel counted as great a foolishness by such, as at the first times of its publishing? Are not the great mysteries of God, and the contrivances of eternity, entertained with coldness, and sometimes with scoffs, and the word, the great instrument of this change, disregarded? Are such new creatures, that contemn the very means to attain it? Surely they are so far from being near the kingdom of God, that they are in the very suburbs of hell. Is a hugging base lusts against the light of nature, a contempt of God's law and authority, the nature of Christ? Were any such spots upon our Saviour's garment? Is this to be like him who was holy, harmless, separate from sin and sinners?

Among professors is there much evidence of a new creation? When men shall say, All that the Lord speaks to us we will do, has not God as great occasion to say as he did of old, "O that there were such a heart in them, that they would fear me, and keep my commandments!" Deut. v. 24. We may find a change of language in some, a change of outward actions in others; but how few are there among many who stand up before God with the breath of life? Here and there a man or woman, wherein God may see the image of his own nature. How few are they with whom Christ can shake hands, and justly call them his fellows! Christ may be in the mouth, and the devil formed in the heart; the name of Christ may be upon them, and the nature of Christ not in them. They may be born of the will of man in a religious education, but not born of the will of God in a spiritual regeneration. Is it not a graceless Christianity in many men, a faith without holiness, a Christianity without Christ? Regeneration is never without faith, love, and righteousness; they depend upon grace as the property upon the form; wherever the new creation is, these are, for they are the qualities created; wherever they are not, there is nothing of a new creature, let the pretences be never so splendid. There may be a nearness to the kingdom of God by profession, when there is no right to it for want of regeneration. Instead of humility, according to our Saviour's pattern, doth not pride compass men as a chain? counting that their ornament which is the strength of their old nature. Instead of patience, roaring passions; instead of meekness, boiling anger; instead of love, a glowing hatred. How few then are renewed! But few shall be saved, and therefore few regenerate. How little is the report of a likeness to God believed by the incredulous world! How few are the strivings of any towards heaven! Most lie quiet without any such motions like the dust on the ground, unless some stormy affliction raise them a little toward heaven, whence they quickly fall back to their old place.

It informs us, that a change of opinion is not this new creature. It is not, if any man change his opinion from Gentilism to Christianity, he is a new creature; but if any man be in Christ, by a vital participation from union with him. As men generally place saving faith in a mere assent, so they place the new creation in a change of opinion, as well from truth to error, as from error to truth, though there be no spiritual knowledge of God, nor internal cordial closing with the Gospel, nor practice of it. Such a change may endue the head with a knowledge which never gently slides down to the affections. It may indeed have some influence upon the life, as this or that principle comes nearest to, or is divine truth, and is settled as an opinion in the soul; yet this great change may not be wrought. That is but a change in the head, this in the heart; that of opinion, this of affection; that perfects the understanding, this both the understanding and will and the whole soul. There is a natural desire of knowledge, but a natural aversion from grace; whence this change becomes easy, the new creature change difficult. A hot contriving head may have a cold and sapless heart. A head informed by the knowledge of truth, may be without a heart enlivened by the Spirit of truth. A head changed in opinion only, will descend into the bottomless pit, when the least grain of renewing grace shall not receive so much as a singe from those flames. A change from error to truth, without a heart framed to the truth, does but more settle a man upon his lees, and makes him not only more regardless, but opposite to a true change to God: it stores up wrath for him, and his very judgment will be a witness for the condemnation of his practice. The knowledge of God will not justify, but condemn a practical denial of him; but for all that, they are abominable. This new creature change is not from one doctrine to another, barely considered as doctrine; but a change to the gospel in the main design of it, as it is "a doctrine according to godliness," 1 Tim. vi. 3, as it may affect purity, and direct the soul in its motion. And by the way, observe this; whenever you are solicited to a change of opinion, consider the truth of it by this rule, whether it have a tendency to encourage and promote internal godliness. Since this doctrine of regeneration was the first gospel-lesson taught, to which all succeeding truths refer as to their end and centre, the apostle tells us what the issue of all such doctrines is, that refer not to this, pride, doting about questions, envy, strife, railings, and evil surmisings. A heap of notions may consist with a body of death in its full strength, but a spirit of grace cannot; a notionalist may speak great things, but a new creature acts them. Great speculations only are but leaves without fruit, like cedars that by their shadows may give a refreshment, but have no fruit to fill the soul hungering after righteousness.

Morality is not this new creature. Moral honesty, freedom from gross vices, &c., I have before spoken something of, showing it insufficient, when I handled the necessity of regeneration; we cannot speak too much against it, it being a soft pillow, from whence many slide insensibly into destruction. How many upon this account think themselves new creatures, who are yet deeply under the image of Satan; and though they have blown off some dust from the law of nature, yet never had a syllable of the law of grace written in their hearts. Nay, the image of the devil may be more deeply engraved in a soul, whose life is free from an outward taint. Profane men express more of the beast; a civil and moral conversation may have more of the devil and serpent within, in spiritual wickedness.

Yet morality is to be valued. It is a comely thing among men, a beauty to human societies, satisfaction to natural conscience, security to the body, example to others; men are to be applauded for it, and encouraged in it. It is a fruit of Christ's mediation, left for the preservation of human societies, without which the world would be a mere bedlam; the works of kindness, justice, mercy, love, pity, &c., are useful and commendable. It is a thing which our Saviour loved, yet not with such a love as eternally to reward it; he looked upon the young man with some affection, Mark x. 21, but scarce upon the Pharisees without anger and disdain.

Yet we must not set the crown belonging to grace upon the head of it, and place it in a throne equal to that of the new creation. It is too amiable for men to be beaten off from it; yet with just reason we may persuade them to arise to a higher elevation. It is a curious paint, a delightful picture, an useful artifice, but not a vital principle: a glow-worm is a lovely light, yet it is not a star. We press not men to throw off morality, but to advance it, to exchange it for Christ, that their moral virtues may commence Christian graces. It is an elevation near the kingdom of God, not a translation into the kingdom of God; it is nature improved, not nature renewed; it is a well coloured picture without a principle of life; an outward resemblance, not an inward power; a form of godliness; as a change that is made upon canvass in the draught of a picture, but no change in it by the conveyance of life. For,

It removes not the body of death. It is a cutting away the outward luxuriances, not the inward root. It removes the stench and putrefaction, not the death; an embalmed carcass is as much dead as a putrefied one, though not so loathsome. It removes not that wherein the strength of sin lies, though it does somewhat of the stench of sin. It may check those degenerate lusts inconsistent with the peace of natural conscience, but not heal the corrupt nature. It may be a change from scandalous to spiritual sins; from vanity in the outward life, to vanity in the mind; from debauched practices, to a vain-glorious and envious spirit. " Henceforth walk not as other Gentiles walk, in the vanity of their minds; having the understanding darkened, being alienated from the life of

God." Eph. iv. 17, 18. By the gentiles from whom
the apostle would have the Ephesians differenced, he
means not the lower sort, but the whole rank, verse
21; there was a truth in Jesus which they had been
taught; he makes no distinction between the looser
rabble, and the professors of wisdom, whom he calls
fools, Rom. i. 22; the followers of the divine (as they
called them) philosophers, were alienated from the
life of God, and walked in the vanity of their minds.
The new man he exhorts them to put on, was another
kind of thing than what the greatest moralists among
the heathen were acquainted with. It was at best
human, not divine; an old nature purified, not a new
implanted; or as the apostle phraseth it, a walking in
the vanity of their mind, in the darkness of their understandings, though not in a vanity of gross actions.
It can never remove that body of death which was
introduced into the world, while this outward morality
stood. What immorality against the light of nature
do you find in Adam? He did break a positive command in eating the forbidden fruit; you find nothing
of drunkenness, lying, swearing; his great sin was inward pride and unbelief; nothing of those sins, the
freedom from which you boast of, and rest on. Some
would make Adam guilty of the breach of every command in the moral law; virtually I confess they may;
expressly I do not see how they can; and also virtually the highest mere moralist is guilty of the breach
of the whole; yet all his morality after the breach of
this one command, could not preserve him in Paradise; nor all the morality without a new nature, restore you to it. You may have Adam's morality with
Adam's corruption; a freedom from gross vices, with
a heap of spiritual sins in your hearts, as Adam had;
but not a true righteousness without the new Adam,
the quickening Spirit.

Therefore the highest morality, without a new creation, is but flesh: all men out of Christ agree in a
fleshly nature. It is the highest thing in the rank of

flesh, but it is not yet mounted to spirit. Water heated to the highest pitch, is but water still; and morality in the greatest elevation of it, is but refined flesh; an old nature in a higher form. A profane man reduced to a philosophical morality, is putrefied flesh reduced to some sweetness, enduced with a fresh colour, but wanting life as much as before: it is an old nature new mended. But a new creature is Christ formed in the soul. Moral virtue colours the skin, renewing grace enlivens the heart; that changes the outward actions, this the inward affections; that paints the man, this quickens him; that is a change indeed in the flesh, not of the flesh into spirit; it is a new action, not a new creation. There is a difference indeed among men in this respect; as there is of cleanly lambs from a filthy swine, or a ravenous wolf, yet both are in the rank of beasts. There seems to be a difference in the wickedness and malice of devils. Our Saviour tells us of a kind that are "not cast out but by fasting and prayer," Matt. xvii. 21; intimating, that there are other kinds of them, not altogether so bad, or so strong; yet all agreeing in one common diabolical nature: as there is a difference in gracious men, one shining like a star, another of a lesser light; yet all agree in the nature of light, and light in the Lord. Although there be a difference among men in point of moral virtue, yet all agree in the nature of flesh; "That which is born of the flesh, is flesh," John iii. 6. Let it be what it will, a Nicodemus as well as Judas, it is flesh, a more refined sensuality, an animal life.

It must needs be differenced from the new creature, because its birth is different. Moral virtue is gained by human industry, natural strength, frequent exercises: it is made up of habits, engendered by frequent acts. But regeneration is an habit infused, which grows not upon the stock of nature, nor is it brought forth by the strength of nature: for man being flesh, cannot prepare himself to it. That may be the fruit of education, example, philosophy, this of the Spirit: that is a fruit of God's common grace, this of his special grace : that grows upon the stock of self-love, not from the root of faith and a divine affection: that is like a wild flower in the field, brought forth by the strength of nature ; this like a flower in the garden, transplanted from heaven, derived from Christ, set and watered by the Spirit. And therefore the other, being but the work of nature, cannot bear the characters of that excellency, which the affections planted by the Spirit do. That is the product of reason, this of the Spirit ; that is the awakening of natural light, this the breaking out of spiritual light and love upon it; that is the excitation of an old principle, this the infusion of a new ; that a rising from sleep by the jog of conscience, this a rising from death by the breath of the Spirit, working a deep contrition, and making all new.

It differs from the new creature in regard of the contractedness of the one, and the extensiveness of the other. That is in part a purifying of the flesh, this a purging both of flesh and spirit ; that binds the hands, this clears the heart ; that purgeth the body, this every part of the soul ; that, at the best, is but oil in the lamp of life, this oil both in lamp and vessel ; that is a change of outward postures, modes, and fashions of walking, this of nature, heart, and spirit ; that seems to be a dislike of some sins, this of all. If any thing in moral honesty be given to God, it is but a certain part ; the greatest and best is kept back from him. That may be a casting away some iniquity, but not making a new heart, when both are commanded together. "Cast away from you all your transgressions, and make you a new heart and a new spirit," Ezek. xviii. 31. That is a casting away the loathsome works of the flesh, this a new root to bring forth the fruits of the Spirit.

It differs from the new creature in the immediate principle of it, and its tendency. That is a cleansing the outward flesh in the fear of man, out of reverence to superiors, as it is said of Jehoash, he did that which was right, while he was under the awful instructions of Jehoiada, 2 Kings xii. 2. This is a "perfecting holiness in the fear of God," 2 Cor. vii. 1. That is an outward reformation from the hearing of the word; some acts materially performed from the newness of the thing, this from a judicious and hearty approbation of the law and will of God: that ariseth from a natural love to reason justice, equity, this consists of love to God; that avoids some sins, because they are loathsome, this because they are sinful; that tends not to God for himself, but for something extraneous to him: it is an acting for self, not for the praise of God. The actions of unregenerate morality, as well as loathsome profaneness, are to gratify the flesh in some part of it; they all meet in that point, as the clearest brooks, as well as the most rapid and muddy streams run to feed the sea.

Well then, deceive not yourselves; conclude not yourselves new creatures by your moral honesty: it will not follow, that because you have some virtues, you have therefore true grace; but it will follow, that if you are new creatures, and have faith and love, you have all graces in the root; and they will appear in time, though they may lie hid awhile in that seminal principle; the greater virtues contain the less, but the less do not infer the greater.

It will certainly follow from hence, that restraints are not this new creature. Restraining grace, and renewing grace, are two different things; the one is a withholding, "I withheld thee from sinning against me." Gen. xx. 6; the other an enlivening, with a free spirit against it. Restraint may be from a chastisement, attended also with something of natural conscience. Abimelech had some natural integrity in his conscience, not to meddle with another man's wife, which God acknowledges; "I know that thou didst this in the integrity of thy heart; for I also withheld thee:" yet without this restraint by a punishment, this natural integrity might have been baffled by the temptation. Restraints may spring from the law in the hand of the magistrate, when it doth not spring from the law of God in the heart. Men may love that which they do not act; at least, they may love it in others, though not in themselves, for some extrinsic considerations; and wish they had as fair a way to commit it as others have. They may hate what they practise. Do all that hear the word, love the word, hide it in their hearts, and let it sink down into the bottom of their souls? Do all that abstain from sin, loathe what they abstain from? the restraints of many being barely outward restraints, are no more arguments of regeneration, than God's withholding the devils by the chain of his powerful Providence, is a sign of the new creation of them. The damned are hindered from committing many of those sins which were their pleasure upon the earth: it is not a change of their disposition, but of their condition. Neither punishments in hell, nor punishments upon the earth, alter the nature: though after lying a thousand years in hell, they should have leave to dwell upon the earth again, they would have the same inclinations, without an inward change. Do we not see it daily in men's afflictions, though the sense of the smart nips a little those inclinations, yet when that sense is extinguished, those inclinations bud forth afresh? The bare pruning a tree, makes it bear more fruit of the same kind, as long as the root remains, rather than diminish it, "Why should ye be stricken any more? ye will revolt more and more: the whole head is sick, and the whole heart is faint." Isa. i. 5. While the head is sick, and the heart faint, though there may be a weakness to act some sins under the stroke, yet afterwards the revoltings are more violent many times than they were before. The best that restraints work of themselves, is but a cautiousness to sin more warily. The act may be repressed, while the habit remains.

A serious fit of melancholy, or a sudden start of

affections, is not this work of the new creature. It is an habit, a law written in the heart: not a transient pang, or a sudden affection; not a skipping of fancy, or a quick sparkling of passion; but a new nature, a divine frame spreading itself over every faculty; knowing God in our understandings, complying with him by our wills, aspiring to him by a settled and perpetual flame of our affections, rising heavenwards, like the fire upon the altar, conforming ourselves to him in the whole man, a denial of whole self for God. It is not a working of the imagination, or a melancholy vapour, which may quickly be removed, or a flash of joy and love; but a serious humility, a constant grief under the remainder of corruption yet unextirpated; a perpetual recourse to God, and delight in him through Jesus Christ. Are your affections raised sometimes to God? and are they not oftentimes raised higher to objects extrinsecal to God? Such affections may arise rather from the constitution of the body, than alteration of the soul. They are but "a taste of the heavenly gift, and the good work of God," Heb. vi. 4, 5; a taste, and no more; and but a transient work. The object about which our affections are stirred, may be divine; yet the operation be merely natural. May not sometimes affections be stirred much at the hearing of the sufferings of our Saviour pathetically expressed, yet only out of a natural compassion, from an agreeable impression upon the fancy? The story of Joseph in the pit, and Christ upon the cross, may be heard with the same workings of passion. And may not the same be done at a well humoured play, or at the hearing a report of the lamentable death of a Turk, or Heathen, pathetically expressed? These are but the workings of natural spirits. Some affections are as movable as quicksilver; upon the least touch, they sweat like marble in moist weather, but resemble it also in hardness. You do not find the affections to be the chief seat of the law. This would be as to write letters upon melted wax, or running water: but the tenor of the covenant runs upon the mind; " I will put my law into their minds," Heb. viii. 8, 10. And when God works upon the mind, the affections will attend the dictates of that, and the motions of the will. But a work upon the affections only, is like water in a spunge, easily sucked up, and upon the least compression, squeezed out. These may be where there is no root of grace; they suddenly rise, and suddenly vanish. When unrooted notions are received only into the fancy, without any illumination of the understanding, or determination of the will, the affections to them will be as volatile as the fancy which entertained them. Those in Matt. xiii. 20, 21, that received the word with a sudden joy, were as suddenly offended for want of a root: Anon with joy he receives it, by and by he is offended. The word translated anon, and by and by, is the same; a lightening of affection, and a sudden vanishing. Therefore this is not the new creature, sudden affections, or a melancholy fit. The law of God seated in the heart, mind and will, through a constant course of affection, is a very good character to judge of the new creature.

It informs us of the excellency of the new creature. How excellent is this new creature! It is a change, a divine nature, a likeness to God, an excellency above that of the greatest moralist under heaven. The apostle calls it a change " from glory to glory," 2 Cor. iii. 18, implying, that the first change wrought upon the soul is glorious, and a new creature excellent in its first make, more glorious in its progress, inconceivably glorious when God shall put his last hand to the completing of it. Regeneration is more excellent than creation. It is more noble to be formed a son of God by grace, than made a man by nature: nature deforms, grace beautifies. By nature we are the sons of Adam; by the new nature the members of Christ. As grace excels nature, and Christ surmounts Adam, so much more excellent is the state of a Christian, a real Christian, above that of a man.

Can there be a greater excellency, than to have a divine beauty, a formation of Christ, a proportion of all graces, suited to the imitable perfections of God? Man is an higher creature than others, because he hath an higher principle: a life of reason is more noble than that of sense. To live by sense, is to play the part, and live the life of brutes: to live by reason, is to live the life of a man: but he that lives by the Spirit, lives the life of God, answers the end of his creation, useth his reason, understanding, will, affection for God, by whom they were first bestowed; acts more nobly, lives more pleasantly, than the greatest angel could do without such a principle. A new creature doth exceed a rational creature, considered only as rational, more than a rational doth a brute. The apostle makes a manifest distinction between the natural, or the rational, and the spiritual man. 1 Cor. ii. 14, 15. A man with the richest endowments, is no more to be compared in excellency, with a regenerate man, than the top of a craggy mountain is with a well-dressed garden. That must needs be excellent, the forming of which is the end of all God's ordinances in the world, the end of the Spirit's being among the sons of men, the end of keeping up of mankind, the end of his patience in forbearing his punishment upon contempt of the gospel. The end of his preserving the world, is to form Christ in the heart: and when the last new creature is formed, God hath no more to do in the world. When all that are given to him, shall come to believe, Christ shall then come "to be admired in them." 2 Thess. i. 10. He doth not come therefore, till all his chosen ones are brought in, to believe in him; for then he would not be admired by all those that are saints in his purpose. This, therefore, must needs be excellent. One new creature is more excellent than the whole unrenewed world, with their choicest ornaments. It was never pronounced of them, that they were partakers of the divine nature.

How much, therefore, should new creatures be esteemed and valued! Is any thing, next to God, more worthy our esteem than that which bears his image? Is any thing, next to a crucified Christ, glorified in heaven, more worthy our valuation, than Christ formed in the heart of a believer? What esteem have men had for those who have had tempers like to some heroes, some generous and useful men in the world? How much more respect should be given to them that bear the character of God upon them, and have communion with God, and Christ, and the Spirit, in their nature! If the dead image of God in a natural man, ought to be respected, much more the living image of God in a renewed man. If a picture is to have respect, much more the life. To slight them, therefore, redounds to the slighting that infinite perfection, whose image it is. They are his living images, sent into the world to represent him. He then that disesteems them for that work, disesteems him that wrought and engraved them, by the same rule, that he that despised the disciples, despised Christ, and the Father that sent him. He therefore that despiseth you, despiseth not man, but God, who hath also given us his Holy Spirit. Luke x. 16. 1 Thess. iv. 8. Yet no better must be expected here: for the contracted spirit of the world, can love no other birth but its own, no other similitude but what draws near unto it: "If ye were of the world, the world would love his own: but because ye are not of the world, therefore the world hates you." John xv. 19. The copy can expect no better usage than the original. The nearer any approach in likeness to Christ, the more they will be exposed to contempt and scorn in the world.

If the new creature be such a thing as you have heard, then the sin of a regenerate man, hath a greater aggravation than the sins of any in the world. If you slip into sin, the sins of the whole unregenerate world have not so great a blackness. It is true, a new creature may, and does sin: for though a new man is created in him with all his members and essential and integral parts, yet the body of death doth remain still with all its members, and a seed-plot still, though not in the same strength and fruitfulness as before: for the apostle Paul doth not complain of a member of death, or a piece of sin, but the whole body of it, and the law of sin in its members. Rom. vii. It seems it did reside there still: and so it doth in all the renewed, though but faint and feeble, an old man indeed, growing older every day, losing its teeth and strength, less able to bite, less able to assault. Yet sometimes a new creature may fall into sin, but not without great aggravation. For other men sin against natural, you against spiritual principles; others sin against a habit of common notion, you against a habit of divine grace. A natural man sins against the light of God in his conscience, a renewed man against the life of God in his heart. Others sin against a Christ crucified, and risen from the grave; he sins against a Christ new formed, and risen in his heart. Others sin against the law of God in the word, he against the law written in his mind and the word too. Such cast dirt upon the Spirit's work, cross the end of so noble a piece, bring a thief into the Spirit's temple, and grieve the Holy Spirit, who instructed him better. Whenever you sin, it must cost you more grief, because your sins are more grievous, and you must grieve the more for them, because the Spirit is grieved by them. Grief for sin is a standing grace in the new creature, and part of a likeness to the Spirit of God, whatsoever some men dream to the contrary.

There is ground of joy unspeakable and full of glory that results from this. Are you of this new creation that I have been discoursing of? Then take your portion of comfort. The jewel of comfort belongs only to the cabinet of grace. It is fit you should have the comforts of heaven in your hearts, who have a fitness for heaven in your nature. The day of the

new birth was a happy day, to be brought from under
the rule of sin and death in it, to the rule of the Spirit
of God and life in it; from bearing fruit to death, to
bringing forth fruit to God and everlasting life; if sin
be a torment to the womb that bears it, no joy can
reside in an unregenerate spirit; if sin be the soul's
rack in its own nature, grace must be its pleasure;
for it carries as much contentment and satisfaction in
its bowels, as sin doth disquietness and sorrow.

You have by the new creation, a relation to the
blessed Trinity. Such are the sons of God, the seed
of Christ, the temple of the Spirit: what a connexion
is there between you and the Three Persons? God in
Christ, and Christ in you, that you may be made perfect in one. God in Christ reconciling the world;
you in Christ reconciled to God. God in Christ, as
a father in a son; you in Christ as members in the
body; the Spirit in you as an informing and enlivening principle. It makes you related to the Father as
his friends, by the ceasing of your enmity: to the Son,
as his property, for then you are his; to the Spirit, as
the tutor of you, and inhabitant in you; all implied,
Rom. viii. 8, 9, 10. By your former birth you were
children of wrath; by this, children of God; by that,
partakers of the nature of the destroyer, by this, partakers of the divine nature of your Creator, and Redeemer; by nature you descended from the loins of
Adam, and thereby were related to all the corruption
of the world; by the new birth, you are descended
from the Son of God, and counted to the Lord for a
generation, and thereby related to all the perfection
of heaven: as really descended from Christ by a
spiritual, as from Adam by a natural generation.
What an overflowing comfort is this! To be a
king's son is a higher privilege than merely to be his
subject; subjects have protection, sons affection; subjects partake of the kindness of the prince, sons of his
nature; as a son he hath a right to the inheritance of
the father, as a subject not. Men are subjects by

covenant, though born of others; sons by generation: by being a new creature, the regenerate man acquires a more noble relation, than by being a creature. That relation that he lost by a prodigal corruption, is restored to him in a more excellent way by his spiritual regeneration.

THIRD GENERAL TOPIC

THE

AUTHOR OF REGENERATION

CHAPTER I

God is the efficient author of Regeneration —Man cannot regenerate himself —His inability generally, does not consist in want
of faculties, or insufficiency of external revelations, but chiefly
in the will, and in innate and acquired habits of sin —Hence, there
is a total moral unfitness for the work, an unwillingness to it,
affections averse to it, and resistance consequent on the aversion —The power of Satan enfeebles him for the work.

Which were born, not of blood, nor of the will of the flesh, nor of
the will of man, but of God—John i. 13.

From the text it appears most evident that God alone
is the prime efficient cause or author of regeneration,
for it will be found upon investigation that man in all
his capacities is too weak to produce the work of
regeneration in himself. This is not the birth of a
darkened wisdom, and an enslaved will. We affect
a kind of divinity, and would centre ourselves in our
own strength; therefore it is good to be sensible of
our own impotency, that God may have the glory of
his own grace, and we the comfort of it, in a higher
principle and higher power than our own. It is not
the bare proposal of grace, and the leaving the will
to an indifferent posture, balanced between good and
evil, undetermined to the one or the other, to incline
and determine itself which way seems best to it. Not
one will, in the whole rank of believers, if left to
themselves. The evangelist excepts not one man
among them; for as many as received Christ, as many

as believed, were the sons of God, who were born; which believers, who had this faith as the means, and this sonship as the privilege, were born, not of the will of the flesh, nor the will of man, but of God.

God challenges this work as his own, excluding the creature from any share as a cause. I will sprinkle clean water upon you, I will cleanse you, I will give you a new heart, I will put a new spirit into you, I will take away the heart of stone, I will give you a heart of flesh, I will put my Spirit into you, Ezek. xxxvi. 25, 26, 27. Here *I will* no less than seven times. Nothing is allowed to man in the production of this work in the least; all that is done by him, is the walking in God's statutes by virtue of this principle. The sanctifying principle, the actual sanctification, the reception of it by the creature, th removal of all the obstructions of it, the principle maintaining it, are not in the least here attributed to the will of man. God appropriates all to himself. He doth not say, he would be man's assistant, as many men do, who tell us only of the assistances of the gospel, as if God in the gospel expected the first motions of the will of man to give him an opportunity for the acting of his grace; you see here he gives not an inch to the creature. To ascribe the first work in any part to the will of man, is to deprive God of half his due, to make him but a partner with his creature. The least of it cannot be transferred to man, but the right of God will be diminished, and the creature go shares with his Creator. What partner was the creature with God in the creation? It is the Father's work alone, without the hand of free-will. None can come, except the Father which sent me, draw them. John vi. 44. The mission of the Mediator, and the attraction of the creature, are by the same hand. Our Saviour could not have come unless the Father had sent him, nor can man come to Christ, unless the Father draw him: what is that which is drawn? the will. The will then is not the agent, it doth not draw itself.

The titles given to regeneration evidence it. It is a creation; what creature can give itself a being? It is a putting in a law and a new heart; what matter can infuse a soul into itself? It is a new birth; what man did ever beget himself? It is an opening the heart; what man can do this who neither hath the key, nor is acquainted with the wards? Not a man knows the heart, it is deceitful above all things, who can know it?

Scripture represents man as exceedingly weak, and unable to do any thing spiritually good, "So then, they that are in the flesh, cannot please God," Rom. viii. 8. He concludes it by his "so then," as an infallible consequence, from what he had discoursed before. If as being in the flesh they cannot please God, therefore not in that which is the highest pleasure to God, a framing themselves to a likeness to him. The very desire and endeavour of the creature after this, is some pleasure to God, to see a creature struggling after holiness; but they that are in the flesh cannot please him. Can any good thing come out of Nazareth, was said of our Saviour? So may we better say, can any good thing come out of the flesh, the enslaved, possessed will of man? If it be free since it was captivated by sin, who set it free? Nothing can, but the law of the Spirit of life, Rom. viii. 2. To be sinners, and to be without strength, is one and the same thing in the apostle's judgment, Rom. v. 6. 8. "While we were yet without strength;" afterwards, "while we were yet sinners." God only is almighty, and man all impotency; God only is all-sufficient, and man all indigent. It is impossible we can have a strength of our own, since our first father was feeble, and conveyed his weakness to us; by the same reason that it is impossible we can have a righteousness of our own, since our father sinned.

This weakness is universal. Sin hath made its sickly impressions in every faculty. The mind is dark, Eph. iv. 18, he cannot know. 1 Cor. ii. 14, there is a hardness in the heart, he cannot bend, Zech. vii. 12, there is enmity in the will, he cannot be subject, Rom. viii. 7. As to faith, he cannot believe, John xii. 39. As to the Spirit, the worker of faith, he cannot receive; that is, of himself, John xiv. 17, acknowledge Christ he cannot. 1 Cor. xii. 3. As to practice, he cannot bring forth fruit, John xv. 4. The unrighteousness introduced by Adam poured a poison into every faculty, and dispossessed it of its strength, as well as of its beauty: what else could be expected from any deadly wound, but weakness as well as defilement? The understanding conceives only such thoughts as are pleasing to the law of sin; the memory is employed in preserving the dictates and decrees of it: the imagination full of fancies imprinted by it; the will wholly submitting to its authority; conscience standing with fingers in its mouth, for the most part not to speak against it; the whole man yielding itself and every member to the commands of it, and undertaking nothing but by its motions.

To evince it, there is not one regenerate man but in his first conversion is chiefly sensible of his own insufficiency. An universal consent is a great argument of the truth of a proposition; it is a ground of the belief of a Deity, it being the sentiment of all nations. I do not speak of disputes about it from the pride of reason, but of the inward experience of it in any heart: what more frequent in the mouths of those that have some preparations to it by conviction, than, I cannot repent, I cannot believe, I find my heart wicked and base, and unable to do any thing that is good? There have been instances of those that would elevate the power of man, and freedom of will in spiritual things, who have been confuted in their reasonings, and acknowledged themselves so, when God hath come to work savingly upon them. Indeed this poverty of spirit, or sense of our own emptiness, insufficiency, and indigence, is the first gospel grace, wrought in the soul, and stands in the front of all those noble qualifications in our Saviour's sermon, as fitting men for the kingdom of God; " Blessed are the poor in spirit, for theirs is the kingdom of heaven," Matt. v. 3. And God in the whole progress of this work keeps believers sensible of their own weakness, thereby to preserve them in a continual dependence on him; and therefore sometimes withdraws his Spirit from them, and lets them fall, that they may adhere more closely to him, and less confide in themselves.

What kind of impotency or insufficiency is there in the soul, to be the cause of this work?

It is not a physical weakness for want of faculties. Understanding we have, but not a spiritual light in it to direct us; will we have, but no freedom to choose that which is spiritually good; though since the fall we have such a free-will left, which pertains to the essential nature of man, yet we have lost that liberty which belongs to the perfection of human nature, which was to exercise acts spiritually good and acceptable to God. Had the faculties been lost, Adam had not been capable of a promise or command, and consequently of ever sinning after. In Adam by creation we were possessed of it; in Adam by his corruption we were stripped of it; we have not lost the physical but the moral nature of these faculties; not the faculties themselves, but the moral goodness of them. As the elementary heat is left in the carcass, which yet is unfit to exercise any animal action for want of a soul to enliven it; so though the faculties remain after this spiritual death, we are unfit to exert any spiritual actions for want of grace to quicken them. If man wanted faculties, this want would excuse him in his most extravagant actions; nay, without those faculties, he could not act as a rational creature, and so were utterly incapable of sinning. Sin hath untuned the strings, but did not unstring the soul; the faculties were still left, but in such a disorder that the wit and will of man can no more tune them than the strings of an untuned lute can dispose themselves for harmony without a musician's hand.

Neither is it a weakness arising from the greatness of the object above the faculty. As when an object is unmeet for a man, because he hath no power in him to comply with it—as to understand the essence of God; this the highest creature in its own nature cannot do, because God dwells in inaccessible light; and it is utterly impossible for any thing but God to comprehend God. If man were required to become an angel, or to rise up and kiss the sun in the firmament; these were impossible things, because man wanted a faculty in his primitive nature for such acts: so if God had commanded Adam to fly without giving him wings, or to speak without giving him a tongue, he had not been guilty of sin in not doing it, because it was not disobedience; for disobedience is only in what a man hath a faculty to do; but to love God, praise him, depend upon him, was in the power of man's original nature, for they were not above those faculties God endued him with, but very correspondent and suitable to him: the objects proposed are in themselves intelligible, credible, capable to be comprehended.

Neither is it a weakness arising from the insufficiency of external revelation. The means of regeneration are clearly revealed in the gospel, the sound is gone into all the earth, Rom. x. 18, and the word of the Lord is an apprehensible object, it is near us, even in our mouths, Rom. x. 8; "the commandment of the Lord is pure, enlightening the eyes," Psa. xix. 8. If the object were hid, the weakness lay not on the part of man, but on the insufficiency of revelation; as if any thing were revealed to man in an unknown tongue, there were an insufficiency in the means of revelation.

But, it is a moral weakness; the disability lies chiefly in the will. Carnal lusts prepossess the heart, and make their party in the will against the things of God: so that inward propensities to embrace sin are as great as the outward temptations to allure to it, whereby the soul is carried down the stream with a wilful violence. In this respect he is called dead, though the death be not of the same nature with a natural death; for such a one hath not the natural faculty to raise himself; but this is an impotency arising from a voluntary obstinacy; yet the iniquity of a man binds him no less powerfully under this spiritual captivity, than a natural death and insensibility keep men in the grave: and those fetters of perversity they can no more knock off, than a dead man can raise himself from the grave. By reason of those bands they are called prisoners, Isa. xlii. 7, and cannot be delivered without the powerful voice of Christ commanding and enabling them to go forth. "That thou mayest say to the prisoner, Go forth." Isa. xlix. 9. The apostle lays the whole fault of men's not receiving the truth, upon their wills. "They received not the love of the truth," 2 Thess. ii. 10; they heard it, they knew it, but they loved not that which courted them. It is not seated in any defect of the will, as it is a power of the soul, for then God who created it would be charged with it, and might as well charge beasts to become men, as men to become gracious. Man as a creature had a power to believe and love God; to resist temptations, to avoid sin, and live according to nature; but man as corrupted by a habit derived to him from his first parents, and increased by a custom in sin, cannot believe, cannot love God, cannot bring himself into a good frame; as a musician cannot play a lesson when he hath the gout in his fingers. When the eyes are full of adultery, when the heart is full of evil habits, it cannot cease to sin, it cannot be gracious, 2 Pet. ii. 14.

Now these habits are either innate, or contracted and increased.

Innate. By nature we have a habit of corruption

fundamental of all others that grow up in us. Man made a covenant with sin, contracted a marriage with it; by virtue of this covenant, sin had a full power over him: what the apostle speaks of the marriage between man and the law, Rom. vii. 1, 2, 3, 4, is applicable to this case: sin, as a husband, by way of covenant, hath a powerful dominion over the will, and binds it as long as sin lives; and the will hath no power to free itself, unless a higher power make a divorce, or by the death of the husband: this is the cause of man's obstinacy against any return to God, the will is held in the cords of sin, Prov. v. 22. The habit hath obtained an absolute sovereignty over it. "They will not frame their doings to turn unto their God: for the spirit of whoredoms is in the midst of them;" Hos. v. 4; that is, in their hearts. This adulterous or idolatrous habit holds their wills in chains, and actuates them, as a man possessed by the devil is actuated according to the pleasure of the devil; the devil speaks in them, moves in them, and does what he pleases by them. And, which binds the will faster, this habit is not in a natural man by way of a tyranny, but a voluntary sovereignty on the part of the will; the will is pleased and tickled with it. As a woman, (to use the similitude of the Holy Ghost in that place,) is so overruled by her affections to other lovers, that she cannot think of returning to her former husband; but her unlawful love plays all its pranks, and riseth with that force against all arguments from honesty and credit, that it keeps her still in the chains of an unlawful lust. So this is not a habit which doth oppress nature, or force it against its will, but by its incorporation, and becoming one with our nature, has quite altered it from that original rectitude and simplicity wherein God at first framed it. It is a law of sin, which having razed out the purity of the law of nature, commands in a greater measure in the stead of it. Hence it is as natural to man, in his lapsed state, to have perverse dispositions against God, as it is essential to him to be rational. And the chariot of that weak remaining reason left us, is overturned by our distempered passions; and the nobler part of man is subject to the rule of these, which bear down the authority both of reason and God too. That one sin of the angels, howsoever complicated we know not, taking place as a habit in them, hath bound them for ever from rising to do any good, or disentangling themselves from it, and may perhaps be meant by those chains of darkness wherein they are reserved and held to the judgment of the great day, having no will to shake them off, though they have light enough to see the torment appointed for them.

New contracted and increased habits upon this foundation. Custom turns sin more into another nature, and completes the first natural disorder. An unrenewed man daily contracts a greater impotency, by adding strength to this habit, and putting power into the hands of sin to exercise its tyranny, and increasing our headstrong natures in their unruliness. It is as impossible of ourselves to shake off the fetters of custom, as to suppress the unruliness of nature. "Can the Ethiopian change his skin, or the leopard his spots? Then may ye also do good that are accustomed to do evil." Jer. xiii. 23. The prophet speaks not here of what they were by nature, but what they were by custom; contracting thereby such a habit of evil, that like a chronic disease, could not be cured by any ordinary means. But may he not accustom himself to do good? No; it is as impossible as for an Ethiopian to change his skin. Those habits draw a man to delight in, and therefore to a necessity of sinning. The pleasure of the heart joined with the sovereignty of sin, are two such strong cords as cannot be untwisted or cut by the soul itself; no, not without an overruling grace: it was a simple wound in Adam, but such as all nature could not cure, much less when we have added a world of putrefaction to it. Te stronger the habit, the greater the impotency:

if we could not raze out the stump of mere nature upon our wills, how can we raze out the deeper impressions made by the addition of custom? If Adam, who committed but one sin, and that in a moment, did not seek to regain his lost integrity; how can any other man, who by a multitude of sinful acts has made his habit of a giant-like stature, completed many parts of wickedness, and scoffed at the rebukes of conscience?

Let us now see wherein this weakness to renew ourselves appears.

In a total moral unfitness for this work. Grace being said to make us meet for our master's use, it implies an utter unfitness for God's use, of ourselves, before grace. There is a passive capability, a stump left in nature, but no fitness for any activity in nature, no fitness in nature for receiving grace before grace; there is nothing in us naturally which doth suit or correspond with that which is good in the sight of God; that which is natural is found more or less in all men. But the gospel, which is the instrument of regeneration, finds nothing in the nature of man to comply with the main design of it: there is indeed some compliance of moral nature with the moral precepts in the gospel, upon which account it hath been commended by some heathen; but nothing to answer the main intendment of it, which is faith, the top-grace in regeneration: this hath nothing to commend itself to mere nature, nor finds an internal principle in man that is pleased with it, as other graces do, as love, meekness, patience, &c. For faith strips a man of all his own glory, brings him from himself to live dependently upon another, and makes him act for another, not for himself; and therefore meets not with any one principle in man to show it countenance. No good thing dwells in the flesh, Rom. vii. 18, there may be some motions lighting there, as a fly upon a man's face; but they have no settled abode, and spring not up from nature. If the apostle, who was renewed, found an unfitness in himself to do that which was good, how great is that unfitness in a mere natural will, which is wholly under the power of the flesh, and hath no principle in it correspondent to spiritual truth to renew itself? If this regeneration had any foundation in nature, it would be then in most men that hear the gospel, because there is not a general contradiction in men to those things which are natural: but since there is no good thing dwells in any flesh, how can it be fit of itself to be raised into a conformity to God, which is the highest pitch of the creature's excellency? The Scripture represents us not as earth, which is fit to suck in showers from heaven, but as stones, which only are moistened in the superficies by the rain, but answer not the intendment of it. Adamants are unfit to receive impressions; and the best natural heart is no better—like a stone, cold and hard. The soul with its faculties is like a bird with its wings, but clogged with slime and clay, unfit to fly. A barren wilderness is absolutely unfit to make a pleasant and fruitful garden. There is a contractedness of the heart till God enlarge and open it, and that in the best nature. Acts xvi. 14. Lydia, it is said, worshipped God, there was religion in her, yet the Lord opened her heart for the gospel. Can any thing be more indisposed than a fountain that is always bubbling up poison? so is the heart of man, Gen. vi. 5. The least imagination, rising up in the heart, is evil, and can be no better, since the heart itself is a mass of venom. If renewed natures find so much indisposition in the progress of sanctification, though their sails be filled with grace, how great must it be where corrupt nature alone sits at the stern? As when Satan came to tempt our Saviour, he found nothing in him, no touchwood in his nature to take fire by a temptation: so when the Spirit comes, he finds no tinder in man to receive readily any spark of grace. This unfitness is in the best mere nature, that seems to have but a drop of corruption; a drop of water is as unfit to ascend as a greater quantity.

There is not only an unfitness, but an unwillingness; a senseless drowsiness of soul, loath to be moved. No man doth readily hold out his arms to embrace the offers of the gospel. What folding of the arms! yet a little more slumber, a little more sin. Man is mere darkness, before his effectual calling: "who hath called us out of darkness." 1 Pet. ii. 9. His understanding is darkened; the will cannot embrace a thing offered, unless it have powerful arguments to persuade it of the goodness of that thing which is offered; which arguments are modelled in the understanding; but that being darkened, hath wrong notions of divine things, therefore cannot represent them to the will to be pursued and followed. Adam's running away from God to hide himself, after the loss of his original righteousness, discovers how unwilling man is to implore God's favour. How deplorable is the condition of man by sin! since we find not one prayer put up by Adam, nor can we suppose any till the promise of recovery was made, though he was sensible of his nakedness, and haunted by his conscience: "I was afraid, because I was naked: and I hid myself," Gen. iii. 10. He had no mind, no heart to turn suppliant unto God, he runs from God; and when God finds him out, instead of begging pardon by humble prayer, he stands upon his justification, accuses God to be the cause, by giving him the woman, by whose persuasion he was induced to sin. What glass will better discover the good will of nature to God, than the first motions after the fall?

There is not only an unfitness and unwillingness, but an affection to something contrary to the gospel. The nature of outward objects is such, that they attract the sensitive appetite, corrupted by sin, to prefer them before that which is more excellent: the heart is forestalled by an inordinate love of the world, and a pleasure in unrighteousness, "they believed not the truth, but had pleasure in unrighteousness," 2 Thess. xii. 12, a singular pleasure. Where the heart and the devil agree so well, what liking can there be to God or his will? Where the amity between sin and the soul is so great, that sin is self, and self is sin, how can so delightful a friend be discarded, to receive one he thinks his enemy? This weakness ariseth from a love to something different or contrary to what is proposed. When a man is so tied to that object which he loves, that he minds not that contrary object which is revealed by a fit light: as a man that hath his eyes or his heart fixed upon a fair picture, cannot observe many things that occur about him : or if he doth consider it, he is taken so much with the things he loves, that he seems to hate the other; that though he doth count it good, yet compared with what he loved before, he apprehends it as evil, and judges it evil, merely by the error of his mind, a practical, affected and voluntary ignorance. So, though a man may sometimes judge that there is a goodness in the gospel, and the things proposed, yet his affection to other pleasures, which he prefers before the gospel, causes him to shake off any thoughts of compliance with it. Now all natural men in the irons of sin, are not weary, but in love with their fetters, and prize their slavery as if it were the most glorious liberty.

There is not only unfitness, and unwillingness, and a contrary affection to the gospel, but according to the degrees of this affection to other things, there is a strong aversion and enmity to the tenders of the gospel. This enmity is more or less in the heart of every unrenewed man, though in some it is more restrained and kept down by education, yet it will appear more or less upon the approaches of grace, which is contrary to nature : as a spark as well as a flame will burn, though one hath less heat than the other; there is the same nature, the same seminal principles in all. The carnal mind, let it be ever so well polished by education, is enmity to God, and therefore unable, because unwilling to be subject to his law, Rom. viii. 7. By nature he is of the devil's party, and hath no mind the castle of his heart should ever come into the hands of the right owner. It is in every faculty. Not one part of the soul will make a mutiny within against sin, or take part with God, when he comes to lay siege to it; when he stretches out his hands, he meets with a rebellious and gainsaying people, Rom. x. 21. It can converse with any thing but God; look with delight upon any thing but that which is the only true object of delight. It can have no desire to have that law written in his heart, whose character he hates. All the expressions in the Scripture, denoting the work of grace, import man's distaste of it: it is to deny himself, crucify the flesh. What man has not an aversion to deny what is dearest to him, his self; to crucify what is incorporated with him, his Isaac, his flesh? The bent of a natural heart, and the design of the gospel, which is to lay man as low as the dust, can never agree. A corrupt heart, and the propositions of grace, meet together as fire and water, with hissing. The language of man, at the proposals of the gospel, is much like that of the devils, "what have we to do with thee? Art thou come to destroy us?" Luke iv. 34.

This aversion proceeds on to a resistance. No rebels were ever stouter against their prince, than an unrenewed soul against the Spirit of God; not a moment without arms in his hand: he acts in defence of his sin, and resistance of grace, and combats with the Spirit, as his deadly enemy; "Ye always resist the Holy Ghost: as your fathers did, so do ye." Acts vii. 51. The animosity runs in the whole blood of nature. Neither the breathings of love, nor the thunders of threatenings, are listened to. All natural men are hewed out of one quarry of stone. The highest rock, and the hardest adamant may be dissolved with less pains than the heart of man; they all, like a stone, resist the force of the hammer, and fly back upon it. All the faculties are full of this resistance: the mind with stout reasoning gives a repulse to grace; the imagination harbours foolish conceits of it: in the heart, hardness and refusing to hear; in the affections, disgust and displeasure with God's ways, disaffection to his interests, the heart is locked, and will not of itself shoot one bolt to let the king of glory enter: what party is like to be made for God, by bare nature thus possessed? Nature indeed does what it can, though it cannot do what it would; for though it resist the outward means, and inward motions, yet it cannot efficaciously resist the determined grace of God, any more than the matter of the creation could resist the all-powerful voice of God, commanding it to receive this or that form; or Lazarus resist the receiving that life Christ conveyed to him by his mighty word; God finds a contradiction in our wills; and we are not regenerate, because our will hath consented to the persuasions of grace, for that it doth not do of itself; but the grace of God disarms our will of all that is capable of making resistance, and determines it to accept and rejoice in what is offered. Nature of itself is of an unyielding temper, and removes not one scale from the eye, nor any splinter from the stone in the heart; for how can we be the authors of that which we most resist and labour to destroy.

Add to all this, the power of Satan in every natural man, whose interest lies in enfeebling the creature. The devil, since his first impression upon Adam, hath had the universal possession of nature, unless any natural man free himself from the rank of the children of disobedience. "The spirit that now works in the children of disobedience;" Eph. ii. 2; where the same word is used for the acting of Satan, and likewise for the acting of sin, in Rom. vii. 5, as for the acting of the Spirit, Phil. ii. 13; in whom Satan works as a spirit, as powerfully according to his created strength,

as the Holy Ghost works in the children of disobedience.   As the Spirit fills the soul with gracious
habits to move freely in God's ways, so Satan fills the
soul (as much as in him lies) with sinful habits, as so
many chains to keep it under his own dominion.   He
cannot indeed work immediately upon the will, but he
uses all the skill and power that he hath to keep men
captive for the performance of his own pleasure, " who
are taken captive by him at his will," 2 Tim. ii. 26, or
for his will; it is in that place a dreadful judgment
which God gives some men up to, for opposing the
gospel, taking away his restraints, both from the devil
and their own hearts; but more or less he works in
every one that opposes the gospel, which every unrenewed man under the preaching of the gospel does:
he is the strong man that keeps the palace, Luke xi.
21.   Can the will of man make a surrender of it, at
God's demand, in spite of its governor?   What power
have we to throw off the shackles he loads us with?
We are as weak in his hand as birds in a fowler's;
what will have we, since we are his willing slaves?
The darkness of nature is never likely by its own
free motion to disagree with the prince of darkness,
without an overpowering grace, able to contest with
the lord as well as the slave: for by the fall he is become prince of the lower creation, and holds it in
chains too strong for weakness to break.   How great
then is man's inability!   How unreasonable it is to
think, that the will of man, possessed with such unfitness, unwillingness, affection to other things, aversion
to the gospel, resistance of it, and in the devil's net,
can of itself do any thing towards its recovery, from
that which it counts no disease, or to turn to that which
it accounts its burden?   If unspotted and sound nature
did not preserve Adam in innocence, how can filthy
and crazy nature recover us from corruption?   If it
did not keep him alive when he was living, how can
it convey life to us when we have not a spark of spiritual life in us?   Man was planted a noble vine, but

turned himself into a degenerate plant; nothing that hath decayed, can by its own strength recover itself, because it hath lost that strength whereby it could only preserve itself.

CHAPTER II

The means of grace do not effect Regeneration —Neither the law or the gospel can effect it — Man's own moral works do not produce the change —He does not actively co-operate with God in producing it. The inability of man not to be pleaded as an excuse for unregeneracy, because wilful and criminal — How the means of grace are to be used.

MAN by the help of instituted privileges doth not produce this work of regeneration in himself, without a supernatural grace attending them. Ordinances cannot renew a man, but the arm of God which doth manage them, renders them effectual: as the arm that wields the sword, gives the blow. Means are the showers of heaven, but they can no more make the heart fruitful, till some gracious principle be put in, than the beams of the sun, the dews of heaven, and the water pots of the clouds, can make a barren ground bring forth flowers without a change of the soil, and new roots planted in it. All the spectacles in the world cannot cure a man's eyes, he must have a visive faculty to make use of them; our faculty must be cured, before we can exercise it about objects, or use means proper to that faculty. All persuasions will not prevail with a dead man: the fairest discourses, the most undeniable arguments, the most moving rhetoric, will not stir or affect him, till God take away the stone from the grave and raise him to life. The report of the prophets will do no good without the revelation of God's arm, Isa. liii. 1, because all those things do not work in a physical way, as medicines,

which attain their end without any active concurrence
of the patient; but in a moral way. The will and nature
must first be changed before those can do any good.
You can never by all your teaching teach a sheep to
provide for winter, as an ant does, because it has no
such instinct in its nature. If any thing were likely
to work upon a man, the most stupendous miracles
were most likely to produce such an effect upon the
reason of man; yet those supernatual demonstrations
without a man only, cannot make him believe a truth.
Miracles are a demonstration to the eye, as well as
preaching to the ear: though they be confessed to be
above the strength of nature, yet all the spectators of
them are not believers, "But though he had done so
many miracles before them, yet they believed not:"
John xii. 37; many of those that saw our Saviour's
works did not believe his doctrine; nay, they irra-
tionally ascribed them to the devil, when they could
find no reason in the nature of them to charge them
upon such a score. The raising Lazarus from the dead,
was as high a miracle as ever was wrought; yet
though many of them believed, yet others did not, but
accused him to the Pharisees, who thereupon more
vigorously took counsel to put him to death, John
ii. 45—53, they acknowledged that he did many
miracles; they had reason as well as others; the
miracles were undeniable, as being performed before
many witnesses: the natural force of them upon all
reasons was equal, the considerations arising from
them unanswerable; and yet they did not believe.
There were evil habits in the will not removed by
grace, which resisted the unanswerable reason of the
miracles. What made the difference between them
and those that believed? Why did not the wills of
the enemies follow the undeniable reason, as well as
the wills of others? Miracles may astonish men, but
cannot convert them, without a divine touch upon
the heart, 2 Kings xviii. 39. The people were astonished by that wonderful miracle of fire falling from

heaven, and consuming the sacrifice, and licking up the water in the trench; and some reverential resolutions were produced in them, they fell upon their faces and said, The Lord he is God; they showed their zeal in taking Baal's prophets, and helping, or at least suffering Elijah to slay them; yet those people revolted to idolatry, and continued so till their captivity. The easiness of faith upon the appearance and instruction of one risen from the dead, was the opinion of one of the damned, "If one went to them from the dead, they will repent;" Luke xvi. 30: but this opinion was contradicted by Abraham, ver. 31, who positively asserts, "If they hear not Moses and the prophets, they will not be persuaded though one rose from the dead." If their wills were obstinate against the means God has appointed for their conversion, the same wills so corrupted would be as obstinate against the highest sort of miracles. If that then which is above the hand of nature to perform, and bears the characters of omnipotence upon the breasts of it, does not work upon men's hearts and wills of themselves, surely nature itself cannot turn the heart to God.

The two great dispensations of God are law and gospel; neither of these can of themselves work this.

The law will instruct, not heal. It acquaints us with our duty, not our remedy; it irritates sin, not allays it; exasperates our venom, but does not tame it; though it shows man his miserable condition, yet a man by it does not gain one drop of repentance. It tells us what we should do, but corrects not the enmity of our nature whereby we may do it. The apostle takes notice of the enmity of man to the law, Rom. v. 6, 7, yet enemies, yet sinners. That *yet*, may refer to what he had spoken of the law in the chapter before. Though men had had so much time from the fall to recover themselves, and had so many advantages by the law and the ceremonies of it, yet all those years spent from the foundation of the world, had produced no other effect than the weakening of them: as creatures that are wounded, by their strugglings waste their own strength. *Yet* sinners, till this time sinners, whereby the load of sin which lay upon the world, was made more heavy by the continual addition made to those heaps. The offence did rather abound by the law, than diminish. " The law was given, that sin might abound:" Rom. v. 20, though it made a clear discovery of the will of God, yet it rather aggravated sin; it added no power to perform that will. The motions of sin were exasperated by it, and brought forth fruit unto death: all the means by the law for the repression of sin, did rather inflame it; sin could not be overcome by it, because the law was weak through the flesh, that is, had not so much power as sin had; it was like a little water put upon fire, which did rather enrage than quell it. Rom. vii. 8, 9. Sin revived when the law came, it had a new life; and the apostle found himself utterly unable to overpower it. There were motions of sin, not only a power in sin, but an enraged power, which adds to the strength of a person; sin slew him; taking occasion by the commandment, and a dead man is wholly at the disposing of his conquerors. The law was holy, it had an impression of God's holiness upon it, Rom. vii. 12— 14, there was also equity and conveniency in it, it was just and good: and though these were considerations enough to spur men on to rid themselves of this tyrant sin, yet they could not, they had not strength enough to do it, though it was holy, just, and good, yet it was not strong enough to rescue them; and the reason of it, the apostle lays upon the difference in the nature of both. " We know that the law is spiritual, but I am carnal, sold under sin;" there was an enmity in his nature to it, and therefore he must lie under the power of it, till a mighty deliverer stepped in to conquer it. Do we find any better effect of the ceremonial law, which was the gospel in a mask, and which was the instrument of all the regenerations among the Jews? How few do we find renewed among them under that means which they enjoyed solely, and no other nation in the world partners with them in it? How frequent were their revolts, and rebellions, and idolatries, inconsistent with regeneration, we may read in Joshua and Judges. The inefficacy of means appears evidently in that nation which had greater advantages than any in the world besides: the covenants, sacrifices, oracles of God, warnings by prophets, yet so frequently overgrown with idolatry from the time of their coming out of Egypt to the Babylonish captivity, and ten tribes wholly cashiered for it.

The gospel cannot effect this change of heart. Though the veil of ceremonies be taken off from it, and it appears open faced; yet till the veil be taken off the understandings of men, it will produce little fruit among them, 2 Cor. iii. 14. The gospel is plain, but only to him that understands, Prov. viii. 9. As the sun is clear, but only to him that hath an eye to see it. The gospel itself cannot remove the blindness from the mind. The proposal of the object works no alteration in the faculty, without some acting on the faculty itself. The beams of the sun shining upon a blind man, make no alteration in him. The Jews, to whom the gospel was preached by our Saviour himself, could not believe, because God blinded their eyes, &c. John xii. 39, 40. There must be a supernatural power besides the proposal of the object, to take away this blindness and hardness which is the obstruction to the work of the gospel: though the Son of God is come, and the gospel be preached, yet the understanding whereby we know, is given us by him. " And we know that the Son of God is come, and hath given us an understanding, that we may know him that is true :" 1 John v. 20. The light of the gospel shines upon all, but all have not an eye given them to see it, and a will given them to embrace it. The mere doctrine of it doth not regenerate any man; some have tasted of the heavenly gift, that is, have had some understanding of Christ, who is the heavenly gift, and are partakers of some common illumination of the Holy Ghost, yet are not regenerate. Was not the gospel preached to the Jews, even by the mouth of our Saviour, whom they crucified? And was it not preached to the Gentiles by the mouths of those apostles whom they persecuted? Were there not proposals that suited the natural desires of men for happiness? yet did not many that seemed to receive it, receive it not in the love of it? If God himself should appear to us in the likeness of a man, and preach to us as he did to Adam, if he did not overpower our hearts with an inward grace, he would do us no good at all by his declarations. We do not read of any work immediately upon Adam, at the promulgation of the gospel by God himself; though it appears, that afterwards there was, by his instructing his sons to sacrifice, and his expectations of a Messiah. But we certainly know that our Saviour, God manifested in the flesh, declared the gospel in his own person, and found no success, but where he touched the heart inwardly by the grace of his Spirit. All mere outward declarations are but suasions, and mere suasion cannot change and cure a disease or habit in nature. You may exhort an Ethiopian, to turn himself white, or a lame man to go but the most pathetical exhortations cannot procure such an effect, without a greater power than that of the tongue to cure nature : you may as well think to raise a dead man by blowing in his mouth with a pair of bellows. Judas had enjoyed the best means that ever were, yet went out of the world unrenewed : and the thief upon the cross, who never perhaps was in any good company in his life till he came to the cross, nor ever heard Christ speak before, was renewed by the grace of God in the last hour.

Neither can a man renew himself, by all his moral works, before faith. Our calling is not according to our works but " according to God's own purpose and grace," 2 Tim. i. 9. Paul, before his conversion, was " blameless as to the righteousness of the law," Phil.

iii. 6, yet this was loss; a bar rather to regeneration, than a means to further it. For all this legal come-liness, he ranks himself before his conversion, in the number of the dead. "When we were dead in sins," Eph. ii. 5; not you, but we; putting himself into the register of the dead. Whatsoever works a man can morally do before faith, cannot be the cause of spiritual life; they are not vital operations; if they were, they were then the effects of life; not the cause: the Scripture makes them the effects of grace; "created to good works," Eph. ii. 10. What is an effect cannot be the cause. The best works before grace are but a refined sensuality, they arise from self-love, centre in self-satisfaction, are therefore works of a different strain from those of grace, which are referred to a higher end, and to God's well pleasing. In all works before grace, there is no resignation of the soul to God in obedience; no self-denial of what stands in opposition to God in the heart; no clear view of the evil of sin; no sound humiliation under the corruption of nature; no inward purification of the heart, but only a diligence in an external polishing. All those acts cannot produce an habit of a different kind from them. Let a man be stilted up with the highest natural excellency; let him be taller by the head and shoulders, than all his neighbours in morality, this no more confers life upon him, than the setting a statue upon a high pinnacle, near the beams of the sun, in-spireth it with a principle of motion. The increasing the perfection of one species, can never mount the thing so increased, to the perfection of another species. If you could vastly increase the heat of fire, you could never make it ascend to the perfection of a star. If you could increase mere moral works to the highest pitch they are capable of, they can never make you gracious, because grace is another species; and the nature of them must be changed to make them of another kind. All the moral actions in the world, will never make our hearts of themselves, of another kind than moral. Works make not the heart good, but a good heart makes the works good. It is not our walking in God's statutes materially, which procures us a new heart; but a new heart is in order before walking in God's statutes, Ezek. xxxvi. 27. Our regeneration is no more wrought by works of our own, than our justification. The rule of the apostle will hold good in this as well as in the other. If it be of grace it is not of works; otherwise grace is no more grace, Rom. xi. 6; and faith is the gift of God, not of works, lest any man should boast, Ephes. ii. 9. And the apostle, Titus iii. 5, opposes the renewing of the Holy Ghost to works of righteousness. He excludes works from being the cause of salvation: and would they not be the cause of salvation, if they were the cause of the necessary condition of salvation?

As man cannot prepare himself to this work, nor produce it, so he cannot co-operate with God in the first production of it. We are no more co-workers with God in the first regeneration, than we were joint purchasers with Christ in redemption. The conversion of the will to God is a voluntary act; but the regeneration of the will, or the planting new habits in the will, whereby it is enabled to turn to God, is without any concurrence of the will. Some say, the habit of faith is never created separate from an act; as the trees at the creation of the world were created with ripe fruit on them, but the tree, with the power of bearing fruit, and the fruit itself, were created at one and the same time by God. Yet though the habit be not separate at first from the act, yet there is no co-operation of the creature to the infusion of that habit, but there is to the act immediately flowing from that habit: for either that act of grace is voluntary or involuntary: if involuntary it is not a gracious act; if voluntary, as it must needs be, since the tone of the will is changed, then the creature concurs in that act: for the act of believing and repenting is the act of the creature: it is not God that repents and believes in us; but we repent and believe by virtue of that power which God hath given us. In the first act therefore, there is a concurrence of the creature; otherwise the creature could not be said to repent and believe, but something in the creature, without or against the will of the creature But in the first power of believing and repenting, God is the sole agent. Jesus Christ is the sun that heals our natures, Mal. iv. 2; the rain that moistens our hearts. "He shall come down like rain upon the mown grass," Psa. lxxii. 6. What co-operation is there in the earth with the sun, to the production of flowers, but by the softness it hath received from the rain? It would else be parched up, and its fruits wither. The Holy Ghost doth by his own power make us good trees; but we afterwards, by virtue of that power, work together with him, in bringing forth good fruit. Yet this is also a subordinate, not a co-ordinate working; rather a sub-operation than a co-operation.

The state wherein man is at his first renewal, excludes any co-working with God. The description the apostle gives of a state of nature, excludes all co-operation of the creature in the first renewal. "For we ourselves were sometimes foolish, disobedient, deceived, serving divers lusts and pleasures, living in malice and envy, hateful, and hating one another." Tit. iii. 3. And "among whom we all had our conversations in time past, in the lusts of our flesh, fulfilling the desires of the flesh, and of the mind." Ephes. ii. 2, 3. Every man is naturally taken up in the fulfilling the desires of the flesh; not only the Gentiles, to whom Paul writes, but himself, for he puts himself, and the rest of the Jews, in the number. In the second verse it was "ye walked," in ver. 3, it is "we all," and in Tit. iii. 3, "we ourselves." We who had the oracles of God, that had greater privileges than others, were carried out with as strong an impetus naturally, till grace stopped the tide, and after stopping, turned it against nature. When the mind was thus prepossessed, and the will made the lusts of the flesh its work and trade, there was no likelihood of any co-operation with God, in fulfilling his desires, till the bent of the heart was changed from the flesh and its principles. The heart is stone before grace. No stone can co-operate with any that would turn it into flesh, since it has no seed, causes, or principles of any fleshly nature in it. Since we are overwhelmed by the rubbish of our corrupted estate, we can no more co-operate to the removal of it, than a man buried under the ruins of a fallen house, can contribute to the removal of that great weight that lies upon him. Neither would a man in that state help such a work, because his lusts are pleasures; he serves his lusts, which are pleasures as well as lusts, and therefore served with delight. There is naturally in man a greater resistance against the work of grace, than there is in the natural coldness of water against the heat of fire, which yet penetrates into all parts of the water.

But the impotence of man does not excuse him; because the commands of the gospel are not difficult in themselves to be believed and obeyed. If we were commanded things that were impossible in their own nature, as to shoot an arrow as high as the sun, or leap up to the top of the highest mountain at one start; the very command carries its excuse with it, in the impossibility of the thing enjoined : but the precept of regeneration, and restoring to righteousness, is easy to be comprehended; it is backed with clear and manifest reason, and proposed with a promise of happiness, which is very suitable to the natural appetite of our souls. To command a thing simply impossible, is not congruous to the wisdom, holiness, and righteousness of God : it would not be justice but cruelty: no wise man will invite another by any promises to do that which is simply impossible ; no just judge will punish a man for not observing such a precept; no righteous and merciful person would impose such a command. But these commands of the gospel are not impossible in their own nature, but in regard of our perversity and contumacy. The command of righteousness was possible when first given, and impossible since, by our own folly; impossible in our voluntarily corrupted nature, and by reason of our voluntarily cherished corruption: the change is not in the nature of the law, but in the nature of the creature; and what is impossible to nature, is possible to grace; and grace may be sought for the performance of them.

Because we have a foundation in our natures for such commands, therefore man's weakness does not excuse him. It had been unjust for God to have commanded Adam in innocence to fly, and give him no wings: this had been above Adam's natural power, he could not have done it, though he would fain have obeyed God, because his nature was destitute of all force for such a command. It would be strange if God should invite the trees or beasts to repent, because they have no foundation in their nature to entertain commands and invitations to obedience and repentance; for trees have no sense, and beasts have no reason to discern the difference between good and evil. If God commanded a man that never had eyes, to contemplate the sun, we might wonder, since such a man never had organs for such an action. But God addresses himself to men that have senses open to objects, and understandings to know, and wills to move, affections to embrace objects. These understandings are open to any thing but that which God commands; their wills can will any thing but that which God proposes. This command is proportioned to the natural faculty, and the natural faculty proportioned to the excellency of the command. We have affections, as love and desire. In the command of loving God, and loving our neighbour, there is only a

change of the object of our affections required. The
faculties are not weak by nature, but by the vicious-
ness of nature which is of our own introduction. It
is strange therefore, that we should excuse ourselves,
and pretend we are not to be blamed, because God's
command is impossible to be observed, when the
defect lies not in the want of a natural foundation, but
in our own giving up ourselves to the flesh, and the
love of it, and in a wilful refusal to apply our faculties
to their proper objects, when we can employ those
faculties with all vehemence about those things which
have no commerce with the gospel.

Because the means God gives, are not simply insufficient in themselves. God doth afford men beams
of light: he makes clear discoveries, as it is, Rom. i.
19, he "hath showed it to them;" "it is manifest in
them." He displays in their hearts some motions of
his Spirit, produces some faint desires. The standing
of the world under the cries of so many hideous sins,
is a daily sermon of God's kindness and patience, in
bearing up the pillars of it, and is a standing exhortation to repentance. The forbearance, long-suffer-
ing, and goodness of God, lead to repentance. The
object is intelligible: the word is near us, in our
mouths, in our hearts: it is apprehensible in itself.
The revelation is as plain as the surface of the Heavens. That men are not renewed, and turned to God,
is not for want of a sufficient external revelation, but
from the hardness of the heart; not from any insufficiency of the means, but the depravity and wickedness
of the soul, to whom those means are offered. The
commands and means of the gospel, are no more
weak in themselves, than the law was; but weak
through the flesh, by reason of the inherent corruption
man hath fastened in himself. Would not the hun-
dredth part of any revelation of some worldly object,
agreeable to man's corrupt heart, be sufficient in itself
to put him upon motion to it, and embraces of it?
The insufficiency does not lie in the external means·

for the gospel is an act of mercy and grace; the call is an act of kindness: it is clear to man, that God offers; it is clear that God will accept, if man will embrace his counsel; and shall this be said to be insufficient, because man will reject it?

Because this impotence in man, is rather a wilfulness than a simple weakness, therefore man's pretended weakness doth not excuse him from the command. It is not a weakness arising from a necessity of nature, but an enmity of will, whereby some other apparent good is beloved above God, and some creature preferred before him. The deeper the habit of obstinacy, the more inexcusable the person. What a ridiculous excuse would this be, to say to God, that I ought not to be obliged to restore myself to righteousness, and obey the command of the gospel, because I am of so perverse a disposition that I will not obey, and will not be restored: or that God is bound to restore to him that will to obey and renew himself; otherwise he is guilty of no crime. The first would be ridiculous, and both impious. What hinders any man from being regenerate under the call of the gospel, but a moral weakness, which consists in an imperious inclination to evil, and a rooted indisposition in corrupt reason and will, to believe and repent? And hence the Scripture lays it upon the hardness of the heart, Rom. ii. 5; and a rebellious walking after our own thoughts. "I have spread out my hands all the day unto a rebellious people, which walketh in a way that was not good, after their own thoughts," Isa. lxv. 2. We are impotent and cannot, because we are rebellious and will not.

This weakness does not excuse from obedience to this command, because God denies no man strength to perform what he commands, if he seek it at his hands. No man can plead, that he would have been regenerate, and turned to God, and could not; for though we have not power to renew ourselves, yet God is ready to confer power upon us, if we seek it.

Where did God ever deny any man sufficient strength, that waited upon him in serious and humble supplications, and conscientiously used the means to procure it? A man cannot indeed merit grace, or dispose himself for it, so that it must by a natural necessity come into his soul, as a form doth into matter upon dispositions to it. But if a man will put no obstacle to grace, by a course of sin, would not God out of his infinite bounty to his creatures, and out of that general love whereby he would have all men saved, and come to the knowledge of the truth, give him special grace? Has not our Saviour made a promise in his first sermon to the multitude, that God will "give good things to them that ask him," with a "much more" than men give good gifts to their children? Matt. vii. 11. They were not only his disciples that he preached that sermon to, but the multitude; compare it with Matt. v. 1, and Matt. vii. 28. Has not God declared, that he delights not in the death of a sinner, Ezek. xxxiii. 11, and does he not, out of his infinite goodness, condescend to beseech us to be reconciled to him? Will not the same infinite goodness bow itself down to form a new image in them that use the means to be reconciled and conformed to him? Has not our blessed Saviour already given a testimony of his affection to such endeavours, in loving the young man for his outward observation of the law, Mark x. 21, who wanted but one thing only to pass him into a gracious state, the refusal whereof barred him of it? And shall not he have a choicer affection to those that strive to observe the rules he has left in his gospel? Will he not be pleased with such motions in his creatures towards their own happiness? Will he not further that wherein he delights? Think not therefore to justify yourselves at the bar of God for your sloth, because you are too weak to renew yourselves. It will not help you then. The question will then be asked, Did you ever seriously beg it, as for your lives? Did God ever desert you when you would fight against sin, when you set yourselves seriously and dependently on him for grace? God gives us talents, but by our sloth we embezzle them. It is upon that score Christ lays it, "Thou wicked and slothful servant," Matt. xxv. 26; God has not promised to furnish you with more talents, when you improve not the talents you have already; non-improvement of them cuts off all pleas men may make against God upon the account of their impotence. As there never was a renewed man, but acknowledged his regeneration as a fruit of God's grace: so there was never any man that can say, he did use his greatest industry in trading with the talents God intrusted him with, and God refused him the supply of his special grace. If you have not a new heart and a heart of flesh, ask your own hearts, whether you ever did seriously inquire of God to do it for you? God never fails them that diligently seek him.

Use the means fervently. With as much ardour as you set upon any thing of worldly concern: do it with all your might, since the eternal blessedness of your soul depends upon it; "Whatsoever thy hand findeth to do, do it with thy might," Eccles. ix. 10; stir up your souls to hear and meditate, as David does to bless, "Bless the Lord, O my soul; and all that is within me, bless his holy name." Psa. ciii. 1, 2. Employ all your faculties in this useful work; bring your hearts as near to the word as you can, spur up your affections to what you meditate upon, check your hearts when they begin to rove. Consider your own particular case in any thing you hear; and let the word be as a delightful picture in the view of your minds continually; let every evangelical object excite your inbred affections.

Use the means dependently. Objective proposals are not useless, because God has ordained them, though they are not always successful, unless God influences them. The means do not work naturally, as a plaster cures a wound, or a hatchet cleaves wood; nor necessarily as fire burns; for then they should produce the same effects in all, as fire doth in combustible matter; but as God pleases to accompany them with his grace, and edge them with efficacy. They must be used with an eye to God; building with one hand, and wrestling with God with the other: men speed best in ordinances as they strive in prayer. There are promises to plead before you come to hear. "In all places where I record my name, I will come unto thee, and bless thee," Exod. xx. 24. The promise was made to the whole nation of Israel, the visible church, therefore, may be pleaded by every one of them; and fix it upon your hearts, that as the death of Christ alone takes away the guilt of sin, so the grace of Christ alone takes away the life of sin, and the death of nature.

Pray earnestly. Intreat God to send his grace; beg of him to issue out a divine force and a quickening power, to enlighten your minds and incline your wills. Lie at his feet, groan, wait till this work be wrought in your soul: how do you know, but while you are looking up to God, God may come down to you? Can a man be wounded and not cry for a healing remedy? Can he be shipwrecked and not cry out for some vessel to relieve him? Let such a voice frequently issue from you, "What shall I do to be saved?" Is there no balm for a wounded soul, no hope for a distressed sinner? No city of refuge for one pursued by wrath and vengeance? Do you pray for daily bread? Why do you not for special grace? Are there no rational pleas you can urge? Is there not a fulness of arguments in the word? Why do you not then use those arguments God hath put into your hands? Why do you not spread his own word before him? Put him in mind how his thoughts were busy about the work of redemption, and that the regeneration you desire of him, was the great end of that, and a thing pleasing to him? Why do you not reason with God? To what purpose he sent his Spirit into the world, but to do this work in the hearts of men, which you are now soliciting him for; and that you come not to beg any alms of him, but what he freely offers himself? You may daily read such arguments in the word, where a revelation is made of them; you may daily plead them: if you do not, it is not your cannot, but your will not. Cry out of the blind eyes you cannot unscale; the iron sinews you cannot bend; the false heart that will not go right; and the fallen nature which cannot reach so high as a holy thought. God gives the Spirit to them that ask him, not to the idle, lazy, and peevish resister of him and his grace. If you have power to regenerate your-selves, why do you not do it? If you have not, why do you not seek it? Is the way of heaven shut to you; or rather, do you not shut your own hearts against it? have you sought it earnestly, and can you say God denies it to you? No man can say so; there is a pro-mise for it. "Draw near to God and he will draw near to you," James iv. 8; he speaks it to sinners, as it follows: "Cleanse your hands, ye sinners." You can pray for other mercies, why not principally for this particular determination of your wills to God, above all other things? Lord, give me to will and to do. Never leave off praying till God hath crowned your petitions with success: and be encouraged to seek to him, whose great business in the world was to destroy the works of the devil, whose principal work was the spiritual death of man. If you have such earnest desires in your souls that you would rather have it than the whole world, and esteem it above all worldly wealth or honours; be of good comfort, some of the rubbish of nature is removed: the steam of such desires shall be welcome to God; and the Spirit's commission shall be renewed to breathe further upon your souls. Desire as vehement as hunger and thirst shall be satisfied, if our blessed Saviour's promise be true, who never deceived any, or broke his word. "Blessed are they that hunger and thirst after righteousness, for they shall be filled," Matt. v. 6; a fulness attends a sense of emptiness, accompanied with hungering desires. But I am afraid few people put up their petitions to God for it; that I may say, as Daniel of his nation: All this evil of unrighteousness and sin is come upon us by our depraved natures, yet made we not our prayer before the Lord our God, that we might turn from our iniquities, and understand thy truth, Dan. ix. 13.

Nourish every motion and desire you find in your hearts towards it. Have you not sometimes motions to go to the throne of grace, and beg renewing grace of God? Do you not find such drawings in your consciences? Is there not something within you spurs you on? Kick not against it, nor resist it, no, nor smother any spark of an honest desire in your hearts; be constant observers of the lessons, your natural consciences, or whatever any other principle sets you; natural notions are not so blotted, but they remain legible, would men be more inward with themselves, than abroad with the objects of sense, which draw their minds from pondering that decalogue writ in their souls. There is not the wickedest man under the gospel, but hath sometimes more bright irradiations in his conscience than at other times, but they are damped by a noisome sensuality: he hath some strugglings against the solicitations of unrighteousness, some assents upon the presenting of virtue: for as grace is not always so powerful in a good man as to stifle temptation, so neither is corruption so powerful in a wicked man as always to beat back those motions to good, which rise up in his soul, whether he will or no: as the law of the mind is not always so sovereign in a gracious man, but that it is affronted by the law of the members: so neither is the law of the members so absolute in a wicked man, but that it is somewhat checked by the law of nature in the mind. Are there not upon hearing the word, or reflecting upon yourselves, some wishings, some inward desires which partake of reason, and the nature of that faculty which represent the necessity of it to you? As there is some kind of weak knowledge left in us since the fall, there is also something of a weak desire; cannot these desires be improved and represented to God? Why is not the grace of God fulfilled in you? Because you persevere not in these desires, you quench the sparks of the Spirit, and willingly give admission to Satan to chase them out. Shut not your eyes then against any light, either without or within you, which may provoke God to withdraw this grace from you. How do you know but upon using the means, praying earnestly, observing inward motions, God may give you an actual regeneration? The neglect of these is a just reason for God to refuse you any further gift; and may take off all things which you may think to bring against him in your own defence. The use of them has been beneficial to many, and no example can ever be brought, that God hath condemned any that conscientiously used the means of salvation. Therefore I say again, if any man uses the means, prays earnestly for this grace, observes the motions of the Spirit in him; he will not want a superadded grace from an infinitely good, tender, and merciful God.

CHAPTER III

God's exclusive agency in Regeneration demonstrated —The Scriptures attribute the whole work to God.—God prepares the heart for it, inspires faith, calls forth the acts of the new creature —The subject and end of regeneration show its authorship, so the weakness of means. It is evinced also by the peculiar differences observable in the work.

FROM the foregoing considerations, it is fully proved that man in all his capacities, is too weak to produce in himself the work of regeneration; therefore *God alone is the prime efficient cause of this glorious work.*

It is subjectively in the creature, efficiently from God. Ezekiel's dry bones met not together of their own accord, or by chance, but were gathered by God, and inspired with life; and not only the last act of life, but the whole formation of them in every part, he particularly owns as the act of his own power; and doing every part of it by degrees, they should know by that admirable work upon them, that he was God. " I will cause breath to enter into you, and you shall live. And I will lay sinews upon you, and will bring flesh upon you, and cover you with skin, and put breath in you, and you shall live, and you shall know that I am the Lord." Ezek. xxxvii. 5, 6. This work as much discovers the glory of his deity, and speaks him God in a more illustrious manner than the creation of the world. We know him to be the Lord Jehovah by his creation of the world; but a clearer knowledge of him in his power is added by his regeneration of the soul. The sinews, flesh, skin, all the preparations to grace are from God, as all the preparation of that mass of clay, for the breath of life in Adam, were from the power of God, as well as the living soul itself. Most understand it of the recovery of the Jews from the captivity of Babylon: but certainly it has a higher import, and respects the time of the gospel, and the renewing of life in the soul of all the Israel of God.

Christ appropriates the work to God, and acknowledges it to depend only upon his will. Had any other cause been in conjunction with God, our Saviour would not have deprived it of its due praise, nor with so much thankfulness and amazement admired the gracious pleasure of his Father, as he did, " At that time Jesus answered, and said, I thank thee, O Father, Lord of heaven and earth, because thou hast hid these things from the wise and prudent, and hast revealed them unto babes; even so, Father, for so it seemed good in thy sight." Matt. xi. 25. "At that time," after he had been discoursing of the judgments upon them for their refusal of the gospel, worse than upon Sodom and Gomorrah. It was God's pleasure not to reveal it to them; and God's justice to punish them for refusal, because they wilfully refused it; the outward teaching was to all in the ministry of Christ; the inward revelation only to few, according to the good pleasure of God: Christ was the outward teacher, but God the inward inspirer; that others are not renewed by him is not because he cannot, for he is Lord of heaven and earth; but because he will renew some and not others: our Saviour refers it here only to the good pleasure of God: he had erred much in ascribing it to God, if he had had the assistance of any other cause. Why this part of the clay he had created was formed into the body of Adam and not another, had no other cause but his pleasure: why this part of corrupted Adam is formed into a temple, a divine image, and not another, can be ascribed to no other but the same cause. He that formed Adam in the earthly paradise, forms every believer in the church, the spiritual paradise, and neither hath a co-worker nor motive without himself.

The Scripture every where appropriates the work to God. They are therefore called his Saints, Psa. xxxiii. 9, as being sanctified by him, as well as belonging to him; his people, "the branch of my planting, the work of my hands," peculiarly his, as being created for his glory, "That I may be glorified," Isa. lx. 21. Their fitness by grace for glory is the work of his hands. The vessels of wrath are fitted for destruction, not by God, but by themselves, Rom. ix. 22. But the vessels of mercy are prepared by him, verse 23. "He had before prepared unto glory." Adam lost himself, but whosoever of his posterity are recovered, are wrought by God for glory, 1 Cor. v. 5. It is observable that the apostle ascribes this in the whole frame of it to God, "But of him are ye in

Christ Jesus, who of God is made unto us wisdom, righteousness," &c. 1 Cor. i. 30, because he would remove all cause of boasting in the creature. Union with Christ, engrafting in him, a new creation, putting into another state, are all purely the work of God. He hath no sharer in it. As Christ trod the wine press alone, in the work of redemption: so God engrafts men alone into this vine. As Christ was the sole worker of redemption, so is God the sole worker of regeneration; in him we are created, but solely by God's skill; Christ the vine, and believers the branches; the one planted, and the other engrafted by the same husbandman. It is by his own will, not any other, that he begat us, James i. 18. Of his own will; his own good pleasure was the motive, his own strength the efficient cause: hence he is called the father of spirits, Heb. xii. 9, not so much (as some interpret it, and that most probably) as he is the Father of souls by creation, as by regeneration, which adds a greater strength to the apostle's argument for submission to him, and patience under his strokes.

And the Scripture affirms that,

All preparations to this work, as well as the work itself, are of God. The removing indisposition, and the putting in good inclinations, is the work of the same hand: the taking away the heart of stone, as well as the giving a heart of flesh. He removes the rubbish, as well as rears the building; razeth out the old stamp, and imprints a new; destroys sin, which is called the old man, and restores the new by the quickening of the Spirit. The preparations of the dust of the ground to become a human body, had the same author, as the divine soul wherewith he was inspired.

All the parts of the new creature are of God. Faith which is the principal part of it, is "the faith of the operation of God," Col. ii. 12, not but that love and other graces are wrought by God; but in this grace which is a constitutive part of the new creature, God comes in with a greater irradiation upon the soul, because it hath not one fragment or point in nature to stand upon, carnal reason and mere moral righteousness being enemies to it : where all other graces are but the rectifying the passions, and setting them upon right objects. Our knowledge of God is a light growing from his knowledge of us ; we know God because we are known of him, Gal. iv. 9. The elective act of our wills is but a fruit of his choice of us, " Ye have not chosen me, but I have chosen you ;" John xv. 16 ; our willing of him, is a birth of his willing us ; our love, a spark kindled by his love to us. God first calls us " my people," before any of us call him, " my God," Hos. ii. 23. The moon shines not upon the sun, till it be first illuminated by it. God first shines upon us, before we can reflect upon him : he calls us, before we can speak to him in his own dialect : our coming is an effect of his drawing ; and our power of coming, an effect of his quickening. Every member in Adam was a fruit of his power as well as the whole body ; every line drawn in the new creature, is done by his pencil, as well as the whole frame.

The acts of the new creature are of God. God doth not only give us the habit of faith, but the act of faith, " Unto you it is given in the behalf of Christ, not only to believe, but also to suffer for his sake :" Phil. i. 29 ; by believing, is meant the act of believing ; as by suffering is meant not only the power of suffering, but actual suffering : as the fruits upon the trees, at the first creation, were created, as well as the trees which had a power to bear. The very attention of Lydia to the gospel preached by Paul, was wrought by God, as well as the opening of her heart, Acts xvi. 14. Our walking in his statutes is a fruit of his grace, as well as the putting in his Spirit to enable us thereunto : the very act of motion is made by the head and heart : if there be a failing of spirits there, if any obstruction that they cannot reach the indigent part, the motion ceaseth. David acknowledged God his continual strength in his holy pursuits, " my soul

follows hard after thee," Psa. lxiii. 8, but what was
the cause ? "thy right hand upholds me ;" his life and
power issued out from the right hand of God.   The
graces of God's people stand in need of the irradiations of God, like the Urim and Thummim, before any
counsel could be given by them.

God is the author of this work if we regard the
subject simply considered ; the heart of man.   None
can work upon it but God, or have any influence to
cause it to exercise its vital acts.   Angels, though of
vast power, cannot work immediately upon the heart
and will of any other creature, to incline and change
it by an immediate touch.   All that they can do
towards moving the will, is by presenting some external objects, or stirring up the inward sensitive appetite to some passion, as anger, desire ; whereby the
will is inclined to will something.   But the stirring
up those natural affections in an unregenerate man,
can never incline his will to good ; for being the affections of the flesh, they are to be crucified.   Angels
also may enlighten the understanding, not immediately, but by presenting similitudes of sensible things,
and conforming them in the fancy: but to remove
one ill habit from the will, or incline it to any good,
is not in their power.   God gave an angel power to
purge the prophet's lips with a coal from the altar,
Isa. vi. 6, 7; but that was done in a vision ; and a
symbol or sign only that his uncleanness was removed.
A coal could have no virtue in it to purge spiritual
pollutions from the spirit of a man.   Neither can man
change the will; men by allurements or threats, may
change, or rather suspend the action of another ; as a
father that threatens to disinherit his son ; or a magistrate, that threatens to punish a subject for his de-
bauchery, may cause a change in the actions of such
persons ; but the heart stands still to the same sinful
point, and may be vicious under a fair disguise.   He
only that made the will, can incline and "turn it as
the rivers of waters ; the heart of the king is in the

hands of the Lord," Prov. xxi. 1; and so is every man's heart kept in the hands of him that created it, both cabinet and key. No man knows the heart; the heart itself knows not every thing which is in it. God knows all the wards in the heart, and knows how to move it. If a man could turn the heart of another, it could only be in one or two points; it cannot be conceived how he should alter the whole frame of it, make it quite another than it was before. The spirit of man being the candle of the Lord, Prov. xx. 27; not to give light to him but lighted by him, can only when it is out, be relighted, and when it burns dim, be renewed by the same hand. Or, suppose for the present, he could do this, it must be with much pains and labour, many exhortations and wise management of him upon several occasions. But to do this by a word, in a trice, to put a law into the heart in a moment; and give the hidden man of the heart possession of the will, that a man knows not himself how he came to be changed: this whole work bears the mark and stamp of God in the forehead of it. Men may propose arguments to another, and he may understand them if he hath a capacity: but no man can ever make another have a capacity who is naturally incapable; it is God alone can make the heart capable of understanding, he alone can put a new instinct into it, and make it of another bent: it is he that renews the spirit of the mind to enable it to understand what he proposes, and elevates the faculty to apprehend the reason of it.

The end of regeneration manifests it to be the work of God. It is to display his goodness. Since this was the end of God in the first creation, it is much more his end in the second. What creature can display God's goodness to him, or give him the glory of it, without first receiving it? Goodness must first be communicated to us before it can be displayed or reflected by us. The light that is reflected back upon the sun by any earthly body, beams first from the sun

itself. Both the subject and the end are put together:
" The beasts of the field shall honour me; the dragons
and the owls: because I give waters in the wilderness,
to give drink to my people, my chosen; this people
have I formed for myself, they shall show forth my
praise," Isa. xliii. 20, 21. The Gentiles shall have the
gospel, who are beasts of the field for wildness,
dragons for the poison of their nature, owls for their
blindness and darkness. The waters of the gospel
shall flow to them, to give drink to their souls. This
people have I formed for myself; even beasts, dragons,
owls. If formed for himself, they could not be formed
but by himself, who only understands what is fit for
his own praise. How can such incapable subjects be
formed for such high ends, without a supernatural
power? " The branch of my planting, the work of my
hands, that I may be glorified," Isa. lx. 21. Planted
by God, that God might be glorified by them. As
God only is the proper judge of what may glorify him;
so he is the sole author of what is fitted to glorify him.
Nothing lower than the goodness of God can instil into
us such a goodness, as to be made meet to praise,
serve, and love him; such a holiness as may fit us to
be partakers of the inheritance of the saints in light,
and enjoy him for ever. As infinite wisdom formed
us in Adam, and moulded us with his own hand to be
a model of his perfection; so are we no less his workmanship in Christ by a second creation to good works;
which as they are ordained by the will of God, so they
are wrought in us by the skill and power of God;
what is ordained positively by him and for him, is
wrought by him.

Now since the ends of this work are so high as to
fit us for his praise, his delight, and a fruition of him;
since it is to bring the interest of God into the soul,
set him up highest in the heart, who before was
trampled under our feet: enthrone him as king in the
soul, cause us to oppose all that opposes him, cherish

every thing that is agreeable to him, this must be his work or the work of none.

The weakness of the means manifests it to be the work of God. How could it be possible that such weak means that were used at the first plantation of the gospel, should have that transcendent success in the hearts of men, without a divine power? That a doctrine attended with the cross, resisted by devils with all their subtlety, by the flesh with all its lusts, the world with all its flatteries, the wise with all their craft, the mighty with all their power, should be imprinted upon the hearts of men; a doctrine preached by mean men, without any worldly help, without learning, eloquence, craft, or human prudence; without the force, favour, or friendship of men, should get place in men's hearts, without a divine inspiration, cannot well be imagined. If it be said there were miracles attending it, which wrought upon the minds of men; it is true; but what little force they had in our Saviour's time, the Scripture informs us, when they were ascribed to Beelzebub the prince of devils. Though miracles did attend it after the ascension of our Saviour, yet the apostle ascribes not so much to them as the means, as he does to the foolishness of preaching; it was that which was the power of God, 1 Cor. i. 18; it was that whereby God saved them that believe, 1 Cor. i. 21. But the greatest change that ever was wrought at one time, was at the first descent of the Spirit, by a plain discourse of Peter's, Acts ii; extolling a crucified God before those that had lately taken away his life, those that had seen him die, a doctrine which would find no footing in their reasons, filled with prejudice against him, and had expectations of a temporal kingdom by him: must not this change be ascribed to a higher hand, which removed their rooted prejudices and vain hopes, and brought so many as three thousand over at once? If there be diversities of operations, it is the same God that works all in all," 1 Cor. xii. 6. He conveys this "treasure in earthen vessels, that the power might appear to be of God, and not of men," 2 Cor. iv. 7. Such weak means as earthen vessels, cannot work such miraculous changes. Therefore perhaps it was that the preaching of Christ in his humiliation had so little success attending it, that nothing should be ascribed to the word itself, but to the power of God in it; to evidence that success depended on the good pleasure of God, who would not make his preaching in person so successful as that in his Spirit; which appears by Christ's thanksgiving to his Father for revealing these things to babes, and not to the wise; "even so, Father, for so it seemed good in thy sight," Luke x. 21. Have you never heard of changes wrought in the spirits of men against their worldly interest, when they have been made the scorn of their friends, and a reproach to their neighbours? Can the weakness of means write a law so deep in the heart, that neither sly allurements, nor blustering temptations can raze out? That a law of a day's standing in the heart, should be able to match the powers of hell, the cavils of the flesh, and discouragements from the world, when there are no unanswerable miracles now to seal the gospel, and second the proposals of it with amazement in the minds of men? The weakness of the means, and the greatness of the difficulties, speak it not only to be the finger but the arm of God, which causes the triumphs of the foolishness of preaching. When the proposal crosses the interest of the flesh, restrains the beloved pleasure, teaches a man the necessity of the contempt of the world, and that men should exchange their pride for humility, the pleasure of sin for a life of holiness; for a man not only to cease to love his vice, but extremely to hate it; to have divine flights, when before he could not have a divine thought; to put off earthly affections for heavenly; and all this by the foolishness of preaching;

it is an argument of divine power, rather than any inherent strength in the means themselves.

The differences in the changes of men, evidence this to be the work of God, and that it is from some power superior to the means which are used. As God puts a difference between men in regard of their understandings, revealing that to one man which he doth not to another; so he puts a difference between men in regard of their wills, working upon some that have known less, and not working upon some that have known more; some embracing it, and others rejecting it. We may see

The difference of this change in men under the same means. One is struck at a sermon, when multitudes return unshaken; why is not the case equal in all, if it were from the power of the word? How successful is Peter's discourse, closely accusing the Jews of the murdering of their Lord and Saviour, which is the occasion of pricking three thousand hearts? Yet Stephen using the same method, and close application of the same doctrine, Acts vii. 52, had not one convert upon record. While Peter's hearers were pricked in their hearts, these gnashed with their teeth. The corruption of the former was drawn out by the pricking of their souls; the malice of the latter exasperated by the cut of their hearts. What reason can be rendered of so different an event from one and the same means in several hands, but the over-ruling pleasure of God? The reasons were the same, set off with the same human power; the hearers were many of the same nation, brought up in the reading of the prophets, full of the expectations of a Messiah; they had both reasons and natural desires for happiness, as well as the other; yet the one are turned lambs, and the others worse lions than before; the bloody fury of the one is calmed, and the mad rage of the other is increased. The grace of God wrought powerfully in the one, and lighted not upon the other. Two are grinding at the same mill of ordinances, one is taken, and another left. Man breathes into the ears, and God into what heart he pleases.

The differences in the changes of men under less means. One is changed by weaker means; another remains in his unregeneracy under means in themselves more powerful and likely; some are wrought upon by whispers, when others are stiff under thunders: the Ninevites by one single sermon from a prophet are moved to repentance; the inhabitants of Capernaum, by many admonitions from a greater than all the prophets, seconded with miracles, are not persuaded; some remain refractory under great blasts, while others bend at lighter breathings. One man may be more acute than another, of a more apprehensive reason: yet this man remains obstinate, while another becomes pliable. Whence does this difference arise, but from the will of God drawing the one, and leaving the other to the conduct of his own will, since both will acknowledge what they are advised to, to be their interest, to be true in itself, necessary for their good, yet their affections and entertainment are not the same? Some of those Jews who had heard the doctrine of Christ, seen the purity of his life, and the power of his miracles, admired his wisdom, yet crucified his person; they expected a Messiah, yet contemned him when he came; when the poor thief, who perhaps had never seen one miracle nor heard one sermon of our Saviour, believes in him, acknowledges him to be the Son of God, whom he saw condemned to the same death with himself, and dies a regenerate man under great disadvantages. A figure, says one, of all the elect, who shall only be saved by grace, and a clear testimony of an outstretched arm of grace. Those that our blessed Saviour admonished only as a doctor and teacher, were unmoved, none stirred but those he wrought upon as a Creator.

Difference of the success of the same means in different places. How various was the success of the apostles in several parts of their circuits? Paul finds a great door of faith opened at Corinth, and in Macedonia, and his nets empty at Athens; multitudes flocking in at one place, and few at another. He is entertained at Corinth, stoned at Lystra, in danger of his life at Jerusalem; while the Galatians were so affected with the gospel, that they could have pulled out their eyes for him. The apostle was the same person in all places; the gospel was the same, and had a like power in itself; men had the same reasons, they were all fragments from the lump of Adam; the difference must be then from the influence of the divine Spirit, who rained down his grace in one place and not in another; on one heart, and not on another; who left darkness in Egypt, while he diffused light in Goshen.

Difference in the same person. What is the reason that a man believes at one time under the proposal of weak arguments, and not at another under stronger? Perhaps God hath stricken a man's conscience before, and he hath undergone that work, shaken off those convictions: he hath contended with his Maker, and mustered up the power of nature against the alarms of conscience; struggled like a wild bull in a net, and broke it, and blunted those darts which stuck in his soul; he hath afterwards been screwed up again, and the arrow shot so deep, that with all his pulling he could not draw it out: but what a divine hand holds it in, in spite of all the former triumphs of nature? How come convictions at last to be fixed upon men, which many a time before did but flutter about the soul, and were soon chased away? And God by such a method keeps up the honour of his grace in men after regeneration, and teaches them the constant acknowledgment of his power in the whole management. Do we not daily find, that the same reasonings and considerations which quicken us at one time in the ways of God, stir us not at another, no more than a child can a mill-stone? That we are quickened by the same word at one time, under which we were dull and stupid at another? And the same truth is deliciously swallowed by us, which seemed unsavoury at another, because God edgeth it with a secret virtue at one time more than another? Hereby God would mind us to own him as the author of all our grace, the second grace as well as the first. Upon all these considerations this can be no other than the work of God. Can a corrupt creature elevate himself from a state of being hated by God, to a state of being delighted in by him? Satan's work none can judge it to be; the destroyer of mankind would never be the restorer; the most malicious enemy to God would never contribute to the rearing a temple to God in the soul, who hath usurped God's worship in all parts of the world. Good angels could never do it, they wonder at it; the wisdom of God in thus creating all things in Jesus Christ, is made known to them by it. Eph. iii. 9, 10. They never ascribed it to themselves; if they did, they could never have been good, their goodness consisting in praising God, and giving him his due. Good men never did it; the first planters of the gospel, (whereby it is wrought,) always gave God the praise of it, and acknowledged both their own action, and the success, to be the effect of the grace of God, and upon every occasion admired it. "It was the hand of the Lord, and the grace of God." Acts xi. 21—23.

CHAPTER IV

The origin of Regeneration —It manifests God's mercy and goodness—his Sovereignty—his Truth—his Wisdom—his Holiness—his Power —Inferences from the whole.

WE now proceed to inquire from what principles in God regeneration flows, or what perfections of God are eminent in this work of regeneration.

Mercy and goodness are the principal perfections of God manifested in this work. Born not of the will of man, but of God; of the will of his mercy. Plato thought that heroes were born of the love of God; divine love brings forth an heroic Christian into the world; all outward mercies are streams of God's goodness; but those are but trifles if compared with this. There is as much of God in imparting the holiness of his nature, as in imputing the righteousness of his Son. We are justified by Christ, quickened by grace, saved by grace; grace is the womb of every spiritual blessing. To be delivered from places and company wherein we have occasions and temptations to sin, is an act which God owns as the fruit of his mercy: " I brought thee out of the land of Ur of the Chaldees," Gen. xv. 7, an idolatrous place; it is a greater fruit of his goodness to be delivered from a nature which is the seed-plot of sin. He heals our back-slidden nature, because he loves us freely. It is therefore called grace, which is not only goodness and mercy, but goodness with a more beautiful varnish and ornamental dress.

Therefore, in this take notice of the peculiarity of mercy. Such a goodness that not one fallen angel ever had, or ever shall have a mite of: neither did mercy excite one good thought in God of new polishing any of those rebellious creatures; mercy cast no eye upon them, but justice left them to their malicious obstinacy.

That singular love which chose Christ for the head, chose some men in him to be his members: "chosen us in him." Eph. i. 4. And the anointing which is upon the head, is poured out by such a peculiarity of love upon the members, not only by an act of his power as God, but by an act of appropriated goodness, "thy God," Heb. i. 9. God anoints his fellows with that holy gracious unction, as their God, not only as God; for anointing him as the head, under that particular consideration, he anoints also his fellows, his members, under the same consideration because he is as well their God, the God of the members, as well as the God of the head, for they are his fellows in that unction: the difference lies in the greater portion of grace given to the human nature of Christ. And the apostle Peter, 1 Pet. i. 3, intimates in his thanksgiving to God, that God begat us as the Father of our Lord Jesus Christ; blessed be the God and Father of our Lord Jesus Christ; the paternal affection he bears to Christ, being the ground of the regeneration of his people. Indeed it is a peculiar, fatherly affection. In his mercy to the world he acts as a rector, or governor; in that relation he proposes laws, makes offers of peace, urges them in his word, strives with men by his Spirit, enduing them with reason, and deals with them as rational creatures; he uses afflictions and mercies, which might soften their hearts, did they not wilfully indulge themselves in their hardness. This is his rectoral mercy, or his mercy as a governor, and as much as his relation of a governor can oblige him to. If men will not change their lives, is God bound as a governor to force them to it, or not rather to punish them for it? But in regeneration there is a choicer affection, whereby besides the relation of a governor, he puts on that of a Father, and makes an inward and thorough change in some which he hath chosen into the relation of children: as a father, who cannot persuade his son lying under a mortal distemper, to take that physic which is necessary for saving his life, will compel him to it, open his mouth, and pour it in; but as he is a governor of his servant, he will provide it for him, and propose it to him; to do thus is kindness to his servant, though he doth not manifest so peculiar an affection as he doth to his son. God governs men as he is the Author of nature; he renews men as he is the Author of grace: he is the lawgiver and governor; it doth not follow that where he is so, he should be the new Creator too; this is a peculiar indulgence.

As there is a peculiarity of mercy, so there is the largeness of his mercy and goodness in this work. It was his goodness to create us, but a full sea of goodness made us new creatures, "Who according to his abundant mercy hath begotten us again to a lively hope." 1 Pet. i. 3. His own mercy, without any other motive; much mercy, without any parsimony; not an act of ordinary goodness, but the deepest bowels of kindness, an everlasting spring of goodness, an exuberance of goodness. The choice love he bears to them in election, cannot be without some real act; it is a vain love that doth not operate: one great part of affection is to imitate the party beloved: but since that is unworthy of God to imitate a corrupt creature, he performs the other act of love, which is to assimilate us to himself, and bring us into a state of imitation of him, endowing us with principles of resemblance to him. It is abundant mercy to love them; it is much more goodness to render them worthy of his love, and inspire them with those qualities, as effects of his love of benevolence, which may be an occasion of his love of complacency.

All the grace and goodness God has are employed in it. In the creation you cannot say, all the goodness of God was displayed, as not all his power, nor all his wisdom: for as to his power, he might have made millions of worlds inconceivably more beautiful and more wisely contrived; for though there be no defect of wisdom and power, yet neither of those attributes was exerted to that height that it might have been: so for his goodness, he might have made millions more angels and men than he did create, with more illustrious natures; for a man may conceive something more than God has displayed in the creation, as to the extensiveness of his perfections at least. But in this God has displayed, as it may seem, the utmost of his grace: for no man or angel can conceive a higher grace than what God shows in this, of beginning in man a likeness to himself, and perfecting it hereafter to as high a pitch as a creature is capable of; therefore called "unsearchable riches of Christ," Eph. iii. 7. A further good cannot be imagined or found out than what is there displayed. Therefore, the apostle Peter speaks of God, as effectually calling us into his eternal glory by Christ, under the title of "the God of all grace," 1 Pet. v. 10, which calling includes all preparation for glory. All grace doth not less fit us for it, than call us to it; there is more grace in fitting us for it than barely in calling us to it; and the call itself hath more of grace in it, than the giving the possession of that inheritance you are called unto. It is not so high a favour in a prince, actually to set his royal bride in the throne with him, as to call her to, and prepare her for so high a dignity. To prepare a soul for it by regeneration, is an act of pure grace; to give it after a preparation for it, is an act of truth as well as grace; nothing obliged him to the first, his promise binds him to the latter.

The freeness of his mercy is manifested in it. It is as free as election, "who hath blessed us with all spiritual blessings (of which regeneration is none of the meanest) according as he hath chosen us in him." Eph. i. 3, 4. It is as free in the stream as it is in the fountain. Jesus Christ is as freely formed in us, as we were freely chosen in him. It is his own mercy not moved by any other; as we do many things by the will of others when our own are not free, in which are mixed acts. It is in regard of this freeness called

grace. Supposing God would create man, and for
such an end as to enjoy blessedness, he could not
create him otherwise than with an universal rectitude;
because had God created him with a temper contrary
to his law, he had been the author of his sin. But
there was no necessity upon God to bestow new
creating grace, after he had stripped himself of the
righteousness of his first creation. And also supposing God will restore man to that end from which he
fell, and refit him for that blessedness; he cannot fit
him otherwise than by restoring him to that righteousness, as a means of obtaining that blessedness. Yet
both these are free, because the original foundation
of both is free. God might choose whether he would
create man when he was nothing, and choose whether
he would restore man when he was fallen. Yet there
is more freedom in this latter than in the former, in
regard of the measures of the new created righteousness, and in regard of the immutability of it; in regard also of demerit. Adam's dust, before creation,
as it could merit nothing, so it had an advantage
above us, that it could not lie under demerit. But we
after the fall are in a state of damnation, children of
wrath: so that regeneration is not a creating us from
nothing, but recovering us from a state worse than
nothing. In regard that man was miserable, he was
capable of mercy; but, as he was a criminal, he was
an object of severity; that is free mercy to renew any
man by grace, when he might have damned him by
justice, to work him for glory, when he had wrought
himself for damnation: the apostle therefore excludes
all works whatsoever from any meritoriousness in
this case, "Not by works of righteousness, which we
have done, but according to his mercy he saved us
by the washing of regeneration, and renewing of the
Holy Ghost." Tit. iii. 5.

As mercy and goodness, so the sovereignty of God
is illustrious in this work. The covenant runs in a
royal style: I will put my Spirit into them; I will

give a heart of flesh, of my own free motion, and good pleasure, like the patents of princes. God reserves this in his own power, to give to whom he pleases. God renews when he pleases; " The wind blows where it listeth," John iii. 8. To some he affords means, to others not : he deals not with every nation as he dealt with Israel. In some he works by means ; to others he gives only the means without any inward work ; it is his pleasure that he works upon any one to will ; his good pleasure that he gives to any one to do. Some hear the word ; others the Spirit in the word : some feel the striking of the air upon their ear ; others the stamp of the Spirit upon their hearts. Who chose this rough stone to hew and polish, and let others lie in the quarry ? Who frames this for a statue, a representation of himself, and leaves another upon the pavement ? What does all this result from, but from his sovereign pleasure ?

No ultimate reason can be rendered for this distinction, but God's sovereignty. We can render an immediate reason of some actions of God : why the heavens are round, because it is the most capacious figure, and fittest for motion : why the sun is the centre of the world, as some think, because it may at a convenient distance, enlighten the stars above, and quicken the things below : why our hearts are in the midst of our bodies, because they may more commodiously afford heat to all the members : so also, why God loved Adam, because he saw his own image in him : why he sends judgments upon the world, because of sin : why he saves believers, and condemns unbelievers, because they receive the grace of Christ, those reject it. We have not recourse immediately to God's will for a reason ; the nature of the things themselves affords us one, obvious to us. But no reason can be rendered of other actions of God but his good pleasure : why he chose Abraham above other men, and delivered him from Ur of the Chaldees ; why Israel above other nations ; since all other men and nations descended from Adam and Noah, and they were in their natures equally corrupt with others; they were not in themselves better than others; nor other nations worse than they. So in Esau and Jacob, why the elder should serve the younger, since they both issued from the same parents, were equally depraved in their nature, had original sin equally conveyed to them by their parents; no reason can be rendered, but the will of God. So if it be asked, why men are condemned? Because they do not believe. Why do they not believe? Because they will not. God hath given them means and faculties. If you ask, why God did not give them grace to believe and turn their wills? No other answer can be given, but because he will not. It is his free will to choose some and not others. Election is put upon his pleasure, "predestinated according to the good pleasure of his will," Eph. i. 5, and the making known the mystery of his will is put upon his pleasure, "Having made known unto us the mystery of his will, according to his good pleasure:" Eph. i. 9, as God regards us absolutely, it is rather mercy than his good pleasure. Why hath he changed our wills? Because he loved us, and bare good will to us in his everlasting purpose, to which he was incited by his own mercy; but if we compare ourselves with others, and ask why he renews this man and not that? Then it is rather an act of the sovereign liberty of his will; for there cannot be the result of any reason from any thing else: he extends his compassions to whom he pleases. The apostle joins mercy and this sovereignty of his will together, "I will have mercy on whom I will have mercy, and I will have compassion on whom I will have compassion:" Rom. ix. 15, he is so absolute a sovereign that he will give no account of these matters, but his own good pleasure. Why he renews any man, is merely voluntary; why he saves renewed men, is just; why he justifies those that believe, is justice to Christ, and mercy to them; but why he bestows faith on any, is merely the good pleasure of his will. The Pharisees believed not, because they were not of Christ's sheep, John x. 26, that is, they were not given to Christ by the Father, as is intimated, verse 29. And the prosperity of those which are given to Christ is resolved wholly into the pleasure of God; " the pleasure of the Lord shall prosper in his hand," Isa. liii. 10. In all our searches into the cause of this, we must rest in his sovereign pleasure; our Saviour himself renders this only as a reason of his distinguishing mercy, wherein himself doth, and therefore we must acquiesce. Even so, O Father, for so it pleaseth thee. Matt. xi. 27.

He may well do so, because he is no debtor to any man in the way of grace. There is nothing due to man but death, that is his wages; the other is a gift, Rom. vi. 23. " To you it is given to know the mysteries of the kingdom of heaven, to them it is not given," Matt. xiii. 11. Who shall control him in the disposal of his own goods? Who shall say unto him, what dost thou? Grace is his own treasure; if he gives the riches of it to any, it is his pleasure: if he will not bestow a mite on any man, it is no wrong. If any man hath given to him, it shall be recompensed to him again, Rom. xi. 35. It is not unjust with God to deny every man grace; it is not then unjust to deny a great part of men this grace: Who hath enjoined his way? saith Job; or, who can say, thou hast wrought iniquity? Job xxvi. 23. He is not to be taught by man how to govern the world: neither can any man justly blame him, if they judge aright of his actions. Though every man is bound to endeavour the conversion of others; and every good man hath so much charity, that he would turn all to righteousness if he could; and though the love of God is infinitely greater than man's, it cannot be argued from thence that, therefore, God should renew every man. This charity in man is a debt he owes to his neighbour by communion of blood, upon which the law of

charity is founded, which obliges him to endeavour
the happiness and welfare of his neighbour: but God
is free from the engagements of any law, but the
liberty of his own will; he is under no government
but his own; he has no superior, none equal with him,
to enjoin him his way, and to prescribe him rules and
methods. If he gives any favour to man it is his
pleasure; if man improves it well, God is not indebt-
ed to him, and obliged to give him more; no more
than a father is bound to give his son a new stock,
because he has improved well the first he has intrusted him with; it depends only upon his pleasure.

God's proceedings in this case do wholly declare
it. In the first gift of his people to Christ he acted
like a God greater than all in a way of supereminent
sovereignty; "My father which gave them me, is
greater than all," John x. 29. He acts as a potter
with his clay; he softens one heart and leaves another to its natural hardness. He converts Paul, a
persecutor; but none of the other Pharisees who
spurred him on in that fury, and commissioned him
to it; he snatches some from the embraces of lust,
while he suffers others to run their race to hell.
David, by grace, is made a man after God's own
heart; and Saul left to be a man after his own will:
some he changes in the heat of their pursuit of sinful
pleasures; others he wounds to death by his judgments: the reason of the latter is deserved justice;
the reason of the other is undeserved pleasure. He
chooses the mean things of the world to be the highest in his favour, and passes over those that the
world esteems most excellent. Not many wise, not
many mighty, is his sovereign method. The amiable
endowments esteemed by the men of the world, have
no influence upon him. He acts in this way with
his own people: he gives sometimes to will, when he
doth not give presently to do: he distributes greater
measures of grace to one than to another: he sometimes excites them by his grace, sometimes lets them

lie as logs before him, that he may be owned by them to be a free agent. And further, it must needs be thus, because God does not work in regeneration as a natural agent, and put forth his strength to the utmost: as the sun shines, and the fire burns, unless a cloud interpose to hinder the one, or water quench the other; but as an arbitrary agent, who exerts his power according to his own will, and withholds it according to his pleasure. For there are two acts of his sovereign will, one whereby he commands men to do their duty, promises rewards, and threatens punishment: but the subject is to be disposed to do God's will of precept. Here comes in another act of his sovereignty, whereby he wills the disposing such and such hearts to the accepting of his grace, and does not will to give others that grace, but leaves them to themselves; this we see practised by God almost in every day's experience.

The truth of God is apparent in this work; truth to his own purpose. "Who hath called us with a holy calling, according to his own purpose and grace, which was given us in Jesus Christ before the world began," 1 Tim. i. 9. Sovereignty first singles this or that man out; and truth to that firm and immutable counsel, and that resolve in his own mind, steps in to excite his holiness, wisdom, and power, to make every such person conformed to the image of his Son. It was not from any truth respecting any condition annexed to any promise he had made, which he might find in the creature: for the apostle plainly excludes it, "not according to our work:" for what motion can our work in a state of nature cause in God, but that of anger and aversion arising from truth to this threatening, the condition whereof is fulfilled by us; but not one mite of good fruit that could as a condition challenge this great work at the hands of the truth of God by virtue of his promise. His truth to his threatening, would have raised up thoughts of destroying men; his truth to his promise carried on his design of effectually calling them. It is not an engagement of truth to his creature, but of truth to himself. So that if you ask why he hath called Peter, Paul, and others, since many better conditioned than they have rejected the gospel, the answer is, because he had so purposed in himself; and he is faithful and cannot deny his own counsel, for that were to deny himself, and that eternal idea in his own mind. "He is faithful and cannot deny himself," 2 Tim. ii. 13; in regard to his purpose, in regard of his absolute promise. Truth to his promise; his promise to his Son, for so Tit. i. 2, is principally to be understood, "In hope of eternal life, which God that cannot lie, promised before the world began:" there was a donation of some, made to Christ, and a donation of grace to Christ for them, deposited in his hands as a treasure to be dispensed to every one of them in their proper time.

The wisdom of God appears in this work. The secrets of wisdom shine forth in the great concerns of the soul in Christ, who is made wisdom principally to us in our sanctification, as well as righteousness and redemption. Wisdom in the imputation of righteousness, in the draught of sanctification, and in the perfection of it in a complete redemption, wisdom, like a thread, runs through every part of the web. The new birth is the great wisdom of the creature; by this he becomes wise, since the Scripture entitles all fools without it. The inspiration of this wisdom can own no other but divine wisdom for the author. It is his own wisdom; for "Who hath been his counsellor?" Rom. xi. 34. He works all things according to the counsel of his own will, freely, wisely; a work of his will, a work of his understanding, "Who works all things according to the counsel of his own will," Eph. i. 11, "That we should be to the praise of his glory," ver. 12, that the glory of the Father may shine out in us. If all things are thus wrought with the choicest counsel, much more the rarest work of God in the world. If all things are wrought with counsel, because he will have a praise from them much more that from whence he expects to gather the greatest crop of glory. The bringing us to trust in Christ, is for the praise of his glory; a glory redounds to him, because there is nothing of our own in it, but all his; a further glory redounds to him, because it is in the wisest manner. It is to the praise and glory of his goodness in the act of his will: to the praise of the glory of his wisdom in the act of his counsel. There was a mystery of wisdom in the first selection and singling out this or that person; a revelation of wisdom in the preparations to it, and formation of it. If there be much of his counsel in the minute passages of his providence, in the lowest creatures, which are the subjects of that providence, much more must there be in the framing the soul to be a living monument of his glory. It is not a new moulding the outward case of the body, but the inward jewel wrapped up from the view of men: the spirit of the mind, which being more excellent, requires more of skill for the new forming of it.

The nature of the new birth declares it to be an effect of his wisdom. It is a building, a divine temple, a spiritual tabernacle, for his own residence; "ye are God's building," 1 Cor. iii. 9. Strength will not build a house without art to contrive and proportion the materials; skill is the chief requisite of an architect. The highest pieces of art, come from the most excellent idea in the creature. The beautiful fabric of grace is modeled by the wisest idea in God: that which is glorious in the erection, supposes excellent skill in the contrivance. Every renewed man is a lively stone, polished and carved by the wise Creator for an everlasting statue; it is he that hath "wrought us up to the self same thing," 2 Cor. v. 5, polished us and curiously wrought us, who were rough stones, covered with the rubbish of sin. As a wise builder, he lays the foundation in sound habits, whereon to raise a superstructure of gracious actions. The counterpart in the heart is no less a fruit of his wisdom, than the law in the tables of stone; wisdom in the first framing of the law, wisdom also in the deep imprinting of it. That which enlightens the eyes, and makes wise to salvation, can be entitled to no other original cause than divine wisdom. The soul is a rational work of God. Surely then that which is the soul of the soul, the glory of the creature, the preparation for happiness, more pleasing to God than the brightest nature, than the natural frame of the highest soul, that which is the pleasure and delight, must be the fruit too of infinite wisdom. Bare effects of power are not the immediate objects of God's special delight.

The means of it declare it to be a fruit of his wisdom. Christ, the exemplar, has the treasures of wisdom; grace copied from it, is part of those treasures. The gospel, the instrument, is the "wisdom of God," as well as the "power of God," 1 Cor. ii. 7. Divine skill framed the model, reared the building; what did partake of wisdom in the contrivance, progress, all the parts and methods of it, partakes of the same in the inward operations of it upon the soul.

The manner of it speaks it to be so. In regard of the enemies he has to deal with, there must be prudence to countermine the deep and unsearchable plots of the powers of darkness. As there is the strength of sin within, the might of Satan without, as fit subjects for his power; so there are the stratagems of Satan, the subtleties and deceits of the flesh, as a fit occasion for his Almighty skill against hellish policy. In regard also of his workings upon the soul; he works upon those that are so contrary to his design, without imposing upon their faculties; he moves them according to their physical nature, though contrary to their moral nature: he makes us do willingly what we would not: he so tunes the strings, that they speak out willingly, what naturally they are most unfit for. The Spirit acts wisely in the revealing to us the knowledge of Christ. "The spirit of wisdom and revelation in the knowledge of him;" Eph. i. 17; which may note the manner of his acting in the revelation, which is the first work in the soul, as well as the effect it produces, though I suppose the effect is principally meant. Some question the wisdom of God in acting so upon the will, as not to leave it to its own indifference in this change. What reason is there to question his wisdom? Do not angels in heaven admire God's wisdom as well as his grace, who hath immutably fixed them to that which is good? Do they question the wisdom of God for so happy a confirmation of them against that indifference which destroyed some of their fellows by creation? But is there not an evident art in this work, to make the will willing, that had no affection to this change? To fit the key so to all the wards, that not one is disordered? To move us contrary to our corrupt reason, yet bring us to that pass to acknowledge we had reason to be so moved? To move our faculties one by another as wheels in a watch? To present spiritual things with such an evident light, as engages our understandings to believe that which they would not believe before, and our wills to embrace that which our affections gainsay? It must, therefore, be a fruit of divine skill, since it is a fruit of divine teaching. John vi. 45.

There is a greater wisdom in it, than in the creation of the world. The higher the work rises, the more skill appears. It is a divine art to make man live the life of plants in his growth; the life of beasts in his sense; the life of angels in his mind: more it is then to make him live the life of God in his grace. Man in his body, partakes of earth; in his soul, of heaven; in his grace, of the heaven of heavens, of the God of heaven; the grace in the new birth is nearer the likeness of God, than the figure of men in the first birth; God therefore more observes the numbers and measures in the second creation than he did in the first. Man was the most excellent piece in the lower creation; therefore more of art in the framing of him, than in the whole celestial and elementary world; the glorious bodies of sun, moon, and stars, had not such marks upon them; the nearer resemblance any thing hath to God, the more of wisdom, as well as power, is signified in the make of it.

The holiness of God is seen in this work. The day of God's power breaks not upon us in the change of our wills, without his appearance in the beauties of holiness. The Spirit is called a Spirit of holiness, not only as he is the efficient, but as he is the pattern, and like fire transforms into his own nature; for that which is born of the Spirit, is spirit. The law in the tables of stone was an image; the law in the heart is an extract of God's holiness. Our first creation in a mutable state, was according to his own image, Gen. i. 26. Our second creation is more exactly like him in a gracious immutability. The holiness of Christ's human nature was an effect of the holiness of God; the holiness we have then in resemblance to Christ, must be a fruit of the same perfection. If we are renewed according to his image, it must be according to his holiness. To be merciful and just, is to have a moral image; to be holy, is to have a divine; the apostle intimates this in his exhortation, we must be holy in serving him, because he was holy in calling us. "As he which hath called you is holy, so be ye holy," &c., 1 Pet. i. 15. In this respect, God calls himself, not only a holy one, but the holy one of Israel. "I am the Lord your holy one, the Creator of Israel, your king." Isa. xliii. 15. He is not only holy in himself, but displays his holiness in them, by an act of a new creation. By Creator, is not meant, his being the Creator of them, as he is of all, even of wicked men, and devils; but implies a peculiar relation to them, as distinguished from others. He is the Creator of devils, holy in his actions towards devils, but not their holy one by any inward renovation, or consecrating them to himself, as he is the holy one of Israel. As he is a God in covenant, he is our God, therefore our God, as he is a holy God, as well as he is a powerful God, communicating the one as well as the other in a covenant-way: therefore the prophet Habakkuk joins them both together: "O Lord, my God, my holy one," Hab. i. 12. His holiness is no less necessary for the felicity of his people, than his mercy and power. What happiness could his mercy move, his wisdom contrive, or his power effect, without the communication of his holiness? Mercy could not of itself fit a man for it, nor power give a man possession of it, without holiness, attiring him with all those graces which prepare him for it. God, as sovereign, chose us; as merciful, pardons us; as wise, guides us; as powerful, protects us; as true, makes good his promises to us; but as holy, cleanseth us from our old habits, makes us vessels of honour, filled with the savoury and delicious fruits of his Spirit, his pleasant things. The implantation of grace in the heart, is no less an effect of his holiness, than the preservation of it is; which our Saviour intimates. when, in his petition for it, he gives his Father rather the title of holy, than of any other attribute. "Holy Father, keep through thy own name." John xvii. 11.

The power of God appears in this work. "Since the world begun was it not heard that any man opened the eyes of one that was born blind," John ix. 32, neither was it ever heard that any man could open the understanding of one that was born dark. Every thing that pertains to life and godliness, of which regeneration is not the meanest, is the work of Divine power, "According as his divine power hath given to us all things that pertain to life and godliness, through the knowledge of him who hath called us to glory and virtue," 2 Pet. i. 3; glory and virtue, that is a glorious virtue: and the apostle adds, that this calling was an effect of a glorious power. When God hardens a man, he only withdraws his grace. But a

divine virtue is necessary for the cure of our hereditary disease. There is no great force required to cut a
dead man; but to raise him, requires an extraordinary power. We may as well deny this work to be
a new creation, a resurrection, as deny it to be an act
of divine power. There is a word that calls; there is
also a power to work, "Our gospel came not unto
you in word only, but also in power, and in the
Holy Ghost," 1 Thess. i. 5; that is, the power of the
Holy Ghost. There was not only grace in the word,
to invite, but the power of the Holy Ghost in it, to
overcome the heart. There is not only an act of an
almighty Spirit, but an act of his almighty power.
The hand of the Lord created the world, " the heavens
are the work of his fingers," Psa. viii. 3, but grace
is the work of his arms, Isa. liii. 1. It may be said of
the first grace in the new birth, as it was of Reuben,
"Thou art my might, the beginning of my strength,
and the excellency of power," Gen. xlix 3. Though
ministerial gifts were as excellent as Paul's, whose
preaching was with demonstration and power, and
who knew the readiest way to men's hearts, if a man
ever did; yet the "excellency of the power was of
God:" and when he brandished his spiritual weapons,
they were only "mighty through God," 2 Cor. x. 4.
Though the declaration was his, yet the working was
Christ's, Rom. xv. 18, none of his people are willing,
till the day of his power, Psa. cx. 3.

It is as great, yea, greater power, than that put
forth in creation. It is as great, it is the introduction
of another form, not in a way of any action or fashion,
but in such a manner as was in the creation; that is,
by the mighty operation of God; otherwise it could
not be called a new creature, though it might be
called a new thing. You call not that which is made
by the art or power of man, as a watch, a clock, a
house, a new creature; for there is nothing of creation in them, but art and industry, setting the pieces
of matter, created to their hands, together in such a

form or figure. But this is called a new creature, not so much in regard of the newness of the thing, but in regard of the power that wrought it, and the manner of working it, being the same with that of creation. And being termed so, it implies the exerting an efficacious power; for creation is not wrought by a cessation of action but the employment of an active virtue. God does not hold his hand in his bosom, but spreads it open, and applies it to an efficacious action; since it is a new creation, it implies a creator, and a creative power; creation cannot be without both. It is a greater power expended in regeneration, than in creation; more power morally in this, than physically in that: one word created the world; many words are combined for the new preparation of the heart. It is easier to make a thousand glasses, than to set together one that is dashed to pieces. It is easier with God to make a world, (as to our conception, for all things are alike easy to God,) and create thousands of men with his image, as bright as Adam's, than to bring that into form which is so miserably defaced.

First in regard of the subject. Sin hath turned man into a beast; and Omnipotence can alone turn a bestial man into angelical and divine. There is a less distance between the least dust and the glorious God, than there is between the Holy God and an impure sinner; sin and grace are more contrary to one another, than something and nothing. A straw may with less power be made a star than a corrupted sinner be made a saint. In creation God was only to put in nature, here he is to put off one that is strong, and to bring in another altogether strange and new; it is hard to bring a man from off his old stock, and as hard to make him nakedly to trust Christ: it is more difficult to make a man leave his sin, than to change his opinion: men are more in love with habitual wickedness, than with any opinion whatsoever. In regard of the indisposedness of the soul. There is some foundation for a natural religion, there

being general notions of God and his attributes, which
would administer some conclusions that he was to be
feared and reverenced; and according to these notions many checks of conscience, which would induce
men to some moral behaviour towards God: but in
the setting our hearts right to God, and creating them
in a Mediator, there was not the least dust in nature
to build upon. In the creating of Adam's body, there
was some pre-existent matter; the dust of the ground,
whereof his body was by a divine power made and
organized; but we meet with no pre-existent matter
for the formation of the soul, which made him a rational creature; that indeed was the breath of God,
not engendered by any concurring cause in nature:
there is no pre-existent matter in the creature, of
which this image is formed, though there be a pre-
existent subject to receive the impression of it; it is
not the rearing any thing upon the foundation of nature; but introducing a nature wholly new, which
speaks almighty power. In regard of the contradiction in the subject. The stream of man's natural reason, the principles of self, whereby he is guided, run
counter to it; there is a pride of reason which will
not stoop to the gospel, which in man's wisdom is
counted foolishness. Man is an untamed heifer, a
wild ass that snuffs up the wind, full of hatred to the
ways of God, guided by gigantic lusts, which make
as great a resistance as a mountain of brass; stoutness of heart, strong prejudices against the law of God;
fierceness of affection, drinking iniquity like water;
universal madness, resisting the Spirit; wild imaginations; frowardness in the will, forwardness to evil,
perversity against good: can any thing less than an
almighty power make an universal cure? It is more
easy to make men stoop to some victorious prince,
and become his vassals, than to bring men to a submission to God and his laws, which they entertain
with contempt and scorn. Nothing obeyed God's
word in the creation; though it contributed not to his

design, yet it could not oppose him ; it could not swell against him, because it was nothing. But every sinner is rebellious, disputes God's commands, fortifies himself against his entrance, gives not up himself without a contest. This pride is hereditary, it bore sway in the heart ever since Adam's fall, and hath prescription of as long a standing as the world, to plead for possession. What, but infinite power, can fling down this pride at the foot of the cross, make the heart strike its swelling sail to Christ, and become nothing in itself, that Christ may be all life in him, and all righteousness to him? It is only possible to God to make a camel with this hunch on its back, pass through a needle's eye: no less than divine power can bring down these armies of opposite imaginations, which have both multitude and strength, (and no man knows either their number or strength,) and the whole frame of contradiction against the grace of Christ. Our Saviour intimates this creative power in that thanksgiving to his Father. " I thank thee, O Father, Lord of heaven and earth," &c., Matt. xi. 25. Christ, in all his addresses to his Father, used attributes and titles suitable to the business he insisted on. The revelation of divine knowledge to babes, the moulding their hearts to receive it, was an act of God as he is the Lord of heaven, and earth, putting forth an infinite power in the forming of it. If God were the author of grace in the hearts of those babes, persons better disposed, and nearer the kingdom of heaven, as he was Lord of heaven and earth ; then there must be some greater power than that of the creation of the world, put forth to conquer the wise and prudent, whose wisdom and prudence stand armed in the breaches of nature to beat off the assaults of the gospel.

In regard to the opposition of the present possessors. The chasing out an armed devil that hath kept the palace in peace so long, must be by a power superior to his own, Luke xi. 21, 22. This great

Goliath has his armour about him, has had long possession and dearest affections: the impulses of natural concupiscence take his part: he has his alluring baits, his pleasing proposals: the world and the flesh are linked with him in a league, to hinder the restoration of the soul to Christ, and the restoration of God's image to the soul. A threefold cord is not easily broken. It must be a power superior to those three great powers in conjunction, that must bind the strong man: and casting him out, and spoiling his goods, are acts of power, Matt. xii. 29. Satan is too strong to be easily cast out, and the flesh loves him too dearly to be easily divorced from him; he is never likely to lay down his arms by persuasions; though all the angels in heaven should intreat him, he would not give up one foot of his empire. Nay, though what God proposes has a greater weight of goodness, pleasure and profit in itself, than what those three great impostors can offer, yet since reason is weak and mightily corrupted under the conduct of sense, which has an alliance with Satan's proposals, and first sucks them in, it is not likely to meet with any entertainment, as being against the interest of the flesh; and the will being backed with two such powerful seconds as Satan and the world, to assist in its refusals. Indeed, if he that is in the regenerate, were not greater and more powerful than he that is in the world, they would not be able to resist his allurements and subtleties, 1 John iv. 4. The triumphs of Christ at his ascension declare his power in his acquisition; with a strong hand he broke the chain of sinners, and led captivity captive before he gave gifts to men, Psa. xlviii. 18. He does the like in giving grace to the heart: he rides upon his white horse in the power of Almighty grace, when he conquers the enmity in the soul, as well as when he overcomes the enemies of his church, Rev. vi. 2.

It is a power as great as that which wrought in the resurrection of Christ. It is remarkable how loftily the apostle sets it out, " And what is the exceeding greatness of his power to us-ward who believe according to the working of his mighty power: which he wrought in Christ, when he raised him from the dead, and set him at his own right hand in heavenly places," Eph. i. 19, 20. " Exceeding greatness of his power," with an hyperbole, according to the working or efficacy of his mighty power, noting the infusion of faith in the soul by a powerful impression. "According to the working of the might of strength;" one word was not enough to signify the great power working: it is strength with a greater edge upon it, as when a man would fetch a mighty blow, he stirs up all his strength, sets his teeth on edge to summon all his spirits to assist his arm. The power of God in the creation of nature is never in the whole Scripture set forth so magnificently as his power in the creation of grace is in this place. The apostle picks not out any examples of God's power in his ordinary works, or that power in less miracles which exceeded the power of nature, to illustrate this power by. He doth not say, it is that power whereby we work miracles, or speak with tongues: no; neither is it that power whereby our Saviour wrought such miracles when he was in the world. It is a more illustrious power than the giving sight to the blind, speech to the dumb, hearing to the deaf, yea, or life to a putrefied carcass; this is an extraordinary power; but yet this gracious power is higher than all this; for it is as great as that which wrought the two greatest miracles that ever were acted in the creation; as great as the raising Jesus Christ, perfectly dead in the grave, and having the weight of the sin of the world upon him; and as great as that power, which after the raising of him, set him in his human nature at his right hand, above principalities and powers, above the whole angelic state: as much as to say, as great as all that which wrought the whole scene of the redemption, from the foundation-stone to the top-stone. It is such an unconquerable power, whereby God brings about all his decrees which terminated in Christ. Some say, this power is not exercised in the begetting faith, but in the faithful after faith is begun. It is very strange that a less power is necessary to beget, than to preserve a thing after it is brought into being. And the same power is requisite to raise the heart of the most moral man under heaven out of the grave of corrupted nature, as well as those that are furthest in their dispositions from God. Had not our Saviour the weight of the sins of men upon him, had he been dead but an hour or two, lain in the grave with a little loose earth, or light sand cast upon him, it would have required infinite power to have restored him to life. The apostle mentions this in other places, though not so highly as in this, " That like as Christ was raised up by the glory of the Father, even so we should walk in newness of life." Rom. vi. 4. It must be understood thus: even so we, being raised up from sin by the glory of the Father, should walk in newness of life. And it may be partly the meaning of the apostle Peter, "Who hath begotten us again to a lively hope by (or through) the resurrection of Jesus Christ from the dead," 1 Pet. i. 3, not only as the foundation of our hopes, but by a power conformable to that which raised Christ from the dead. I would only, by the way, note, that this infers a higher operation than merely an exhortation and suasion ; for would any one say of a philosopher that had taught him morality, that he had displayed in him the exceeding greatness of his power, only upon the account of advising and counselling him to reform his manners, and live more soberly and honestly in the world! Our Saviour esteemed this one thing greater than all the other miracles he wrought, and declared himself to be the Christ more by this than by any other. When John sent to know who he was, he returns no other account than the list of his miracles, " The blind see, the lame walk, the lepers are cleansed, the deaf hear, the dead are raised, to the poor the gospel is preached," Luke vii. 20. That which brings up the rear, as the greatest, is " the poor are evangelized ;" it is not to be taken actively of the preaching of the gospel, but passively, that they were wrought upon by the gospel, and become a renewed people, transformed into the mould of it, else it would bear no analogy to the other miracles; the deaf hear, and the dead are raised ; they had not exhortations to hear and live, but the effects were wrought in them; so those words import not only the preaching of the gospel to them, but the powerful operation of the gospel in them. This greatest miracle in the catalogue is the only miracle our Saviour has left in the world since the cessation of all the rest.

I have insisted the longer upon these perfections of God apparent in this work :

To stir up every renewed person to a thankful frame toward God; that he should engage his choicest attributes for the good of a poor creature. To what purpose did the apostle so long and so highly speak of the power of God in raising them from a spiritual death, but that they should acknowledge it, and admire God for it ? It cannot but raise high admiration and adoration of God, to consider how mercy moved for them, sovereignty called them out, wisdom modelled them, holiness cleansed them, and power framed them.

To stir up deep humility. It is a plain declaration of our miserable estate by nature, and the difficulty of emerging out of it; impossible for any creature to effect. Had not God been infinitely merciful, wise, holy, true, and omnipotent, and put forth his power to free men from a slavery to sin, not a man had been able to escape out of it ; and these two, admiration of God, and humiliation of self, are the two great acts of a Christian, which set all other graces to work. Mercy speaks us very miserable, wisdom declares us fools, holiness unclean, and power extremely weak.

How mightily will it give a ground to the exercise of faith ! He that is deeply sensible of this work of holiness and power in him, cannot but trust God upon his deed, as well as before he did upon his word. As you go to the promises without you, consider also the counterpart of the promise within you, and the efficacy of that power which wrought it; you have a ground of faith within you: the power extends to every one wherein this work is wrought: "What is the exceeding greatness of his power to usward who believe:" this the apostle speaks to all the believing Ephesians.

Therefore look much into yourselves by way of examination, to observe the actings of God's wisdom, holiness, and power, within you. The want of this makes many gracious persons live disconsolate. Paul was certainly diligent in his observation, since he speaks so feelingly and experimentally of it. It is the way to answer Satan's objections, silence unbelieving thoughts, when you can trace the steps and operations of them in you: it would make you strive for an increase of this work of regeneration, that you may feel in yourselves more evidences of the holiness and power of God.

Those that want it, may well despair of attaining it by themselves and their own strength. Divine wisdom and power are exerted in this work; and men may as well think themselves able to raise a dead man, yea, Christ from the grave, and set him at the right hand of God, as do this by their own strength: if we want an eye or a hand, all the creation cannot furnish us with either. How can any power but that which is infinite, give us an eye to look to Christ within the veil, and a hand to clasp him in heaven?

It directs men where to seek it, and to seek it earnestly. At the hands of God; since infinite wisdom, holiness and power, are necessary for the production of it. With earnestness, because it is so transcendent a work, has so many perfections of God shining in it, that creature-strength and wisdom are utterly unable to frame and raise it; and with hopes too, if they earnestly seek it, since God has hereby declared himself infinitely loving in the combination of so many attributes for effecting it. Plead therefore the glory of God in these his attributes; and if God give you a heart to seek it, it is a probable argument he will give you that grace, which he has given you a heart to desire.

CHAPTER V

In what way Regeneration is effected—It is a secret work—It is rational—It is a work wrought in the *understanding*, removing its indisposition, fixing the attention, stimulating the reasoning faculties, and thus producing conviction—It is a work wrought in the *will*—The will being depraved, it is wrought on by an immediate supernatural influence—not compulsive, but free, gentle, and yet insuperably victorious—Inferences.

This work is secret, and therefore difficult to be described. The effects are as obvious to a spiritual sense, as the methods of it are obscure to our understandings, secret as the origin of winds, sensible as the sound and bluster of them, John iii. 8. If a dead man were raised, he would not know the manner how his soul returned into the body, how it took its former place, and made up a new union; he would know that he lives and moves. A gracious soul knows that he was carnal, and now spiritual; blind, and that he now sees; he finds strength instead of weakness; inclinations to good, instead of opposition; sweetness in the ways of God, instead of bitterness. The methods of grace are obscure, as those of nature, " Who knows the way of the Spirit, or how the bones grow in the womb of her that is with child? even so thou knowest not the works of God who makes all." Eccles. xi. 5. The manner of the formation of Christ in the soul, is as undiscernible as the formation of a child, or the manner of Christ's conception in the womb of the virgin; both which are fearful and wonderful, as it is said of the first, "Who can declare his generation?" Isa. liii. 8; that is, the generation of Christ, either in his person, or in his people. We cannot give a satisfactory account of the natural motions of our souls, how one faculty commands another, how the soul governs the several parts of the body; what the nature of the action of our mind is in contemplation and reflection; how our wills move the spirits in the body whereby the members are influenced in their motion, and the functions of life performed: much more undiscernible are the supernatural methods of the Spirit of God. We know ourselves heirs to the corruption of the first Adam, by the inbeing of it; the light of the grace of the second Adam discovers itself in the soul; but the manner of the descent of either is not easily to be determined. The loadstone attracting iron is the best representation of this work; the soul, like that, moves sensibly, cleaves strongly to God; but wherein this virtue consists, how communicated both in that of nature, and this of spirit, dazzles the eye of reason.

Yet this is evident, that it is rational; that is, congruous to the essential nature of man. God does not deal with us as beasts, or as creatures destitute of sense, but as creatures of an intelligent order. Who is there that believes in Christ in such a manner, as heavy things fall to the earth. or light things fly up to the air, or as beasts run at the beck of their sensual appetite, without rule or reason? If the Spirit of God wrought so upon man, this were to lay our faculties asleep, not to influence them, but to act only upon them; this were to invert the natural order by creation, to raze out the foundations of virtue, and deny the creature the pleasure of his condition, who according to such a manner of operation could not understand his own state, no more than a brute can the harmony of music, or the pleasing variety of colours: but grace perfects our souls, possesses them with new principles, moves one faculty by another, like the motions of the wheels in a clock or watch; like the common course of providence, wherein he orders all affairs according to the dependence of them one upon another by creation, without making any inroad upon the natural rights of any creature; but preserving them entire, unless in some miraculous action. He diffuses a supernatural virtue into the soul, not to thwart it in that course of working he appointed it in the creation, but to move it agreeably to its nature as a rational being. As the sun conveys a celestial virtue upon the plants, drawing them forth by its influence according to their several natures; so the Holy Ghost introduces a supernatural principle into men, whereby they act as reasonable creatures in a higher strain. What methods our Saviour used in the first declaration of the gospel, he uses in the propagation of it in the hearts of men. The same reason that is used in writing the indenture, is used in writing the counterpart. He might by his omniscient wisdom have found the way to the most secret corner of every man's heart, and by his power have set up what standard he pleased in every part of the castle, without proposing the gospel in the way of miracles and arguments; but he transacts all that affair in such a manner, that men might be moved in a rational way to their own happiness. He required a rational belief, as he gave rational evidences. "If I do not the works of my Father, believe me not," John x. 37, that is, the works that none but one empowered by God could do. God that requires of us a reasonable service, would work upon us by a reasonable operation. God therefore works by way of a spiritual illumination of the understanding, in propounding the creature's happiness by arguments and reasons, and in a way of a spiritual impression upon the will, moving it sweetly to embrace that happiness, and the means to it which he proposes and indeed without this work preceding, the motion of the will could never be regular.

God does this by a double work: upon the understanding, and upon the will.

Upon the understanding. The opening the eyes precedes the conversion from darkness to light, in God's operation, as well as in the apostle's commission, Acts xxvi. 18. The first appearance of life when God raises the soul, is in the clearness and distinctness of its knowledge of God, Hos. vi. 2, 3. And the apostle in his exhortation to the Romans, tells them, the way for the transformation of their souls, was by the renewing of their minds; "Be ye transformed by the renewing of your minds," Rom. xii. 2. The light of the sun is seen breaking out at the dawning of the day, before the heat of the sun is felt. As the action of our sense is to sensible objects, so is that of our soul to spiritual; our eye first sees an object, before our hearts desire it, or our members move to it; so there is an apprehension of the goodness of the thing proposed, before there is any motion of our wills to it. So God begins his work in our minds, and terminates it in our wills. In regard of this, as a state of nature is set forth under the term of darkness, so a state of grace is often termed light, that being the first work in the new creation, as it was the first word of command in the old; "Let there be light," 2 Cor. iv. 6; Col. iii. 10; and is therefore called a renewing in knowledge. If you consider the Scripture, you will find most of the terms whereby this is set forth to us, have relation to the understanding. The Gospel itself is called knowledge, Luke i. 77; wisdom, 1 Cor. i. 30. What faculty in man is appointed for the apprehending of a science to gain wisdom but the understanding? That whereby we receive the gospel, is called the spirit of the mind, the eyes of the understanding and sight, which is put before believing. "Every one which sees the Son and believes on him," John vi. 40. The work of grace is called revelation, Gal. i. 16; illumination, Ephes. i. 18; translation from darkness to light; opening the heart. The action of our minds being enlightened, is called comprehending, Eph. iii. 18; and knowledge, 2 Pet. i. 2. All respect the understanding, as the original wheel which God primarily sets in order, from whence he influences secondarily all the other faculties which depend upon its guidance, God preserving hereby the order which he instituted in nature: therefore when the understanding savingly apprehends the deformity of sin, the will must hate it: when it apprehends the mercy of God, and the beauty of holiness, the will must love him; and the higher the degrees of this saving illumination are in the mind, the stronger and firmer are the habits and acts of grace in the will. This illuminative act of the Spirit is before the other of inclining the will: for the understanding is first exercised about the word as true, before the will is concerned in it as good. The understanding takes in the light of the gospel, which by the working of the Spirit is reflected upon the will, whereby it is changed into the image of Christ whose gospel it is. " Beholding as in a glass the glory of the Lord, we are changed into the same image," 2 Cor. iii. 18. The first act is of the mind, which is the eye of the soul; where the apostle intimates, that the whole progress as well as the first change, is wrought in this manner.

This is wrought,

By removing the indisposition and prejudices which naturally are in the mind. As a wise physician which orders his medicines for the removing of the principal humour. Chains of darkness must be broken, films upon the eye must be removed, which hinder the act of vision; for what the eye is to the body, that the understanding is to the soul. The darkness of ignorance is promised in the covenant to be scattered. " They shall all know me from the least to the greatest of them." Jer. xxxi. 34. This being a law in the inward parts, the eye must be cleared to read it, as well as the heart cleansed to obey it. The object being spiritual, requires a spiritual disposition in the faculty for the reception of it.   This is called in Scripture a giving eyes to see, and ears to hear, Deut. xxix. 4, and the revealing things not only by the word, but by the Spirit, 1 Cor. ii. 10, which in regard of rectifying the reasons and judgments of men, is called a spirit of judgment; "and shall have purged the blood of Jerusalem from the midst thereof, by the spirit of judgment, and the spirit of burning;" Isa. iv. 4; a spirit of judgment, as it is light in the understanding, removing the darkness; a spirit of burning, as it is heat in the heart, thawing the hardness.   It reduces the mind into a right order, and teaches it to judge between truth and falsehood, between good and evil; the want of which is the cause of sin, whence sins are called, Heb. ix. 7, errors, as arising from error in judgment.   Since the mind is filled with fogs, and incapable of perceiving the splendour of divine truths, God acts upon the mind by an inward virtue, causing the word proposed to be mixed with an act of faith, which he begets in the soul, whereby it apprehends the excellency of that state presented to it in the gospel.   As there is a manifestation of his name in the word, so there is an operation of his grace; an internal teaching by God, as well as an external by the gospel; the proposal of the word by man, the opening and fitting the heart by God.   "Every man that hath heard, and hath learned of the Father, cometh unto me."   John vi. 45.   Christ taught all by his ministry, the Father only some by his Spirit. Learning of God goes before coming to Christ: and those two acts are plainly distinguished; "hear, and not understand;" Isa. vi. 9, 10.   The lock of their minds was to be opened, as well as that of their ears; the prophet's voice could unlock the one, the Spirit alone had the key of the other.   Men may enlighten as moral causes, God only as the efficient cause, to root out the inward indisposition.   The Spirit also removes the prejudices against Christ as undesirable, against holiness as troublesome; takes down the strength of corrupt reasonings, pulls down those idols of the mind, and false notions of happiness; out-reasons men out of their inward thoughts of a happiness in sensual pleasures, pride of life, mammon of honour or wealth, which are the root of our spiritual disease, and first to be cured. In this there is a manifest difference between the working of Satan, and the operation of God; he sets his battery against the affections, because the entry is there easiest; God breaks in upon the understanding, which being the chief fort, will quickly be a means to reduce the less citadels. And when the work begins in removing the blindness, it is the way to a true conversion; when it begins only in the affections, it is a prognostic of a quick starting aside. In our outward exhortation, God acts suitably to our nature, since we are endued with understanding and will; but in acting upon us within, he remedies the vice of our nature, since our reason and will are corrupted.

It is wrought by bringing the mind and the object close together. Sight is produced in a blind man by drawing off the scales from his eyes, and the recourse of spirits to the eye necessary for sight; besides this, there must be outward light, and objects coloured by that light; and from the eye so disposed within, and the thing discovered without, ariseth the action of sight: so from the preparation of the understanding, and the application of the object, arises this action of spiritual vision. There is a double opening, one of the gospel, the other of the understanding; our Saviour did both, " he opened the Scriptures," Luke iv. 32, and opened their understandings, ver. 45, that there might be a mutual entrance, that the word might dwell in their hearts, and their hearts have admission into the word. The Spirit shows the great things of the gospel to the soul. " He shall receive of mine, and show it unto you;" John xvi. 14; not in general, but bring them near to them, to make them view, " and know the things that are freely given to them

of God," 1 Cor. ii. 12, the benefits of the death and
resurrection of Christ; he repeats them again and
again, that there may be an evidence in the mind
that they are the royal gifts of God. There is a knowledge before this work of the Spirit, but as of things
at a distance; many know the things proposed in the
gospel, but they know it not as a glorious gospel, nor
see the wonders in this law, till the Spirit brings that
and the faculty close together. As a man may discern a statue or picture at a distance, but till the eye
and the objects meet closer together, it cannot discern
the beautiful workmanship upon them, with any affection to them. Not that a man knew nothing, or knows
new reasons of those things which he knew before; but
there is a nearer, and therefore clearer representation
of them, which is a manifest demonstration, whereby
he knows them in another manner than he did before.
As a man may know the promises before, but they
were not brought so near to him as to taste them;
taste being an addition to knowledge, whereby a man
knows that sensibly, which before he only knew no-
tionally. It is one thing to know a mechanical instrument, and another to know it in the operation of it, when
it is applied to its proper use. It is like a man that
has his understanding more cleared by seeing mathematical demonstrations, and lines drawn, than by all
the rules of art in his head.

By fixing the mind upon the object so closely presented. The Spirit settles that light and the object so
in the mind, that it can no more blow it out than puff
out the sparklings of a diamond, or than an artist
endued with the habit of some art, can divest himself
of his skill. Many men have some convictions of
truth, but flashy and uncertain, and which slip from
their minds: but when the Spirit opens the heart, it
holds the object to the mind, and the mind to the object; starts one holy thought after another about the
truth it hath darted in, makes the mind think about it,
and take notice of every lineament of that truth that

we see, and those thoughts lie down, rise up, and walk with us. When Lydia's heart was opened, she attended to the things spoken by Paul, Acts xvi. 14; her whole heart cleaved to them. In this respect the Spirit is a remembrancer, making the soul ponder, and beat over again with all intenseness of mind, the goodness and truth of those things in the gospel which are brought unto it; that the heart is, as Paul was, bound in spirit to Jerusalem, Acts xx. 22. The thoughts of that journey so haunted him and followed him, as the shadow does the body, that no arguments of friends, nor fear of danger, could divert him; the soul is bound by them, one consideration overtaking another, and all at work beating upon the mind. Hence consideration is put before conversion, "because he considers, and turns away from all his transgressions," Ezek. xviii. 28. And it is called the ingrafted word, fastened to the soul as a graft to the stock; when the heart is opened by the Spirit, the word is inserted in and bound to it, and at last the heart becomes one with the word and grows up with it.

By bringing the soul to an actual reasoning and discourse upon the sight of the evidence. God convinces the judgment with reasons proper to evidence the truth and goodness of what he proposes, and that with pregnant and prevailing demonstrations, which give a competent satisfaction; therefore called the "demonstration of the Spirit and power," 1 Cor. ii. 4; that is, a spiritual and powerful demonstration. When the eye is opened, and the revelation made, and held close and fast to the soul with a divine demonstration, that this is the only means to elevate him to a high condition, and at last bring him to a blessed immortality; the understanding is moved to compare the force of those arguments, and consequently judge that true which before it counted false and foolishness: and comes by the help of this spiritual light to reason spiritually and spiritually to discern the proposition made to it. It compares its natural state with the happy state offered to it; its own ignorance with that light, its own misery with that mercy. God will not have man, who is so far above a beast, do any thing without reason; for this would be to do it brutishly, though the thing done were ever so good; when men act as men, they follow the judgment of the best reason they can; and shall man that was created a rational creature, be renewed without reason, when the very work is to advance him to the true state of a reasonable creature, and his reason is enlightened by the Spirit, that it may rightly judge of the demonstrative arguments it offers to him? Is there not as much reason for the guidance of the will in the highest concern, as for the conduct of it in affairs of a lower sphere? Man was first endued with reason, that he might rationally serve God; and his depraved reason is reformed, that he may rationally return to God. If, therefore, he act like a man in other things, he does not surely act like a brute in this; but the Spirit excites the reason he has enlightened, to judge of those excellent things he proposes and the strength of the arguments he backs them with, which are so clear and undeniable, that they cannot be refused by a mind divested of those indispositions which drew out before a contempt of them. The change in the will being an election and choice, cannot be made without convincing and satisfying reasons which induce it to that choice, and justify the election it has made; that can hardly be called faith, when a man believes that which he does not think upon the highest reason was his duty to believe. And indeed what man is there that cannot allege some reason why he is induced to this or that act? God moves men by presenting things to the understanding, under the notion of good, honest, profitable; and when the understanding is enlightened to judge of things in some measure under the same notion that God proposes them, a man's own reason cannot but upon a view of them assent unto them;

and that assent is followed with a change, according to the degrees of that illumination, if it be a saving one. Upon this account that our own reason is excited to judge of the proposal, our faith can no more be said to be a human faith, or the work to proceed from our own power, than it can be said to be sensitive, because it comes by hearing: for though faith depends upon hearing and reasoning, as upon natural powers; yet the light whereby the faculties are actuated, is wholly supernatural, and from the Spirit of God.

Hence follows a full conviction of the soul; both the knowledge of its own misery, and the amiableness of the gospel offer, whence issues a weariness under the one, and desires for the other. By this enlightening, the soul sees sin in its empire, God in his wrath, Satan in his tyranny, and the hardness of the stone within him; he sees the law accusing, sin triumphing, heaven shut, and hell open, God ready to judge him, and his soul every way deplorable. He sees also in the gospel how Christ has expiated sin, answered the demands of the law, stills the clamours of conscience, satisfied the justice of God by bearing his wrath; hereupon the soul closes with Christ, and is born again. Here are heaps of sin that cannot be numbered; on the other side are riches of mercy that cannot be reckoned; there is sin to damn, here is a Christ to save; heaven and hell, sin and Christ, damnation and salvation, are presented in their proper colours, and pressed upon the understanding, which beholds all by a clear light. And thus by the illuminative virtue of the Spirit, the soul is laid at God's feet in a sense of its misery, and then drawn into Christ's arms by a sense of his grace. This is wrought by a convictive persuasion, for so the word signifies, John xvi. 8, which causes both a sight of sin, and a sense of righteousness, and produces a full assent in the understanding.

The next faculty wrought upon, is the will. The

will is inclined as well as the understanding enlightened, whereby spiritual things are approved with a spiritual affection; the same hand that darts light into the mind, puts heat into the will. After the act of understanding hath preceded in a serious consideration, and thorough conviction, the act of the will by virtue of the same Spirit, follows in a delightful motion to the object proposed to it; it is conducted by light, and spirited by love; the understanding hands the object to the will as necessary to be embraced; and the arms of the will are opened to receive it, as the eyes of the mind are to behold it.

For the understanding of this, take these propositions.

There seems to me to be an immediate supernatural work upon the will, as well as upon the understanding; not that the understanding is only enlightened, and the will follows the dictate of that, without any further touch of the Spirit upon it; but the will as it is the will, and therefore cannot be forced, there is need of a moral cause which may determine it according to its nature, and draw it by the cords of a man. When a master instructs a youth in his trade, he does it by arguments, morally; when he holds his hand with the instrument in it, and directs the motion, he acts physically; so does the Spirit exhort us to spiritual motion, telling us inwardly which is the way, that we may walk in it, and takes our wills by the hand, as it were, and leads them in the way they are to go. A nurse's tongue and exhortation is not enough to make a child to go, because of the weakness of its limbs; nor the light in the understanding sufficient to move the will, wherein there is an habitual weakness and contradiction. How did God work up the wills of the Egyptians to lend their jewels to the Israelites, but by some immediate touch. Their reason might have furnished them with many more arguments against it, than it could for it: they knew the Israelites had been highly injured, and that very lately too; that they could not but have a deep sense of their oppression, and intentions of revenge, as far as their power extended. They knew that the Israelites prepared for flight, and might more than conjecture that they intended never to return or send their jewels to them; for what need had they of so many goods barely to sacrifice in the wilderness? How were their wills thus bended against so many arguments against this action, and without any strong reasons to move them to consent to such a desire of the Israelites? How must this be, but by the efficacious power of God, not forcing their wills, but taming their fierceness, softening them by a secret influence, and exciting them to grant the Israelites' request. The apostle says, God gives us to will. If there were not a particular act upon the will, it had better been said, God gives us to understand and know, and man to will and do. After the evidence set up in the understanding, there is a secret touch upon the will, opening and enlarging it to run the way that is proposed in an excellent and charming manner. As the power of God raises every part of Christ, so the same power raises every faculty of the soul; it was also a supernatural power, since mere exhortation would never have effected it.

The Scripture intimates this in the terms whereby it signifies this work to us; as creation, resurrection, regeneration, new birth, all which denote some supernatural operation distinct in each faculty in the new creation, as there was in the first; not only the law in the mind to direct, but the heart of flesh to comply, is God's act. The fleshy heart is wrought by him, as well as the knowledge of the mind lighted by him. In regeneration there is an eradication of corrupt habits, and an implantation of gracious ones. It is called a giving a heart, a circumcision of the heart to love God. Deut. xxx. 6. Love is an act of the will, though it supposes a knowledge of the amiable object in the understanding. If faith be principally in the will, as I think it is, as to consent? and the words leaning, resting, coming, rather denote an act of the will than an act of the understanding; there is then an operation of God upon the subject, viz. the will in the implanting of it.

The will is corrupted as well as the understanding. The works of the flesh issue from both; if the corruption were only in the understanding, then that being removed, the will would be regenerated. As in a watch, if the fault be only in one wheel, that being mended, the whole frame is rectified; but if there be a flaw in all, the mending of one, though the principal one, which moves the rest, will not set every wheel right, without a particular application of art to restore them to their due frame. Was not original righteousness subjectively in the will, as well as in the mind? Did not a stoutness in the will succeed in the place of that righteousness, as well as darkness in the place of light? Must there not then be a habit of mollifying grace bestowed upon the one, as well as a habit of enlightening truth set up in the other; an inclination to good in the will, and an aversion from evil, as well as the knowledge of both? The corrupt proneness in the will, is the cause that it is easily excited to evil by the persuasion of the devil and the world; and is there not need of an inward rectitude in the will to bias it to a free embracing and close adherence to the good proposed to it by God, that his grace may be efficacious in every part? This work is the quickening of a man under an universal spiritual death; the will was dead, as well as the mind dark, which must have life instead of its darkness, as the other has light instead of its deadness: and if they be two distinct faculties, then there are two distinct acts of the Spirit, though they depend one upon another. There is no less power requisite to make us spiritually willing, than to make us spiritually knowing; since the corrupt habits in our wills are rather stronger than the prejudices in our understandings: therefore there seems to be a distinct act in removing the resistance from the one, as well as expelling the darkness from the other. As the Spirit takes away the wisdom that was sensual, earthly, and devilish, so it divests the will of that disposition whereby it was enamoured of that devilish wisdom of the flesh, and makes it willing to cut off the right hand, to pluck out the right eye, to deny sin, which is the very self, and engage in an irreconcilable quarrel against all that engrossed its choicest affections.

If the understanding has such power, by virtue of its illumination, without an act also of the Spirit upon the will, and a particular application of the understanding to the will, and the will to the understanding, why did not Adam's will follow his understanding? His understanding was clear, without darkness; his affections first made the rebellion; sense was the leader and the will the follower. Eve's understanding was not silent under the temptation of Satan; her knowledge was evinced in that speech, "God hath said, Ye shall not eat of it, neither shall ye touch it, lest ye die," Gen. iii. 3: she cites the word, her understanding must needs concur with it, unless it were corrupted and darkened before the fall. Where then lay the resistance? In the affections, and the will which sided with them. Why may not the will possessed with those evil habits, resist the understanding imperfectly restored to its primitive light, as well as Adam's will did where there was no scale or film upon the eye of his soul? And likely his affections had kept their due order, if the will had preserved its due dependence upon reason, and its sovereignty over the sensitive part. Do we not find that our wills are oftener in contradiction to the true sentiments of our understanding, and in conjunction with the affections, than in a due subordination to the one, and command over the other? Is it not frequently seen, that men of much light, knowledge, and gifts of reason, answer not the end of that illumination, and are without a will to turn to God? Besides, since corruption came in

by the affections, when the understanding was clear;
how can regeneration of the will come in by the illumination of the understanding, without a particular
operation upon the will and affections? If it be said,
the will follows the dictate of the understanding, why
did it not so in Adam? If we were perfectly restored, as Adam was in innocence, without the
grace of God in our wills, as well as light in our
understanding, we were not likely to keep up in due
order.

If there were not a supernatural operation and habits in the will, what would become of infants, who
cannot in that state be renewed without such a kind
of working? They are not susceptible of moral exhortations; we cannot conceive any other way the
Spirit hath to work upon them, but by such an operation, putting habits into their wills, whereby they
are renewed and sanctified; they are capable of the
habit, though not of the act. We never find our
Saviour spending any exhortations upon infants, but
he took them in his arms and blessed them; and told
us, that of such is the kingdom of heaven; and if the
kingdom of heaven be of such, there is some operation
upon them different from this method of working only
upon their understanding.

If there were not some operations of the Spirit upon
our wills, regeneration and conversion would be more
our work than God's. If the Spirit terminates his
working only upon the understanding, and the will
be moved by the understanding alone, without any
conjunction of the Spirit in the work upon the will,
then the Spirit does not immediately concur in the
chief part of regeneration, but as it illuminates the
mind; for the chief part of renewing grace is in the
will. It was in a less affair than this, wherein David
blessed God for the people's willingness, offering so
freely; acknowledging it indeed the people's act, but
by God's overruling their wills, 1 Chronicles xxix.
13, 14.

God is all in all in glory. When Christ shall have delivered the kingdom to his Father, God then shall be all in all; 1 Cor. xv. 28, all in their understandings, all in their wills; he shall be the immediate cause of all things, and govern and dispose all things by himself, and for himself; binding the souls of all the glorified by everlasting ligatures to himself: all in all to the glorified, all light in their understanding, all love and delight in their will, objectively, efficiently. What efficacy he has in glory, shall we deny him in grace in every particular faculty?

Yet this work, though immediate, is not compulsive and by force. It is a contradiction for the will to be moved unwillingly: any force upon it destroys the nature of it; if it be forced, it ceases to be will. It is not forced, because it is according to reason, and the natural motion of the creature; the understanding proposing, and the will moved to an embracing; the understanding going before with light, the will following after with love. The liberty of the will consists in following the guidance of reason; to have a liberty to go against it, is the greatest misery of the creature: that is properly constraint, when we are compelled to work contrary to the natural way of working: there is no constraint by force, but there is a kind of a constraint by love, because the Spirit accompanies this operation with so much efficacy, that instead of that sadness we should have in a thing we were forced to, there is an unspeakable joy and content in the soul; it not being possible to taste so much of the love of God, to be delivered from so fearful a condemnation, to be brought to so glorious a hope, without being seized with much pleasure and delight. God changes the inclination of the will, but does not force it against its inclination: the will, being a rational faculty, cannot be wrought upon except rationally. Since the main work consists in faith and love, it is impossible there can be any force: no man can be forced to believe against his reason, or love against his will, or desire against his inclinations Belief is wrought by persuasion; no man can be persuaded by force. It cannot be conceived, that the will should will against the will. No man can be happy against his will, all happiness consisting in a suitableness of the object to the faculty: those things that in themselves are the greatest pleasures of the world, if they please not a man, cannot confer any happiness upon him. The Spirit never works thus; because "where the Spirit of the Lord is, there is liberty." 2 Cor. iii. 17, he destroys not the liberty, but induces it to will more nobly than before. Besides, the liberty of the will doth not stand in indifference to this or that thing, for then the will would lose its liberty every time it determined itself to any one thing, because after the determination it would be no longer indifferent to the other. But the liberty of the will consists in being carried out according to the dictate of the practical judgment, and not by a blind instinct. God doth not deal with us as stones, and logs, or slaves, whom the whip makes to do that which they hate in their hearts: but conducts us in ways agreeable to our nature: he calls, saying, "Seek ye my face;" and inclines the will to answer, "Thy face, Lord, will I seek," Psa. xxvii. 8. That God who knows how to make a will with a principle of freedom, knows how to work upon the will, without intrenching upon, or altering the essential privilege he bestowed upon it: he that formed us, as a potter does his vessel, knows very well the handles whereby he may take hold of us, without making any breach in our nature.

It is free and gentle. A constraint, not by force, but love, which is not an extrinsic force, but intrinsic and pleasant to the will; he bends the creature so, that at the very instant wherein the will is savingly wrought upon, it delightfully consents to its own happiness: he draws by the cords of a man, and by a secret touch upon the will, makes it willing to be

drawn, and moves it upon its own hinges. It is sweet
and alluring; the Spirit of grace is called, the " oil
of gladness ;" it is a delightful and ready motion which
it causes in the will; it is a sweet efficacy, and an
efficacious sweetness. At what time God savingly
works upon the will, to draw the soul from sin and
the world, to himself, it does with the greatest willingness, freedom, and delight, follow after God, turn to
him, close with him, and cleave to him, with all the
heart, and with purpose never to depart from him,
" Draw me, and we will run after thee ;" Cant. i. 4;
drawing signifies the efficacious power of grace ; running signifies the delightful motion of grace ; the will
is drawn, as if it would not come ; it comes as if it
were not his creature, nor doth prejudice his absolute
power. As God moves necessary causes, necessarily;
contingent causes, contingently; so he moves free
agents freely, without offering violence to their natures.
The Spirit glides into the heart by the sweet illapses
of grace, and victoriously assures the soul, " I will
allure her, and speak to her heart ;" Hos. ii. 14; not
by crossing, but changing the inclination, by the all
conquering and alluring charms of love ; as a man
doth that person whom he intends for his spouse ; for
to that he alludes ; because in the latter part of the
chapter, he speaks of the consummation of his marriage with the church, " In that day thou shalt call
me Ishi ;" verse 16; in what day ? In the day that
he should allure, and speak to her heart. God puts
on the deportment of a lover in changing the frame
of the will. The Spirit is as one that leads the way
into truth. " The Spirit shall guide you into all
truth," John xvi. 13. Not drags ; he opens the heart,
not by a forcible entry, but as a key that fits every
ward in the lock. The attraction of the will, is much
like that of iron by the loadstone, which had no
motion of itself, till the powerful emissions of the loadstone's virtue reached it, and then it seems to move
with a kind of voluntariness : there is no force used,

but a delicious virtue emitted, which doth, as it were, both persuade and enable it to join itself to its beloved attractor. There is a secret virtue communicated by God, which, as soon as it touches the soul, puts life and delightful motion into it, which before lay like a log. It embraces Christ as its portion, and passes a decree, that it will keep his words, "Thou art my portion, O Lord: I have said, that I will keep thy word." Psa. cxix. 57.

It is insuperably victorious. What the mouth of God speaks, what his will proposes, his hand fulfils, 1 Kings viii. 24. It is not a faint and languishing impression, but a reviving, sprightly, and victorious touch. As the demonstration of the Spirit is clear and undeniable; so the power of the Spirit is sweet and irresistible; both are joined, Cor. ii. 4. An inexpressible sweetness allures the soul, and an unconquerable power draws the soul; there are clear demonstrations, charming persuasions, and invincible efficacy combined together in the work. He leaves not the will in indifference. If God were the author of faith only by putting the will into an indifference, though it be determined by its own proper liberty, why may not he also be said to be the author of unbelief, if by the same liberty of this indifference it be determined to reject the gospel? For in the same manner God is author of one motion of the will as well as of the other, if he doth no more than leave the will in an equilibrium. This irresistibleness takes not away the liberty of the will. Our Saviour's obedience was free and voluntary, yet necessary and irresistible. He could not sin in regard of the hypostatical union, yet he had a greater aversion to sin than all the angels in heaven. Is not God freely and voluntarily good, yet necessarily so? He cannot be otherwise than good, he will not be otherwise than good. So the will is irresistibly drawn, and yet freely comes to its own happiness. The soul is brought over to God, and adheres to him, not by a necessity of compulsion, but of immutability: as the angels necessarily obey God, not by compulsion, but from an immutable love. A sinner is necessarily a servant to sin; a regenerate man necessarily a servant to God; both by a kind of necessity of nature. Our main business then is to see what new enlightenings there are in our minds by the Spirit in the gospel; what tastes and relishes we have of divine truths; how our wills are allured to a sincere and close compliance with the proposals of God in the gospel; what vigour is in them. This is God's method, to work first upon the understanding, then upon the will. That work which begins first in the affections, without light dawning and breaking in upon the mind, and growing up by consideration and inquiries into the gospel, is to be suspected, and is not likely to be durable.

This is the Scripture method, and every regenerate person may find it more or less in himself.

Inferences.—If God be the efficient cause of regeneration, then there is a necessity for the influence of God in all the progress of grace. It is yet imperfect; the same hand that planted it, must also water and dress it. There is a tough sinew left in man's will, which makes him halt, after he hath the new name of Israel put upon him; a weakness of faith, a coldness of love, a faintness of zeal. What God is the Creator of, is nursed by his providence; what he is the new Creator of, is fostered by a succession of grace: the Scripture, therefore, appropriates all to him; he is the God that calls us, the God that anoints us, the God that carries us, the God that establishes us, the God that keeps us, and the God that perfects us. He is the author of grace in its first issue, its fruitful sproutings, its delicious ripenings; it depends upon him in creation, preservation, augmentation, as well as natural things depend upon him in all their progressive motions, from one degree to another, as the author of nature. When nature was most unspotted, grace was necessary to preserve and fix it in that state. Adam needed the assistance of grace with the embellishments of nature. The same power that inspires us with life, inspires us with a perpetual continuation of it. If the tide that turns the stream of the river, desert it, and return to its own channel, the river will return to its natural current. Our hearts will decline, our life languish, unless fed by that supernatural efficacy which did first produce it. The plants cannot grow merely from their own internal form; nor trees bring forth their pleasant fruits without the influence of rain and sun drawing them out to make a show of themselves in flowers and fruits; and when they are brought forth, they stand in need of the same rain to fill them, the same sun to ripen them.

If God be the efficient cause in regeneration, then we see where we are to have recourse in all the exigencies of the new creature; to whom, but to the author of those beginnings of eternal life? God is all, in all parts of this glorious work; " The God of all grace, who hath called us into his eternal glory, make you perfect, strengthen, stablish, settle you," &c. 1 Pet. v. 10. There is need of preserving, strengthening, increasing, quickening, and perfecting grace.

These you need, and these must be sought, and will be had, from the same goodness and power by which you were new born.

God only can give such graces. There is a necessity for it: as God rears it, so he only can keep it from pining away. Plants will wither, if the rain do not descend; the flame will be extinguished, if fuel be not added. There is as much necessity for a constant influence to keep up this new nature, as there is of the sun to preserve the horizon from that darkness which would invade it upon the turning its face to other parts of the world. The perpetual duration of renewing grace, is not essential to grace; for then Adam and the angels would have stood by virtue of their grace, for nothing ever loses its essential property; but it is by additional grace, distinct from the first grace, wherein our regeneration consists; as the preservation of the creatures in their natural beings is by an act of God, distinct from his creative act. The first grace God gives now, is a bounty to his creature, but it is further an obligation upon himself, not as it is grace, or as it is his own work, for Adam's grace which failed, was wrought by his fingers, inspired by his breath; but as it is a new covenant grace, which alters the condition of it. God's finger wrote the law in the heart, and his breath can alone blow the dust off, that would fill the engraved letters.

FOURTH GENERAL TOPIC

THE

INSTRUMENT OF REGENERATION

The gospel is the Instrument of Regeneration — Difference between efficient and instrumental causes—The law and gospel compared in this work—The gospel is the only and necessary instrument, and yet nothing more than an instrument—The mode of its operation—General inferences.

" Of his own will begat he us, with the word of truth, that we should be a kind of first fruits of his creatures."—JAMES i. 18.

FROM this passage, it is very obvious, that the gospel is the instrument whereby God brings the soul forth in a new birth.

The Scripture distinguishes between the efficient and instrumental causes of regeneration. We are said to be born of God, and to be born of the Spirit, but we are no where said to be born of the word, or begotten of the word, but by or with the word. Sin entered into the heart of Eve by the word of the devil; grace enters into the heart by the word of God; that entered by a word of error, this by a word of truth ; " Ye are clean through the word I have spoken to you," John xv. 3, whereby our Saviour means the word outwardly preached by him, for it is the word spoken by him. Not that it had this efficacy of itself, but as an instrument of their sanctification, rendering them ready to every good work. The holiness therefore which it begets, is called the holiness of truth, Eph. iv. 24, opposed to the lusts of deceit, verse 22. Lusts grow up from error and deceit; and holiness of the new man grows up from truth.

For explication, take the following propositions:

The law is not the instrument. The law taken in general for the legal administration prescribed to the Jews, was instrumental in renewing, because there was a typical gospel in that judaical administration, " For to us was the gospel preached as well as unto them ;" Heb. iv. 2 ; they were evangelized, as the word signifies : the judaical administration was compounded of law and gospel; the moral law, as a covenant of works: the ceremonial law, representing the covenant of grace. The law of God, or gospel among them, is said to convert the soul. Psa. xix. 7. But the law, taken as a covenant of works, was not appointed for renewing the soul ; otherwise what need had there been of enacting another law for that work ? And those that say, the law is instrumental in conversion, or inflaming our affections to obedience, say, that all the benefits by it are to be ascribed to the covenant of grace in Christ. It is true, the law considered in itself is preparatory to cast men down, and show them their distance from God, and contrariety to his commands: but the law without the gospel never brought any man to Christ. Whatsoever it doth in this case, is not of itself, but by the mingling the gospel with it, which inspirits it to such an end. Though the law did not encourage sin, yet it gave no help against it, but left the soul under the dominion of it, which is evident by the apostle's inference, " Sin shall not have dominion over you ; for ye are not under the law, but under grace ;" Rom. vi. 14 ; hence the property of the law, which is meant by the letter, 2 Cor. iii. 6, is to kill, but the Spirit gives life ; that leaves under the severity of justice, after sin had entered ; but the spiritual administration wherein the Spirit works, is to quicken and renew the soul, and make it able to get above the guilt and power of sin. The apostle therefore wholly excludes the law : " Received ye the

Spirit by the works of the law, or by the hearing of
faith?" Gal. iii. 2. That is, the word of faith, as the
gospel is called, Rom. x. 8. By *spirit*, is meant saith
Calvin, the grace of regeneration, as by *faith* is meant
the doctrine of faith. I might have preached (as if
the apostle had said) the works of the law till my lungs
had been worn out, and the renewing Spirit would
never have entered into you by that fire, but it descended upon you in the sweet gospel-dew. The gospel
is therefore called the "ministration of the Spirit," and
the "ministration of righteousness," 2 Cor. iii. 8, 9.
It is the chariot or vehicle, wherein the Spirit rides,
the proclamation by which it is declared, the channel
through which it is conveyed. The law discovers the
righteousness of God, as well as the gospel; but that
demands a righteousness *from* the creature, the gospel
confers a righteousness *upon* the creature; the law
shows us God's righteousness in his nature, and grace.
The law is a hammer to break us, the gospel God's oil
to cure us; the law makes sin live and our souls die,
"When the commandment came, sin revived, and I
died;" Rom. vii. 9; the gospel makes sin die and our
souls live. The law awakens the lion, the gospel lets
out his blood. At the best the terrors of the law chain
up our furious affections, but the sweetness of gospel
mercy changes them. The law prepares the matter,
the gospel brings the new form. That was appointed
for the rule of our walk, not for the restoration of our
life. And it is the promises of mercy which are
the motives to return; rebels will not submit to their
prince, as long as they know they shall have no quar-
ter. Hue and cry make the thief fly away the faster.
By the great and precious promises we are made partakers of the divine nature, 2 Pet. i. 4. The promises
of the law being conditional, belong not to us without
fulfilling the condition, of which we are incapable of
ourselves. The law therefore since that fall, is destructive, the gospel restorative, and the promises of
it, the cords whereby God draws us.

The gospel is this instrument. It is an instrument to unlock the prison doors, and take them off the hinges; strike of the fetters, and draw out the soul to a glorious liberty. It is by the voice of the archangel, men shall rise in their bodies: it is by the voice of the Son of God in the word, that men rise in their souls, Nothing else ever wrought such miraculous changes; to make lions become lambs, Isa. xi. 6; Hos. iv. 13, beloved idols to be cast away with indignation; to make its entrance like fire, and consume old lusts in a short time; these have been undeniable realities, which have created both affections and astonishment in some enemies as well as friends. It has a more excellent instrumentality in it, than other providences of God, because it is a higher manifestation. Every creature conducts us to the knowledge of God, by giving us notice of his power, wisdom, and goodness, Rom. i. 20. The declaration of his works in the world, is instrumental to make men seek him, Acts xvii. 27. Every day's providence declares his patience; every shower of rain his merciful provision for mankind, Acts xiv. 17; every day's preservation of the world under a load of sin, manifests his mercy. The heavens have a tongue, and the rod hath a voice; the design of all is to lead men to repentance, Rom. ii. 4. If these, therefore, be some kind of instruments upon the hearts of considering men, the gospel being a discovery superior to all these, in manifesting not only a God of nature, but a God of grace, must be designed to a choicer and nobler work: the heavens and providences are instruments to instruct us, this to renew us.

It is not a natural instrument, to work by any natural efficacy; as food doth nourish, the sun shines, or the air and water cool, or as a sharp knife cuts, if it be applied to fit matter. If it were thus natural, it would not be of grace: though the shining of the sun, or the healing of diseases, are acts of the goodness and mercy of God, yet the Scripture calls them not by that higher title of acts of grace. If the operation were natural, the gospel would never be without its effect, wheresoever it were preached; as the sun, wheresoever it shines in any land, both enlightens and warms. Our Saviour then would have had more success, since the gospel could not have greater natural efficacy than from his lips; yet the number of his converts was probably not much above five hundred, for so many he appeared to after his resurrection, 1 Cor. xv. 6, when many thousands in that land heard his voice, and saw his miracles. Christ, who was always able to give himself success, would not, perhaps for this among many other reasons, to advance his spiritual above his corporeal presence; and to prevent any thoughts of any natural virtue in the word, without the power of the Spirit working by it. Every day teaches us, that though many see the glass of the gospel, yet few see the glory of God in that gospel. Were it natural, then, that all that hear it are not renewed, would be more miraculous than that any are; as it was more a miracle that the sun should stand still in Joshua's time, against its natural course of motion, than that it moves every day in the heavens. If it were a natural instrument, it must then have life in itself; but how can the voice of a man, or the words and syllables in a book, be capable of receiving spiritual life, which they must have before they can naturally convey it to others? Were it a natural instrument, it would have the same effect upon the soul at one time, as at another. But does not daily experience testify, that the word shines at some particular times upon the soul with a clearer ray than at other times, that such a soul has thought itself in another world (as it were,) and that too when it has been much clouded by the weakness of the instrument declaring it? Lastly, were it natural, the wisest men, men of the sharpest understandings, could not resist it; no man can hinder the sun's shining upon him, when he is under the beams of it; it would warm him whether he would or not; yet have not such been the most desperate opposers of it in all ages of the world, as well as in the times of the apostles? It is not then a natural, but a moral instrument, which will follow afterwards, when we come to consider how it works.

It is the only instrument appointed by God to this end in an ordinary way. God has made a combination between hearing and believing, Rom. x. 14—17, so that believing comes not without hearing. The waters of the sanctuary run only through the channels of the gospel; the mines of grace are found only in the climates of the word. Why does not air nourish? because God did not set that, but meat, apart for such an end: though God could, by his Almighty power, bless air to this end, yet in an ordinary way he has fixed his blessing on these natural causes of his own ordaining. God has appointed second causes for natural operations; if we would be warm God has appointed fire and sun to warm us; he could do it immediately, by spreading a lively heat in every member, as well as he gave at first a power to fire to burn; but he uses natural instruments in natural effects, and likewise spiritual instruments in spiritual productions. God may flow in an extraordinary way upon the soul by a divine breath, without any instrument: as he did immediately upon the prophets, or as he gave light to the world the first three days of the creation without a sun, but since only by the sun and stars; but God seems here to have fixed his power. "The gospel is the power of God to salvation." Rom. i. 16. Not that his power shall always attend it, but that he will exert his power, at least ordinarily, only by it; no other organ through which the wind of the Spirit shall blow, no other sword which the Spirit shall manage, but this, Eph. vi. 13. Though our Saviour prayed upon the cross for some of his greatest enemies who had their hands imbrued in his precious blood, though he was heard, yet his prayer was not answered but through Peter's ministry, to grace the first spiritual discovery of the gospel. Nothing else can have that

efficacy. Had every man in Israel made a brazen
serpent, and looked upon it when they had been stung,
they might have looked till they had groaned their
last, before they had met with any cure, because only
one was of God's appointing : to a cast of an eye upon
that, he had alone promised his healing virtue ; in that
only then he had lodged his power.

It is therefore a necessary instrument.

In regard of the reasonable creature there must be
some declaration. God doth not ordinarily work but
by means, and doth not produce any thing without
them which may be done with them. God doth not
maintain the creatures by a daily creation, but by
generation ; he maintains that faculty of generation
in them by the means of health and nourishment, and
that by the means of the fruits of the earth, and doth
all this according to the ordinance he fixed at the
creation. when he appointed every kind of creatures
their proper food, and bestowed his blessing upon
them, " increase and multiply." So according to the
method God hath set of men's actions, it is necessary
that this regeneration should be by some word as an
instrument : for God hath given understanding and
will to man : we cannot understand any thing, or will
any thing, but what is proposed to us by some external objects ; as our eye can see nothing but what is
without us : so it is necessary that God by the word
should set before us those things which our understandings may apprehend, and our wills embrace.
Now we believe things as we conceive them true, or
disbelieve them as we conceive them false : we love,
desire, delight in things, as we conceive them honest
or profitable ; we hate, we refuse, or grieve, as we
conceive them dishonest, or troublesome, or hurtful
to us : whatever we are changed by in our understandings, wills and affections, is represented to us
under some of these considerations. To make an
alteration in us according to our nature of understanding, will and affection, it is necessary there

should be some declaration of things under those considerations of true, good, delightful, &c. in the highest manner, to make a choice change in every faculty of the soul; and without this a man cannot be changed as a rational creature; he will otherwise have a change he knows not why, nor to what end, nor upon what consideration, which is an inconceivable change in a rational creature.

It is necessary the revelation of this gospel we have, should be made. There is a necessity of some revelation; for no man can see that which is not visible, or hear that which has no sound, or know that which is not declared. There is also a necessity of the revelation of this gospel; since faith is a great part of this work. How can any man believe that God is good in Christ, without knowing that he has so declared himself? Since the Spirit takes of Christ's and shows it to us; there must be a revelation of Christ, and the goodness of God in Christ, before we can believe. Though the manner of this revelation may be different, and the Spirit may renew in an extraordinary manner; yet this is the instrument whereby all spiritual begettings are wrought; the manner may be by visions, dreams, by reading or hearing, yet still it is the gospel which is revealed; the matter revealed is the same, though the formal revelation, or manner, may be different. Paul's regeneration was by a vision; for at that vision of the light, and that voice of Christ, I suppose him to be renewed, because of that full resignation of his will to Christ, Acts ix. 6; yet the matter of the revelation was the same, that Christ was the Messiah; for so Paul understands it, in giving him the title of Lord. Though God may communicate himself without the written word, to some that have it not, yet according to his appointment not without a revelation of what is in that word.

This necessity will further appear, if we consider that it always was so. Adam and Eve were the first after the fall, wherein God constituted his church whose regeneration and conversion were wrought by that promise of the seed of the woman, made to them in paradise, God surely putting an enmity in the heart of those to whom his first promise was made; upon which promise a sacrifice followed. What regeneration Adam had, was by this word of the gospel; had not Adam believed it, he would not have delivered it to Abel; and Abel had not sacrificed, unless he had been taught so by his father, or immediately by God; but most likely by his father, because God does not use extraordinary means, when ordinary will serve. And Abel was regenerated; for it is said, by faith he offered this sacrifice, Heb. xi. 4; and it was faith in Christ, faith in the promised seed; for all of them in that catalogue, Heb. xi. did behold Christ by faith, as well as Moses, of whom it is particularly expressed, verse 26; that he esteemed the reproach of Christ greater riches than the treasures of Egypt. Considering all this, it is evident, that the ancient restoration was by the revelation of Christ and the gospel, as the only necessary means. Abraham, it is likely, had some external word in his father Terah's family, by tradition from the patriarchs; and had the revelation of the promise made to him by God, Gen. xviii. 19. And it was wrought then in an ordinary way, by instruction; for that, Abraham is commended, and no doubt but Isaac and Jacob did the same; so that all along this change of the heart was wrought by declaration of the word of the gospel.

It is necessary by God's appointment, for all the degrees of the new birth, and all the appendages to it. When God shows his own glory for a further change, he represents the species of it in the glass of the gospel; "we, beholding as in a glass the glory of the Lord, are changed into the same image from glory to glorh," 2 Cor. iii. 18. It is the ministration of the Spirit in all the acts of the Spirit. If the Spirit quicken, it is by some gospel precept; if it comforts, it is by some gospel promise; if it startles, it is by some threatening in the word; whatsoever working there is in a Christian's heart, it is by some word or other dropping upon it. If any temptation which assaults us, be baffled, it is by the word, which is the sword of the Spirit. The life of a Christian is made up of increasing light, refreshing comforts, choicer inclinations of the heart towards God; by the same law whereby the soul is converted, the heart is rejoiced, and the eyes further enlightened. "The law of the Lord is perfect, converting the soul, making wise the simple, rejoicing the heart, enlightening the eyes," Psa. xix. 7, 8. The Spirit makes the word not only the fire to kindle the soul, but the bellows to blow; it is first life, then liveliness to the soul; it is through the word he begets us, and through the word he quickens us, "thy word hath quickened me," Psa. cxix. 50, 93. It is by the word God gathers a church in the world, by the same word he sanctifies it to greater degrees, Eph. v. 26. It is the seed whereby we are born, the dew whereby we are refreshed. As it is the seed of our birth, so it is the milk of our growth, 1 Pet. ii. 2. Faith comes by hearing, and salvation after faith by the foolishness of preaching, 1 Cor. i. 21. It helps us after we have believed through grace, Acts xviii. 27. Our fruitfulness depends upon our plantation by this river's side. The influence of other ordinances depends upon it. Sacraments that nourish and increase, are not efficacious, but by virtue of the word; they have their dependence on the word, as seals upon the covenant; the word is operative without sacraments, sacraments are not operative without the influence of the word, they are only assistants to it. This quickens and increases habitual grace, as well as it was the instrument first to usher it into the heart, "that he might sanctify and cleanse it with the washing of water by the word," Eph. v. 26. As God will have the mediation of his Son honoured in the whole progress and perfection of grace as the efficient cause, so he will have the word in every step to heaven honoured as the instrumentul cause; that as Jesus Christ is all in all, as the chief, so the word may be all in all as the means. As God created the world by the word of his power. and by the word of his providence bid the creatures increase and multiply, so by the word of the gospel he lays the foundation and rears the building of his spiritual house.

As it is not a natural instrument, but the only instrument appointed by God, and therefore, upon these, and upon other accounts, a necessary instrument; so it is an instrument, which makes mightly for God's glory. The meaner the appearance of the instrument, the more evident the power and skill of the workman. It would be miraculous for a man to raise up another from death, by a composition of medicines syringed down the throat, but a greater miracle to raise him by speaking a word.   In the new birth there is nothing sensible to man but the word, the other causes are secret, like the wind; you know not whence it comes, nor whither it goes. The instrument being weak in itself, none can claim any share with God in the glory of the work. But were there a natural strength in the means, much of the honour would be taken from God, and assumed by the creature. It is like the trumpet in the right hand of Gideon's soldiers, and a pitcher with a lamp in the left, upon the blowing of the trumpet and the breaking the pitcher, the enemies fled, and God would have the means but small, but three hundred of thirty-two thousand, that Israel might not vaunt, and say, mine own arm hath saved me, Judg. vii. 2.   It had not been so admirable for Sampson to have killed so many with a sword or spear, or if the walls of Jericho had fallen flat by the force of some battering engine; but it was wonderful to see them tumble at the blast of rams' horns. Is it not the same to see strong-holds, high thoughts, Goliath-like corruptions, and spiritual death itself fly before the

voice of the word? To see a man, like the Babel
builders, swelling, and rearing up his own confidences
against God, to have all the former language of his
soul confounded by a word; to think of other objects,
speak in another strain, descend from self to dust,
deny pleasure, embrace a crucified Christ: that carnal
reason should be silenced, legions of devils driven out,
a massive Dagon fall before an ark of wood, that hath
nothing in it but the rod of Aaron, and the pot of
manna; in such weak means is the power of God exalted, and no other cry can reasonably be heard, but
This is the Lord's doing, and it is marvellous in our
eyes. So it was more glorious for our Saviour to turn
many of the Jews to him after his death, than in his
life; to bring them to believe by a word, upon a person they had crucified as a malefactor, than if he had
brought them to believe, while he was attended with
a train of miracles: the power of his miracles might
seem in their eyes to be extinct with his death, since
he that delivered others, did not deliver himself from
the hands of his murderers: he now honours both his
own word, and their faith, in bringing them to believe by the preaching of men, who did not believe by
the word from his lips attended with the seals of so
many glorious miracles.

As it is an instrument, so it is but an instrument.
God begets by the word, the chief operation depends
upon the Spirit of God. No sword can cut without a
hand to manage it—no engine batter without a force
to drive it. The word is objective in itself, operative
by the power of the Spirit; instrumental in itself, efficacious by the Holy Ghost. The word of Christ is
first spirit, and then life, " The words that I speak,
unto you they are spirit, and they are life," John vi.
63. The word is the chariot of the Spirit; the Spirit
the guider of the word; there is a gospel comes in
word, and there is a gospel comes in power, 1 Thes.
i. 5. There is a publishing of the gospel, and there
is the "fulness of the blessing of the gospel," Rom.

xv. 29.   There was the truth of God spoken by Peter, and Paul, and God in that truth, working in the heart, " He that wrought effectually in Peter to the apostle-ship of the circumcision, the same was mighty in me towards the gentiles."   Gal. ii. 8.   The gospel in itself is like Christ's voice; the gospel with the Spirit is like Christ's power raising Lazarus; other men might have spoken the same words, but the power of rising must come from above.   It is then successful when an inward unction drops with the outward dew, when the veil is taken from the heart, and the curtain from the word, and both meet together, both word and heart; when Christ kisses with the kisses of his mouth, and the man embraces it with the affections of his heart.   The light in the air is the instrument by which we read, but the principle of that light is in the sun in the heavens.   The word is a rod, a breath, but effica-cious in smiting and slaying the old man, as it is the rod of Christ's mouth, the breath of his lips, Isa. xi. 3.   A rod like that of Moses, to charm us, but as it is the rod of his strength, Psal. cx. 2.   A weapon, but only mighty through God, 2 Cor. x. 4.   A seed, but brings not forth a plant, but by the influence of the sun.   The word hath this efficacy from the bleeding wounds and dying groans of Christ; it is by his making his soul an offering for sin, that he sees the travail of his soul in his new born creatures; by his blood are all the promises of grace confirmed; by his blood they are operative.   The word whereby we are begotten, was appointed by God, confirmed by Christ, and the Spirit which begets us, was purchased by the same blood.   To conclude, the word declares Christ, and the Spirit excites the heart to accept him.   The word shows his excellency, and the Spirit stirs up strong cries after him.   The word declares the promises, and the Spirit helps us to plead them.   The word admin-isters reasons against our reasonings, and the Spirit edgeth them.   The word shows the way, and the Spirit enables to walk in it.   The word is the seed of

the Spirit, and the Spirit the quickener of the word.
The word is the graft, and the Spirit the engrafter;
the word is the pool of water, and the Spirit stirs it
to make it healing.

How doth the word work?

Objectively; as it is a declaration of God's will.
As it doth propose to the understanding what is to be
known in order to salvation hereafter, and practice
here; as it declares the purpose of God to save only
by Jesus Christ the Mediator, and by him to deliver
us from sin, Satan, and whatsoever is contrary to
everlasting happiness; and thus is significative of
something to our minds and understandings. The
Spirit gives us an eye to see, and the word is the
light which discovers the object to the eye. The
Spirit gives us an organ, but something must be proposed for that organ to exercise itself about, otherwise there is no use of the understanding in any
rational operation, which certainly there is; for
though the object is supernatural, and the inward
work upon the mind supernatural, yet the proposal
of the object to the mind is made in a rational manner. The word doth objectively propose life and
death, in a way suitable to the nature of man, that
he may rationally choose life. " I have set before you
life and death, blessing and cursing, therefore choose
life." Deut. xxx. 19. Both the blessings of the gospel, and the curses of the law are presented in the
word, that the one may be chosen, the other avoided.
The word is proposed under various notions; as true,
and so it is the object of the speculative understanding; as good, so it is the object of the practical understanding and will; as profitable, so it is the object of
the appetite and affections. When it is received into
the speculative understanding, it is a preparation to
the new birth; when it is received into the practical
understanding and will, it is the new birth. It discovers the wonders in God's own heart, his Son, and
his promise; the Spirit demonstrates it, and gives

power to embrace it; it first presents the promise, and then answers the pleas the stubborn heart makes against it, yet by the same gospel; it fetches demonstrative arguments from that quiver to satisfy a cavilling understanding, and motives from thence to overcome a resisting will; it silences the fears, points to the way, excites the soul to an acceptance of Christ, all by this gospel; and so draws us, as a man draws a child, by presenting some alluring object to him: the Spirit immediately himself, touches the soul, but by the word, as an instrument proposing the object, and drawing out the soul into an actual believing.

The two chief parts of the work are,

The discovery of our misery by nature. The heart is laid open, our putrefied condition in our own blood evidenced, our deplorable state unfolded, and thereby the conscience awakened to sensible reflections; it dissects the heart, discovers the secret reserves, unravels the thoughts, pursues sin to its recesses, and pulls and brings it out, as Joshua the kings to execution. "And thus are the secrets of his heart made manifest, and so falling down on his face he will worship God, and report that God is in you of a truth." It opens sin to the very secrets, discovers the inward impurity, takes off its beautiful disguise, its silken covering, and shows the odiousness under it. It discovers the forlorn estate by nature, and the insufficiency of flesh and blood to inherit the kingdom of God. Let the word be whispered by the Spirit in the ears of a rebel sinner, and the curtains which obscured his sin from his eye, drawn open, that he may see what a nest of devils he has, what astonishment will it raise in him! how will he stand amazed at his own folly! how will he loathe that self, which before he so vehemently loved!

A second discovery is of the necessity and existence of another foundation. It discovers our misery by nature, and our remedy by Christ, the plague brought upon the world by the first Adam, the cure brought to the world by the second. It proclaims a peace concluded between God and the humbled sinner by his Son the great ambassador, confirmed by his blood, assured by his resurrection. It shows him the fountain of death in his sin, the fountain of life in Christ, the free streams and gracious communications of it. The promise discovers the gracious nature of God, his kindness to man, the openness of his arms to receive him; and thus brings the soul off from itself to the foot of God, and the bottom of the cross. When the world like fire, and the heart like tinder come close together, the heart catches the spark and burns. From the word reconciliation and peace step out, and meet the soul; it finds the kisses of Christ's mouth inspiring it with life, the box of the gospel promises broken open, the window of the gospel ark opened, and the dove flying out of it into the desert heart. The word proposes things as they are in reality, and the soul knows things as it ought to know, 1 Cor. viii. 2. It understands the unavoidable necessity, and the infallible excellency of the things proposed. It sees the rocks and shelves wherein the danger lies, and a compass whereby to steer, a road wherein to lie safe at anchor; whereupon he relents for his sin, is astonished at divine kindness, rejoices at the promise, as before he trembled at the threatening, and has far other thoughts of God than he had before: in which act, divine life is breathed into the soul.

The word seems to have an active force upon the will, though the manner of it be very hard to conceive. It is operative in the hand of God for sanctification the petition of our Saviour, "Sanctify them through thy truth: thy word is truth," John xvii. 17, seems to intimate more than a bare objective relation to this work; it both shows us our spots and cleanses them. It is a seed; seed though small, is active; no part of the plant retains a greater efficacy; all the glory and strength of the plant in its buds, blossoms, and fruit, are hidden in it: the word is this seed, which being settled in the heart, by the power of the Spirit, brings forth this new creature. It is a glass that not only represents the image of God, but by the Spirit changes us into it, 2 Cor. iii. 18. A sword that pierceth the heart, Heb. iv. 12, yea, sharper than a two edged sword, dividing asunder the soul and spirit; it is a fire to burn. The Spirit does so edge the word, that it cuts to the quick, discerns the very thoughts, insinuates into the depths of the heart, and rakes up the small sands from the bottom, as a fierce wind does from the bowels of the sea. It is God's ordnance to batter down strong holds; though it be not a natural instrument to work necessarily, yet it is likened to natural instruments, which are active under the efficiency of the agent which manages them; and this also, in the hand of the Spirit, works mighty effects. The sanctification of the Spirit, and belief of the truth, are joined together, one subordinate to another, 2 Thess. ii. 13. The Spirit efficiently infusing holy habits; the word objectively and actively: objectively as outwardly proposed; actively as inwardly engrafted: it at least excites the new infused gracious principle, and produces our actual conversion and believing. As the pronouncing excommunication, in the primitive times, filled the person with terror; and no question, but upon the same account, the authoritative pronouncing the pardon of sin by the apostles, though only declarative, might have a mighty operation upon the soul in filling it with joy: yet both, as managed by the Spirit, concurring with his own ordnance. So that the word is mighty in operation, as well as clear in representation; for an activity seems to be ascribed to it by the Scripture metaphors. The chief activity of it is seen in the likeness which it produces in the soul to itself. Seeds have an efficacious virtue to produce plants of the same kind with that whose seeds they are: so the word produces qualities in the heart like itself. The law in the heart, is the law in the word transcribed in the soul; a graft which changes a crabbed stock into a sweet tree, James i. 21; like a seal, it leaves a likeness and impression of itself; it works a likeness to God as he is revealed in the gospel : for we are changed into the same image ;—what image ? The same image which we behold in that glass, 2 Cor. iii. 18, not his essential image, but the image of his glory represented in the gospel for our imitation. The word is the glory of God in a glass, and imprints the image of the glory of God in the heart. It is a softening word, and produces a mollified heart; an enlightening word, and causes an enlightened soul; a divine word, and engenders a divine nature ; it is a spiritual word, and produces a spiritual frame ; as it is God's will, it subdues our will; it is a sanctifying truth, and so makes a sink of sin to become the habitation of Christ. To conclude, this is certain, the promise in the word breeds principles in the heart suitable to itself; it shows God a father, and raises up principles of love and reverence; it shows Christ a mediator, and raises up principles of faith and desire. Christ in the word conceives Christ in the heart ; Christ in the word, the beginning of grace, conceives Christ in the soul, the hope of glory.

Use of information.

How admirable then is the power of the gospel ! It is a quickening word, not a dead ; a powerful word, not a weak; a sharp-edged word, not a dull; a piercing word, not cutting only skin-deep, Heb. iv. 12. What welcome work doth it make, when a door of utterance and a door of entrance are both opened together ! It hath a mighty power to outwrestle the principalities of hell, and demolish the strong holds of sin in the heart. It is a word of which it may be said, as the Psalmist of the sun, " his circuit is to the ends of the earth, and there is nothing hid from the heat thereof." Psa. xix. 6. No part of the soul is hidden from a new birth by the warm beams of it, when directed by God to the soul. What a powerful breath is that which can make a dead man stand upon his feet, and walk !

If you should find your faces, by looking in a glass, transformed into angelic beauty, would you not imagine some strange and secret virtue in that glass? How powerful is this gospel word, which changes a beast into a man, a devil into an angel, a clod of earth into a·star of heaven!

It is above the power of all moral philosophy. The wisdom of the heathen never equalled the gospel in such miracles: the political government of the best states never made such alterations in the hearts of men. How excellent is that gospel, which has done that for the renewing of millions of souls, which all the wit and wisdom of the choicest philosophers could never effect upon one heart! All other lectures can do no more than allay the passions, not change them; bring them into an order fit for human society, not beget them for a divine fellowship; not draw them forth out of a principle of love to God, and fix them upon so high an end as the glory of God that is invisible. This is the glorious begetting by the gospel, which enables not only to moral actions, but inspires with divine principles and ends, and makes men highly delight in the ways they formerly abhorred. What are a few sprinklings of changes moral philosophy has wrought in the lives of men, to the innumerable ones the gospel has wrought, which were such undeniable realities, that they were never openly contradicted by any of the most violent persecutors of the Christian religion, and were always the most urged argument for the truth of the gospel in the ancient apologies for it? How long may we read and hear mere moral discourses, and arrive no higher than some reformation of life, with unchanged hearts; have sin beaten from the outworks, yet retain the great fort, the heart?

It is above the power of the law. The natural law sees not Christ; the Mosaic law dimly shows him afar off: the gospel brings him near, to be embraced by us, and us to be divinely changed by him. The natural law makes the model and frame of a man; the Mosaic adds some colours and preparations; and the gospel conveys spirit into them. The natural law begets us for the world; the Mosaic kills us for God; and the gospel raises up to life. The natural law makes us serve God by reason; the Mosaic by fear; and the gospel by love. It is by this, and not by the law, those three graces, which are the main evidences of life, are settled in the soul: it begets *faith*, whereby we are taken off from the stock of Adam, and inserted in Christ; *hope*, whereby we flourish, and *love*, whereby we fructify. By faith we have life; by hope, strength; by love, liveliness and activity: all these are the fruits of the gospel administration.

Its power appears in the subjects it has been instrumental in changing. Souls defiled by sin, have been made miraculously clean: it has changed the hands of rapine into instruments of charity: hearts full of filth, into vessels of purity; it has brought down proud reason to the obedience of faith, and made active lusts to die at the foot of the cross: it has struck off Satan's chains, and snatched away his captives into the liberty of God's service. It has changed the most stubborn hearts. The conversion of a great company of those Jewish priests that were most violent against it and the author of it, is ascribed to the power of the word, "And the word of God increased, and a great company of the priests were obedient to the faith." Acts vi. 7. How many were raised to life by Peter's sermon! More souls turned than words spoken upon record. It subdues the will, which cannot be conquered but by its own consent. Light can dart in upon the understanding whether a man will or no, and flash in his face, though he keep it in unrighteousness: conscience will awaken and rouse them, though men use all the arts they can to still it. The will cannot be forced to any submission against its own consent; the power of the gospel is in the conquest of the will and putting new inclinations into that.

The power of it is seen in the suddenness of its operation. In a moment, in the twinkling of an eye, like the change at the last resurrection. How have troops of unmastered lusts fled at the voice of the gospel trumpet, like a flock of frightened birds, and left their long possessed mansion! How have the affections, which have sheltered so many enemies against God, been on the sudden weary of their residence, and abhorred what they loved, and loved what the moment before they abhorred! How have welcomed temptations been upon this sudden change rejected, a despised Saviour dearly embraced, a furious soul tamed, a darling self crucified, and a soul open to every temptation strongly fortified against it! How frequent are the examples, in the first time of Christianity, of men that have been almost as bad as devils one day, one hour, and joyful martyrs the next; and as soon as ever they have been begotten by it, asserted the power of it in another new birth by flames!

And this has been done many times by one part, one particle of the word. One word of the gospel, a single sentence, has erected a heavenly trophy in a soul, which all the volumes of the choicest mere reason could never erect; one plain scripture has turned a face to heaven, that never looked that way before, and made a man fix his eye there against his carnal interest. One plain scripture has killed a man's sins, and quickened his heart with eternal life; one word of Christ, remembered by Peter, made him weep bitterly; and two or three scriptures pressed by the same Peter upon his hearers, pricked their hearts to the quick. How has hell flashed in the face of a sinner, out of a small cloud of a threatening, and heaven shot into the soul from one little diamond spark of a promise; a little seed of the word, like a grain of mustard seed, changed the soul from a dwarfish to a tall stature! This the experience of every age can testify.

And this power appears in the simplicity of it. Savanarola observes, that when he neglected the preaching of the scripture, and applied himself to discourses of philosophy, he gained little upon the hearts of the people; but when he came to illustrate and explain the scripture, the minds of people were wonderfully inflamed and excited to a serious frame. And that when he discoursed in a philosophical manner, there was inattention, not only of the more ignorant, but the more learned sort too. But when he preached scripture truths, he found the minds of men mightily delighted, stung with divine truth, brought to compunction, and a reformation of their lives; which shows, says he, the power of the word, acting more vigorously than all human reason in the world. And indeed, Scripture and Scripture reason is the wisdom of God; all other reason is the wisdom of man. God will depress man's wisdom, and advance his own. It works as it is "the word of God, which lives and abides for ever," 1 Pet. i. 23. To wrap a fine piece of silk about a sword, or guild a diamond, is to hinder the edge of the one, and the lustre of the other.

The gospel is then certainly of divine authority. Since in this God hath set a tabernacle for the sun of righteousness to move in; as the heavens are the tabernacle for the material sun, Psa. xix. That word that raises the dead, must needs be the word of no less than God. Our Saviour's discovery of men's thoughts argued his deity: the word's discovery of the inward workings of the heart, and the alteration it makes there, evidence a divine stamp upon it. God would never have made a lie so successful in the world, or blessed it in making those alterations in men, so comely in the eye of moral nature, so advantageous to human society as the principles it instils into the minds of men are. A lie would never have been blessed to be an instrument of so much virtue

and truth; it would not consist with the righteousness
of God's government, or his goodness and truth as
governor, to bring the hearts of men into so beautiful
an order by a deceitful gospel. What word ever
had such trophies? What engine ever battered so
many strong-holds? If the lame walk by the strength
of it, if the dead are raised by the power of it, if
lepers are cleansed by the virtue of it, if impure souls
are sanctified, dead souls enlivened, are we to question its divine authority? Should a word work such
wonderful effects for so many ages, that had no stamp
of divine authority upon it? Would all those witnesses be given by God to a mere imposture? Let
the victories it has gained, evidence the arm that
wields it: what sword was used at the first conquest
of the world through grace, but this of the Spirit.
How soon was the devil, with all his heap of idols,
fain to fly before it! How soon was the devil, with
all his pack of lusts, forced to leave his habitation in
the hearts of men! Is not that of divine authority
that so routs the enemies of God, puts sin to flight,
expels spiritual death, breaking the bands of that
worst king of terrors; that had skill to find out sin
in its lurking holes, and power to dispossess that, and
introduce spiritual life into the soul? Can that be a
thing less than divine, that restores man to his due
place as a creature respecting his Creator, referring
all things to his glory? that implants the love, fear,
hope of God in the mind? that makes man of a miserable corrupt creature to become divine? that roots out
the vices of hell, and stores the soul with the virtues
of heaven? Can such a gospel be termed less than a
divine word of truth? If there be any word, that can
so change the nature, and transform wolves into
lambs, let it have the honour and due praise when it is
found out; but whatsoever the atheism of the world is,
that never felt the powerful efficacy of it, you surely
that have felt it a mighty weapon to conquer the devils
that once possessed you, and an instrument to new

beget you when you lay in your blood, should entertain no whisper against the divine authority of it, but count it the power and wisdom of God, as, indeed, it is in itself, and in its effect upon souls, Rom. i. 16. It is said there, to be "the power of God to salvation;" upon that account the apostle was not ashamed of it, neither should we; but conclude as the same apostle says, if I be not an apostle, yet to you I am an apostle; so if the gospel be not in itself the gospel of God, surely it is so to you who have been renewed.

It shows us the reason why the gospel is so much opposed by Satan in the world. It begets those for heaven, whom he had begotten for hell. It pulls down his image and sets up God's: it pulls the crown off his head, the sceptre from his hand, snatches subjects from his empire, straitens his territories, and demolishes his forts, breaks his engines, outwits his subtlety, makes his captives his conquerors, and himself the conqueror, a captive; it pulls men out of the kingdom of darkness, and translates them into a kingdom of light, Col. i. 13. And all this, as it is a word of truth, opposed to his word of deceit, whereby he has cheated mankind, and deceived the nations: that we may well say of him, as the apostle of death, "O death, where is thy sting?" 1 Cor. xv. 55. O hell, where is thy power? O Satan, where is thy victory? This slays Satan, and revives the soul.

We see then how injurious they are to God, who would obstruct the progress of the gospel in the world; who, as the papists, would hinder the reading and preaching of the word. Whose seed are they, but the seed of that dragon, that would as well hinder the new birth, as devour a divinely-begotten babe as soon as it ever were born? Rev. xii. 4. Such would hinder the greatest and most excellent work of God upon the souls of men, would have no spiritual generations for God in the world. Such envy Christ a seed, and God a family, they would despoil him of a family on earth, though they cannot of a family in heaven. In banishing the word, they would banish the grace of God out of the world, and leave no place, in a world drowned with ignorance, where this dove should set her foot. Those that would take away the seed would not have a spiritual harvest, but reduce souls to a deplorable famine, lock them up in the grave, and keep them under the bands of a spiritual death.

It informs us, that the gospel shall then endure in the world, as long as God has any to beget. Men may puff at it, but they cannot extinguish it; it is a word of truth; and truth is mighty, and will prevail. It was a mighty wind wherein the Spirit came upon the apostles, to show not only the quick and speedy progress of the gospel, as upon the wings of the wind, but the mighty force of it, that men can no more silence the sound of the gospel than they can the blustering of the wind. It shall prevail in all places where God has a seed to bring in, a people to beget. Those given to Christ shall come from far: from the east, Isa. xlix. 12, and from the west, and from the land of Sinim. The word, being the instrument, shall sound every where, where he hath sons and daughters to beget for Christ. As long as Christ doth retain his royalty, his mouth shall be a sharp sword, Isa. xlix. 2. That is the first thing concluded on between God and Christ, before they come to any further treaty; which is expressed in that chapter. As Christ shall be his salvation to the ends of the earth, so shall the word be the instrument of it to the end of the world, the polished shaft is hid in his quiver. As he is a light to the Gentiles, so the golden candlestick of this gospel wherein this light is set, shall endure in spite of men and devils. Since his promise of a seed to Christ stands sure, the word, whereby he begets a generation for him, is as sure as the promise, and shall not return void, " but it shall accomplish that which he pleases, and it shall prosper in the thing whereto he sent it."

Isa. lv. 11. Never fear then the removal of the gospel out of the world, though it be removed out of a particular place; since it is a word of truth, and an instrument ordained to so glorious an end.

It is a sign then God has some to regenerate, when he brings his gospel to any place. He has a pleasure to accomplish, and it shall not return unto him void. Prosperity is entailed upon it for the doing the work whereto he sent it. Since then it is appointed an instrument, in the hand of the Spirit, for a new begetting, it will be efficacious upon some souls where it comes; for the wise God would not send it, but to attain its main end upon some hearts. God never sends his word to any place, but it is received and relished by some as the savour of life. It looseth the bands of spiritual death in some, and binds them harder upon obstinate sinners: to them that perish it is the savour of death. In every place the gospel was savoury to some. "God made manifest the savour of his knowledge," by the apostles, "in every place." 2 Cor. ii. 14, 15. Wherever this seed is sown, the harvest has been reaped, either more or less. It is fruitful at Corinth, for there God has much people, Acts xviii. 10. It is not fruitless at Athens, though the harvest was less; most mocked, but some believed, and but one man of learning, and worldly wisdom, Acts xvii. 32, 34. When God sends John in a way of righteousness, if the pharisees believe not, God will make a conquest of publicans harlots. "John came to you in the way of righteousness, and you believed not: but the publicans and harlots believed him." Matt. xxi. 32. The net of the gospel is not cast in vain.

Prize the word of truth, which works such great effects in the soul. Value that as long as you live, which is the cord whereby God has drawn any of you out of the dungeon of death. Never count that foolishness by which God has inspired you with the choicest wisdom; and never count that weakness, which has made any of you of dead, living; of darkness, light; and of miserable, happy by grace. If a soul be worth a world, and therefore to be prized, how precious ought that to be which is an instrument to beget a soul for the felicity of another world! How should the law of God's mouth be better to us, than thousands of gold and silver! Psa. cxix. 72. How should we prize that word whereby any of us have seen the glory of God in his sanctuary, the glory of God in our souls! When corruptions are strong, it is an engine to batter them. When our hearts are hard, it is a hammer to break them. When our hearts are cold, it is a fire to inflame them. When our souls are faint, it is a cordial to refresh them; it begins a new birth, and maintains it. It is the seed from whence we spring, 1 Pet. i. 23, the glass, wherein we see the glory of God, 2 Cor. iii. 18. By the waters of the sanctuary we have both meat for nourishment, and medicines for cure, from the tree that grows by its streams. The fruit thereof shall be for meat, and the leaf for medicine. Ezek. xlvii. 12. Have a great regard to it, keep it in the midst of your hearts, for it is life, Prov. iv. 21, 22.

Wait upon God in the word. When there is a revelation on God's part, there must be a hearing on ours. Sit down therefore at the feet of God, and receive of his words, Deut. xxxiii. 3. Despise it not: he that contemns it, never intends to be new begotten, since he slights the means of God's appointment; he that intends an end, will use all means proportionably to his desires for that end. He that contemns it never was renewed; habitual grace being wrought by it, cannot but in its own nature have a great affection to it. He that loves Christ, cannot but love all the methods of his operations. Despise it not because it is but an instrument. Say not, because God is the chief agent, therefore you need not come to the word. Our Saviour knew that "man did not live by bread alone, but by every word that proceeds out of the mouth of God," Matt. iv. 4. Did he therefore neglect means for preserving this life? Because God gives the increase, should not the husbandman plough and sow? If God does not work upon you by the means, you can have no rational hopes he will do it any other way. What though ministers can only speak to the ear? John Baptist could do no more, whose ministry was notwithstanding glorious in being the forerunner of Christ. To neglect it therefore is to double-bar your hearts against the entrance of grace, and slight the truth which Christ brought down from the bosom of God.

How shall we wait upon the word, so as that we may be new begotten by it?

Wait upon the word frequently. Be often in reading and hearing, and meditating on it. Men set upon these works, as if they were afraid they should be new born too soon, or prejudiced in their concerns and contentments in the world; as if they feared the mighty wind of the Spirit should blow away their beloved dross too fast: as if it were a matter of indifference to be like their Maker. If you had gold not thoroughly refined, would you not cast it again and again into the fire? If the filth be not wholly purged, would you not use the fountain again and again? Those that are in the sun are coloured and heated by it, and have things more visible: those that are much in the word, see more of the wonders, feel more of the warmth, receive deeper impressions, are endued with the grace and holiness of truth, have a purer flame in their affections for heaven. How do you know but an opportunity missed might have been the best market? How do you know but the Spirit might have joined himself to the word, as Phillip to the eunuch's chariot while he was reading? "While Peter yet spake those words, (it is said) the Holy Ghost fell upon all them which heard the word," Acts x. 44. What words? Even the marrow of the gospel; "that through his name, whosoever believes in him shall receive remission of sins," v. 43. God may have a portion ready for us, and we go without it, because we are not ready to receive it. We must not expect a raven to bring us food upon a bed of sluggishness. Do it the rather, because you may live to see such times, wherein Bibles may be as much shut as they are now open, wherein (as in former time) you may be willing to give a large parcel of your goods for one chapter of it. We read of some that have given a load of hay for one chapter of St. James. Be frequent in waiting upon the word.

Let your hearts be fixed upon that which is the great end of the word. New begettings are the end of the gospel; come then with minds fixed upon this end, and desires for it. Regard it not as a mere sound of words, but as an instrument of the noblest operations in the soul. If this be the great work of the gospel, we ought to read and hear it with desires to be enlivened where we are dead, quickened where we are dull; be made new creatures, where we are yet but old; taller creatures where we are yet but of a low stature; not only to have our understandings instructed, but our hearts changed. To "inquire after God, to behold the beauty of the Lord," Psa. xxvii. 4; that we may be transformed into it: to look for God who is in the word of the truth; for the kingdom of God comes nigh to you in the gospel; that was the word, that Christ when he sent his disciples out first to preach, bid them speak unto men, Luke xii. 9. Men usually get no more than they come to seek. He that goes to market, intending only to lay out his money upon some trifle, returns for the most part with no better commodity. Zaccheus got upon the tree to meet Christ, and so noble an end wanted not an excellent success; that day came salvation into his house, Luke xix. 9. When the Jews did not mind the end of sacrifices, and regarded not the things God principally looked for in them, God slighted them, and they went without any divine operations upon their souls by them, Isa. i. 11, 13, 14. When our ends suit the gospel, then we are like to feel gospel influences. We come with wrong ends, and therefore return with unchanged hearts; we come for a sound, and go away with no more. Our end therefore in coming should be to gain this new begetting, or increase the growth of the new creature; our ends are not else conformable to the ends of God in it; therefore, as the earth sucks in the rain, and the roots in the earth attract it unto themselves that they may bring forth fruit; so should we open our hearts to receive the showers of the word with an aim at a new birth, or a further growth.

Mind the word in the simplicity of it, and that in it, which tends to that end. Some men are more taken with colours, than truth; more enamoured with words than matter, fill themselves only with air, and neglect the substance. Such are like those that are pleased with the colours of the rainbow, more than with the light reflected, or the covenant of God represented by it. No man is renewed by phrases and fancies, those are only as the oil to make the nails of the sanctuary drive in the easier, in Eccles. xii. 11, acceptable words joined with words of truth, are as the fastening of the nails, both given by one shepherd. Words then must be to make things intelligible; illustrations to make things delightfully intelligible, but the seminal virtue lies not in the husk and skin, but in the kernel, the rest dies, but the substance of the seed lives, and brings forth fruit; separate therefore between the husk and the seed. The word does not work as it is elegant, but as it is divine, as it is a word of truth. Illustrations are but the ornaments of the temple, the glory of it is in the ark and mercy-seat. It is not the engraving upon the sword cuts, but the edge; nor the key, as it is gilt, opens, but as fitted to the wards. Your "faith must not stand in the wisdom of men, but in the power of God," 1 Cor. ii. 5; it is the juice of the meat, and not the garnishings of the dish, that nourishes. Was it the word as a pleasant song, or as a divine seed that changed the souls of old, made martyrs smile in the midst of flames? It was the knowledge of the excellency of the promise, and not worldly eloquence, made them with so much courage slight gibbets, stakes, and executioners; they had learned the truth as it is in Jesus.

Before you wait upon God in any ordinance, plead with him as Moses did in another case, to what purpose should I go, unless thy presence go with me? What can the letter do without the Spirit, or words without that powerful wind to blow them into my heart? None can have life by the bread of the word, without the blessing of God; as man brings the graft, desire God to insert it. And may we receive the truth with cordial affection, and live under its divine influence to the praise and glory of God through Jesus Christ our Lord. Amen.